INTEGRATION REQUIREMENTS FOR IMMIGRANTS IN EUROPE

Based on legal-philosophical research, and informed by insights gleaned from empirical case studies, this book sets out three central claims about integration requirements as conditions for attaining increased rights (ie family migration, permanent residency and citizenship) in Europe:

(1) That the recent proliferation of these (mandatory) integration requirements is rooted in a shift towards 'individualised' conceptions of integration.
(2) That this shift is counterproductive as it creates barriers to participation and inclusion for newcomers (who will most likely permanently settle); and is normatively problematic insofar as it produces status hierarchies between native-born and immigrant citizens.
(3) That the remedy for this situation is a firewall that disconnects integration policy from access to rights.

The book draws on perspectives on immigrant integration in multiple EU Member States and includes legal and political reactions to the refugee/migrant crisis.

Integration Requirements for Immigrants in Europe

A Legal-Philosophical Inquiry

Tamar de Waal

•HART•
OXFORD • LONDON • NEW YORK • NEW DELHI • SYDNEY

HART PUBLISHING

Bloomsbury Publishing Plc

Kemp House, Chawley Park, Cumnor Hill, Oxford, OX2 9PH, UK

1385 Broadway, New York, NY 10018, USA

29 Earlsfort Terrace, Dublin 2, Ireland

HART PUBLISHING, the Hart/Stag logo, BLOOMSBURY and the Diana logo are trademarks of Bloomsbury Publishing Plc

First published in Great Britain 2021

A catalogue record for this book is available from the British Library.

Library of Congress Cataloging-in-Publication data

Names: Waal, Tamar de, 1988- author.

Title: Integration requirements for immigrants in Europe : a legal-philosophical inquiry / Tamar de Waal.

Description: Oxford, UK ; New York, NY : Hart Publishing, an imprint of Bloomsbury Publishing, 2021. | Based on author's thesis (doctoral – Universiteit van Amsterdam, 2017) issued under title: Conditional belonging : a legal-philosophical inquiry into integration requirements for immigrants in Europe. | Includes bibliographical references and index.

Identifiers: LCCN 2021008480 (print) | LCCN 2021008481 (ebook) | ISBN 9781509931651 (hardback) | ISBN 9781509950072 (paperback) | ISBN 9781509931675 (pdf) | ISBN 9781509931668 (Epub)

Subjects: LCSH: Emigration and immigration law—European Union countries.

Classification: LCC KJE6044 .W33 2021 (print) | LCC KJE6044 (ebook) | DDC 342.2408/2—dc23

LC record available at https://lccn.loc.gov/2021008480

LC ebook record available at https://lccn.loc.gov/2021008481

ISBN: HB: 978-1-50993-165-1
ePDF: 978-1-50993-167-5
ePub: 978-1-50993-166-8

Typeset by Compuscript Ltd, Shannon

To find out more about our authors and books visit www.hartpublishing.co.uk. Here you will find extracts, author information, details of forthcoming events and the option to sign up for our newsletters.

For my parents, Hans and Inge

ACKNOWLEDGEMENTS

I would like to express my gratitude to the Paul Scholten Centre for Jurisprudence of the University of Amsterdam; the Forum for Philosophy and Public Policy of Queen's University (Kingston, Canada); the Centre for the Study of Democratic Citizenship of McGill University; and the Max Planck Institute for the Study of Religious Diversity (Göttingen, Germany) for providing me inspiring environments for conducting the research required for this book. I owe special debt to my PhD supervisors Prof Will Kymlicka (Queen's), Prof Marc de Wilde (UvA) and Dr Roland Pierik (UvA). In addition, I also want to extend my gratitude to my hosts Prof Dietlind Stolle (McGill) and Prof Ayelet Shachar (Max Planck) for their guidance and support.

This book is an extended and updated version of my PhD thesis *Conditional Belonging: A Legal-philosophical Inquiry into Integration Requirements for Immigrants in Europe* defended at 21 September 2017 at the Amsterdam Law School of the University of Amsterdam. The dissertation received the biennial VWR prize for best dissertation in the field of legal theory in the Netherlands and Belgium in 2019.

Chapter 1 is a modified and updated version of '"Make Sure You Belong!": A Critical Assessment of Integration Requirements for Residential and Citizenship Rights in Europe' published in the *Buffalo Human Rights Law Review* (25 *Buff. Hum. Rts. L. Rev.* 37 (2019)).

Chapter 3 is a modified and updated version of 'Conditional Belonging: Evaluating Integration Requirements from a Social Equality Perspective' published in *Journal of Intercultural Studies* (41:2, 231-247, DOI 10.1080/07256868.2020.1724906).

CONTENTS

LIST OF ABBREVIATIONS

CJEU	Court of Justice of the European Union
ECHR	European Convention of Human Rights
ECtHR	European Court of Human Rights
EU	European Union
Family Directive	Council Directive 2003/86/EC of 22 September 2003 *on the right to family reunification* [2003] OJ L21/12
LTR Directive	Council Directive 2003/109/EC of 25 November 2003 *concerning the status of third-country nationals who are long-term residents* [2003] OJ L16/44
TCN	Third Country National

Introduction

Since 1998 there has been a structural growth of standardised integration measures for third country nationals[1] (TCNs) in EU Member States.[2] Statistical indexes of integration requirements across Europe such as 'CIVIX' developed by Sarah Goodman show a drastic change from 1997, when such policies were largely absent, to 2009, when such policies were prevalent (Goodman 2010a). Also the Migrant Integration Policy Index 2011 (MIPEX) observed that in 1999, Germany was the only EU Member State to impose a language requirement as an integration condition for permanent residency but that increasingly '[...] the trend on language and integration conditions extends from Europe's established countries of immigration (DK, DE, UK) to new countries of labour migration in the south and east (CY, CZ, IT, PT)' (Huddleston 2011: 20). Indeed, since 2003 a majority of Member States implemented minimally one integration requirement as a condition for the obtainment of a permanent residency permit in a relatively short time span of ten years; in this period five countries also implemented integration requirements abroad for family migrants (Pascouau 2014; De Vries 2013). Today, according to MIPEX 2020, 17 out of 27 Member States have at least one compulsory language or civic integration requirement for permanent residency and 24 of 27 have at least one for naturalisation (Solano and Huddleston 2020; see also Orgad 2019: 529).

In particular, many Member States require newcomers[3] to undergo civic integration courses, integration contracts, language and citizenship tests, participation declarations and oaths. Such integration measures have proliferated and are often imposed as requirements at different states of the immigration process: initial entry, renewed residency, obtaining permanent residency and/or naturalisation (see, eg, Bauböck and Joppke 2010; Goodman 2010a; Van Oers 2013; Joppke 2017; De Waal 2018). The implementation of these formal requirements for TCNs in the EU has taken place against the backdrop of heated debates about the desirability of immigration, concerns about increasing diversity and the emerging (so-called) refugee crisis (see, eg, Kymlicka 2012; Orgad 2010: 56; Goodman 2012: 659; Guild et al 2009; Hernes 2018). Alarmed by (alleged) acute failures of integration and the fear of uncontrollable 'mass-immigration', the increase of these integration

[1] Individuals who are neither citizens of the EU country in which they are currently living or staying, nor of other Member States of the EU.

[2] The Netherlands was the first country that enacted a 'Newcomer Integration Act', which obliged newcomers to attend language and 'social orientation courses'. See also Goodman 2010a.

[3] I will use this term to refer to recently arrived, non-EU (legal) immigrants in EU states.

policies can be seen as 'among the most visible if not the most significant [...] policy changes' (Goodman 2012: 659) in the context of accommodating migration in the recent history of Europe.

The introduction of these integration measures has generated a range of criticism in both academic and public debate. Initially, the concerns were predominately aimed at the *content* of these new integration education and tests in Europe, questioning the elements they highlight as part of the dominant cultures. For example, a question that provoked quite some ridicule was included in the exercise material for the *Life in the UK*, asking where Father Christmas comes from (Lapland; Iceland; or the North Pole) (Orgad 2010: 103). In the Netherlands, TCNs had to answer questions such as what people should do if they have a severe headache and the doctor tells them to go to bed early and take a pain killer (watch television; see friends at the tea house; or go to bed early). Another question in the Dutch citizenship test concerned that the examination computer produced the sound 'bananas, bananas for sale' followed by the question: 'Where are you?' (in the supermarket; at the marketplace; in a flower shop) (De Groot et al 2009: 64–65). At a later stage, however, the tone of the debate became more serious, as the number of EU states introducing integration requirements kept growing. Moreover, in several countries the penalty for failing to complete these requirements became the impositions of fines, denied renewal of residency or measures to actively revoke visas. Accordingly, an academic debate emerged on how 'liberal' integration and citizenship tests are. In particular, the question was raised whether receiving states may demand a commitment to certain *values* before immigrants are allowed to obtain certain rights, for instance in approving gender equality and LGBT+ rights. In the citizenship scholarship, the consensus that emerged on this matter seems to be that governments are not allowed to require cultural assimilation as a prerequisite of inclusion (that is, prescribe that immigrants, for instance, have to renounce certain cultural or religious identities as a condition for obtaining permanent residency or citizenship). Indeed, several commentators agreed that receiving liberal-democratic states (including EU countries), given their commitments to individual freedom and freedom of conscience, can only require newcomers to 'have knowledge' of liberal-democratic and constitutional values and abide by the law, but cannot require that they personally endorse them (eg, Orgad 2009: 101–102; Joppke 2010: 1–4, 39–41).[4]

In addition, some scholars argued from a broader perspective that the motives behind the rise of integration requirements in Europe have not been genuinely driven by the intention to find the best strategies for incorporating newcomers in society, but are in fact more sinister and coincide 'with Islamophobic campaigns

[4] That said, Ines Michalowski found that this debate was a bit off target, or at least theoretical, in terms of discussing the current proliferation of integration requirements in EU Member States, because the tests in Austria, UK, Germany and the Netherlands in fact do not or rarely ask about 'what is good' but rather about the political system, countries' history, geography, national symbols and, at times, sociocultural norms. See Michalowski 2011.

and the increasing influence of right-wing parties that underpin elites' and concerns to reduce (unwanted) migration as well as reduce the number of naturalisations (Kostakopoulou 2010a: 15). Others, however, emphasised the more positive and emancipatory aspects of integration requirements and assured that they 'equip immigrants with the linguistic, social and political skills that will enable them to take full advantage of the society they are joining' (Miller 2016: 136; see also Kiwan 2008).

The main question of this study is: How to ensure that EU states do not misuse integration measures for TCNs for exclusionary and counterproductive purposes? I consider this question to be relevant and warranting proper discussion, both for the sake of academic and political debate in Europe, as integration and equal citizenship are highly pertinent and topical issues. Moreover, as I realised soon after I started this investigation, most academic debates, for instance those that focus on the permissible *content* of citizenship tests and their degree of liberalness (see, eg, Bauböck and Joppke 2010; Orgad 2009), raise valid points, but often discard important issues pertaining to the legal and conceptual frameworks underpinning the rise of integration requirements in contemporary Europe. Furthermore, existing studies often flag the risk of integration requirements becoming too restrictive, illiberal or exclusionary, but do not reflect or provide insights on how to counterbalance the possibility that EU countries enforce integration policies in illegitimate ways. When I began this study, the sub-questions I therefore had in mind were: How to *explain* the growth of integration requirements in multiple EU Member States over the last two decades? What does it actually mean to 'integrate' a person? What, if anything, is the relationship between integration requirements as conditions for attaining increased rights and the principle of equality before the law? Can immigrants who fail to integrate indeed be sent back to their country of origin on this ground? What impact, if anything, do such integration requirements have on the societal position of newcomers and our notions of citizenship? And what are the (potential) side effects of integration requirements targeted at newcomers on the path to secure residency or citizenship?

Working on this book, I found answers to most of these questions. Most importantly, I found that the integration requirements for TCNs to obtain increased rights (that is, family migration, permanent residency and citizenship) in EU Member States are increasingly legally misapprehended, misused and are prone to have counterproductive policy outcomes, often contradicting their formal objectives. More particularly, I established that they structurally carry the risk of being used to serve exclusionary purposes, which prevent rather than enable successful integration. In addition, I observed that they also often reinforce problematic status hierarchies between *citizens*, as they facilitate a perceived distinction between two kinds of citizenship: the unrestricted citizenship of non-immigrants versus the status of immigrant citizenship, which may only be achieved under certain constraints and conditions. To be more specific, certain integration requirements nurture the perception that the entitlement of citizens with immigrant backgrounds to their legal citizenship is conditional and contingent on certain desirable competences while citizens without immigrant backgrounds are perceived as natural possessors of their unconditional form of legal citizenship.

Due to these developments and the overall implications thereof, I see little reason to evaluate the proliferation of integration requirements in Europe positively. However, my research also shows that this does not mean that all possible integration strategies for EU states should be denounced. The problem with these relatively novel integration requirements in EU Member States, I will argue, is *not* that receiving liberal-democratic countries have no legitimate interests in providing (mandatory) integration trajectories to newcomers. What is problematic is their precise legal positioning, as these measures are predominately targeted at TCNs with relatively strong rights to inclusion but also imposed as conditions for obtaining secure rights and citizenship. Indeed, one of the roots of a variety of problems with the integration requirements for TCNs in EU countries today lies in their current legal configuration. In this regard, I suggest we should carefully examine alternative institutional set-ups for integration strategies in EU countries.

The upshot of these alternatives must be: (a) that receiving states must be able to implement integration policies that are effective; and (b) that TCNs (who lack secure residency rights, direct political voice, strong political and social networks and equal constitutional protection) are treated as legally vulnerable individuals who deserve special protection against possible abuses of state power. In that context, I will propose such an alternative in the final chapter of this book. In particular, I will argue that while states have legitimate interests to establish public integration strategies to facilitate desirable societal outcomes, states should not impose integration requirements for TCNs, and especially not if they are family migrants or refugees,[5] as a condition for determining if, and when, they are allowed to receive residency or citizenship rights. Put differently, I suggest that European states should install a so-called institutional 'firewall' between, on the one hand, laws that regulate the residential inclusion and naturalisation of TCNs and, on the other hand, public strategies and policy schemes that promote integration. Both – so laws regulating legal inclusion of immigrants and integration policies – are in principle defendable and acceptable, but only if they operate separately. In this way, receiving EU states continue to have the option to adopt (mandatory) integration strategies for newcomers as a support structure to meet sets of certain societal goals (eg, increase language levels, nurture belonging, promote equal participation in different societal spheres, etc). But they cannot demand of TCNs that they should 'earn' their residence or citizenship by completing and fulfilling certain

[5] I will use the term 'refugee' to describe TCNs who received a refugee status (based on Article 1 of the Convention Relating to the Status of Refugees) or so-called 'subsidiary protection' (based on Article 3 of the European Convention of Human Rights). Even though convention-based protection and this complementary form of humanitarian protection are strictly seen as two different legal statuses, for the purposes of this book I can conflate them because the prohibition of *refoulement* applies to both. This means that a state cannot expel persons who are granted these statuses (for failing an integration requirement, or otherwise) to a territory where he or she faces a real risk of suffering serious harm. See, eg, Oudejans 2011: 15–21.

integration requirements. As will become clear, this firewall could be respected in EU Member States in two ways. The first option would be through legal reforms at the level of EU law. The second option would involve the voluntary commitment of Member States to enact this firewall, as current EU law does not insist that Member States should connect integration requirements to increased rights for TCNs, but only give the option to enact such policies.

I. Methodological Considerations

This is a book in applied legal philosophy. It is also an interdisciplinary work, as it blends traditional legal analysis, political and legal theory and social science research. In this investigation, I draw upon theoretical discussions on liberal nationalism, the ethics of migration and social egalitarianism, together with empirical and legal scholarship on the legal configuration and impact of integration requirements in the EU and possible alternative integration strategies. The general aim of the study is normative but also explanatory. Although I do not conduct empirical research myself, I analytically explain and normatively assess integration policies based on insights gleaned from empirical case studies. As such, one of the objectives of this research project is to show how fruitful the interaction between political theory, legal research and social science can be for all these disciplines. Yet, ultimately, my overarching perspective involves a normative view on positive law. I aim to discover under which legal conditions integration requirements are most likely to be part of an adequate response of EU states to the multi-layered challenge to welcome and incorporate TCNs in their societies. I do not claim to offer final solutions to this multi-layered challenge. But I do hope this study will improve our understanding of what the purposes of public integration policies should be and that it will redirect current perspectives to the main (normative) dilemmas and principles that should be taken into account if integration policies are implemented or assessed.

To achieve such an enhanced understanding and perspective, I believe we should closely examine how current integration and citizenship practices and laws relate to liberal-democratic principles. This approach requires several methodological decisions. First of all, I do not adopt a specific conception of liberal democracy. Instead, my argumentation is grounded in the core values of the EU of 'human dignity, freedom, democracy, equality, the rule of law and respect for human rights including the rights belonging to minorities' that, according to Article 3 of the Treaty of Lisbon 'are common to the Member States in a society in which pluralism, non-discrimination, tolerance, justice, solidarity and equality between women and men prevail'.[6] Consequently, the analysis of this book involves

[6] European Union, *Treaty of Lisbon Amending the Treaty on European Union and the Treaty Establishing the European Community*, 13 December 2007, 2007/C 306/01.

what Will Kymlicka has described as 'mid-level' theory (Kymlicka 2001: 8). It does not address foundational philosophical questions such as the nature of 'human dignity' or 'reason', nor whether the core values of the EU are universal or culturally relative. Moreover, although it builds on empirical and legal research, it does not provide an update or highly detailed case studies of the (lower level) integration and citizenship regimes in EU countries or cities (for the recently emerging literature on cities, see, eg, Manatschal et al 2020). Rather, I examine the standard ways of legally, politically and publicly addressing 'integration' in contemporary Europe and highlight the risks and limits of prevalent trends. Successful argumentation on this method provides a combination of correct legal exegeses of (in this case EU and domestic) laws; sound empirical descriptions of the standard conceptualisations of 'integration' based on policy documents and, more incidentally, political and public debates, and constructive normative analyses of the ways of how these policies potentially impact on core liberal-democratic values (of the EU). With this inquiry, my aim is to identify biases, double standards and confusions in legal and policy documents, public perceptions and everyday discourses on integration, citizenship and belonging. I contend that all these concepts are normatively laden and far-reaching, and although we tend to think we know what they mean, they are ambiguous and often inconsistently applied. Moreover, I hope to convincingly demonstrate that such double standards and inconsistencies are not innocent or inconsequential but can systematically negatively affect the legal, political and public responses to newcomers (who are in precarious legal positions) in EU Member States. Moreover, they can also put EU citizens with immigrant backgrounds in positions of disadvantage. It is necessary, for these reasons and more, that we understand the (biased) dynamics of integration policies and propose strategies as to how these can be overcome.

Based on this methodological strategy, I hope this book will be helpful and provide a substantial contribution to debates within academic circles (see next paragraph), in addition to its relevance for policy makers, governmental bodies and non-governmental organisations. This book illuminates present-day developments regarding how European countries treat TCNs and the normative and empirical effects of integration requirements in Member States. Furthermore, it sheds light on the tenets of the political tradition of liberal democracy, particularly in respect to its notions of inclusive equality, equal citizenship, respect for diversity and national identity.

II. Academic Relevance and Contribution to the Literature

This book attempts to bridge academic discussions on migration, integration and citizenship that often take place in isolation from one another. It confronts theoretical concerns such as social equality and the normative implications of the vulnerable position of legal-noncitizens ('precarity') with concrete issues surrounding public policies to regulate the integration and naturalisation of legal immigrants in EU states. For this reason, the analysis and arguments in this book are, I think, of interest for (at least) two academic audiences. First, they bring insights for legal and political theorists interested in the legitimacy of public institutions and the use of state power in the context of processes of immigration, integration and promoting equal citizenship. Second, they provide insights to scholars that are more practically orientated and seek to better understand the current integration practices applied to TCNs in Member States.

This book aims to further the academic debate by *combining* analyses of domestic and EU legal frameworks concerning the integration of newcomers with normative political and legal theory. These requirements have to date certainly already received considerable attention in a variety of academic discussions – and this research is heavily informed by these existing debates. However, each of these fields of academic research provides relevant points and arguments, but none of them as currently elaborated have, I believe, succeeded in fully integrating the legal, philosophical and empirical debates about the growth of (mandatory) integration requirements for newcomers in European states. This has created a gap in the literature, lacking a comprehensive evaluation of these policies that discusses their legal form, engages in applied normative reasoning and proposes possible and feasible institutional reforms for EU states that have the potential of leading to better 'integration' outcomes.

Accordingly, in this book, I draw upon, but also go beyond, 'liberal nationalists' (eg, Tamir 1995; Kymlicka 1995; Miller 1995) and empirical studies that distinguish under which conditions integration requirements are liberal or more restrictive (eg, Goodman 2010a; Howard 2009; Koopmans et al 2005). I will explain how both these bodies of literature, each in its own way, only highlight when integration requirements should be evaluated as inclusionary or exclusionary (see Chapter 2). As a result, their evaluations can be supplemented with constructive analysis on how such potential exclusionary effects of integration requirements could be *prevented.*

Furthermore, in this book I describe, use and add to the emerging political philosophical academic debates on 'social equality' that aim to envision what a 'community of equals' looks like (see Chapter 3). I observe that the growing group of social equality theorists has not (yet) paid enough attention to the phenomena of migration and how the arrival of newcomers might affect standards of equality (eg, Anderson 1999; Scheffler 2003; Fourie et al 2015). Moreover, I discern that certain integration requirements contribute to social inequalities that evidently should be *avoided* in a community of equals, such as a social division between (non-immigrant) citizens who are perceived as naturally belonging to the community and (immigrant) citizens who are perceived to only conditionally belong. Lastly, I propose that EU states should disconnect integration strategies from laws allocating residency rights and citizenship to TCNs, especially if they are applied to refugees and family migrants (see Chapter 4). To my knowledge, a comparable normative and institutional argument has not been put forward yet in academic migration or citizenship scholarship.

That said, it is also valuable to be explicit about to which academic debates this book does *not* (directly) contribute. First of all, it will not contribute to answering the main questions of the 'ethics of migration' literature, that is, to explore whether states have any normative right to control migration flows. I will write a few words about this, because readers might expect analyses in this book that mainly directly engage, rebut or refine the analyses of theorists working on issues concerning the ethics of migration (eg, Bader 2005; Kostakopoulou 2008; Shachar 2009; Carens 2013; Miller 2016). So far it is seen as the most applicable normative literature to evaluate integration requirements as conditions for attaining increased rights and commentators within the ethics of migration literature have indeed been quick to notice and comment on the recent rise of integration requirements in EU Member States (see, eg, Kostakopoulou 2010a; Carens 2010). However, as I see it, the research agendas and normative ambitions of these theoretical migration commentators and the normative questions generated by the growth of (mandatory) integration requirements in EU Member States that I am interested in are not fully aligned with each other for two reasons.

First, the lion's share of the ethics of migration literature focuses on two key decisions (often based on wide cosmopolitan ideals): decisions about who, under which circumstances, are to be admitted (ie border control, or territorial admittance) and decisions about who, under which circumstances, can obtain citizenship (ie naturalisation, or civic admittance). In effect, this literature predominately evaluates policies based on their impact on initial admission and naturalisation.[7] However, as we will see in Chapter 1, the novel mandatory integration requirements for family migration and permanent residency do not *select* individuals for immigration. Rather, these requirements are targeted at TCNs who already have a legal right to reside (predominately based on either family migration or asylum) and legally must facilitate integration outcomes.[8] In relation to naturalisation, the ethics of migration does provide a powerful analysis (which I will discuss in Chapter 3), but this argument is not new and broadly applies to all requirements for citizenship in all liberal-democratic countries. As a result, to fully disentangle the heart of the real-world dilemmas and practical issues raised by the integration requirements in EU countries, we need additional legal-normative reflections that

[7] To be sure, some migration theorists do reflect on issues beyond legal inclusion such as the importance of the value of equal citizenship in a broader sense, most notably Carens (2013). However, to my knowledge, these analyses never result in fine-grained recommendations on which integration requirements for residence and citizenship are desirable, legitimate or illegitimate.

[8] On a more critical note, one could argue that the often more cosmopolitan reflections on integration requirements for residence as developed in the ethics of migration literature are often not the most subtle. It is hardly surprising that if one's philosophical outlook is that (virtually) all immigration policies are unjust and borders should be open, that one also rejects the current EU integration requirements as conditions for increased residence or citizenship rights for particular immigrant groups. See Lægaard 2012: 41.

do not (only) address questions of sovereignty of states upon decisions of immigration and further legal inclusion. Instead, we must (also) normatively consider integration requirements as they are permitted in the current world order, that is, under the relevant EU directives, taking into account their actual legal and political specificities and official purposes.

On that account, my argumentation also differs from more applied legal and political analyses of integration requirements and tests in EU states, that do not take into account some of their most important legal and constitutional particularities. For example, Liav Orgad has written extensively on both the potential and the risks of imposing integration requirements for immigration and citizenship in response to the rise of such requirements in EU countries. In this research, he focuses for instance on the question of whether EU countries are permitted to *select* immigrants based on cultural and civic requirements and regulate their access to the territory or citizenship based on such integration criteria. He concludes, inter alia, that immigrants may indeed be asked to accept 'some structural liberal-democratic principles as a prerequisite for state admission' (Orgad 2009: 719). However, again, under current EU law, there are no integration requirements that function as *criteria* for immigration, selecting migrants based on values or otherwise. There are 'integration requirements abroad' for family migrants, formally applied to facilitate their territorial inclusion given that they have (already acknowledged) bona fide claims to family reunification. For this reason, Orgad's theory does not neatly apply to – and hence does not evaluate – the integration requirements abroad as implemented by a number of EU countries today (but does provide an answer to the normative question on the possible legitimate grounds for immigrant control).

To be sure, this does not imply that such academic endeavours do not raise important questions or insights. On the contrary, I believe it to be crucial and academically fully legitimised for political theorists to concentrate on principled discussions regarding immigration and integration and rethink the (legal) status quo. Moreover, I base some of my arguments upon analyses developed in the ethics of migration literature. For example, parts of my analyses resonate with the work of Dora Kostakopoulou, in particular in relation to the 'contractual frame' that increasingly underpins the current integration schemes in EU countries (see Chapters 1 and 3). However, her fundamental critique of the novel integration requirements within EU Member States originates from a revolutionary model of 'a-national citizenship' (eg, Kostakopoulou 2008; 2009; 2010b). On that account, her work, grounded in an advanced post-national perspective, challenges the right of nation-states to decide upon any question of immigration and citizenship. Therefore, her work has a fundamentally different research ambition than this book that provides an applied normative analysis of integration requirements within EU law. My aim is to both *understand* the stark growth of these requirements in Europe within their current legal and political frameworks and to *provide an institutional response* that, in principle, is implementable in the short term.

Second, this book will not elaborately reflect on two ongoing academic debates in the citizenship scholarship. First, there is the debate on whether integration policies converged in Europe or whether Member States remain to have very different 'national models'. Second, there is the debate on whether, overall, requirements for citizenship have become more restrictive or in fact liberalised in Europe. For purposes of clarity, I should mention the following on these debates. In relation to the first debate, it is undeniably true that national integration policies still reflect national continuities and have path-dependent reactions on these continuities and cultural differences between Member States (see, eg, Mouritsen 2013; Brochmann and Midtbøen 2020; James and Janmaat 2019). Indeed, the procedures for TCNs to obtain increased residency and citizenship rights (still) vary greatly between Member States: they differ in when they are applied, towards whom, based on what procedure, under which exceptions and at what cost. Furthermore, as always, this is amplified by that the more legal perspective often does not tell the whole story: the concrete implementation of integration requirements in countries also depends on the role of locally embedded 'street-level bureaucrats' (Lipsky 1980). Nevertheless, and crucially, it is also uncontested that integration requirements for TCNs as conditions to attain increased rights have proliferated in Europe – and continue to do so – and are often installed and defended by governments as 'citizen-making policies' (eg, Carrera and Vankova 2019; Orgad 2019: 525; Goodman 2012; Joppke and Eule 2016). In this context, studies categorising integration requirements in Member States observe that this policy field has been 'extremely dynamic and subject to constant changes' (Pascouau 2014: 25) over the last quarter of a century. It is this latter broader trend that this book aims to understand and evaluate, for which the nuanced discussion on under which circumstances we can meaningfully speak of a 'policy converge' or distinct 'national models' is not crucial. I will therefore discuss the growth of integration requirements in different Member States without working with abstract citizenship typologies of integration models of countries – such as 'civic territorial' or 'multicultural' (eg, Brubaker 1992; Koopmans 2005 et al) – as developed in the empirical literature.[9]

In relation to the second debate, I should highlight that in this book I (solely) focus on *integration* requirements in EU Member States, that is, 'integration requirements abroad' for family migrants;[10] integration requirements as conditions for attaining permanent residency;[11] and integration requirements for naturalisation (this latter is Member State competence).[12] Yet, in academic studies regarding the question of whether requirements for citizenship have liberalised or not, other requirements for family migration, permanent residency or citizenship are most often also taken into account, such as economic requirements (income, employment, self-sufficiency), having a clean criminal record or the renunciation of a previous citizenship (eg, Joppke 2008a; Howard 2009; Goodman and

[9] The growing academic consensus seems to be that these models tend to oversimplify the integration policies of countries, exaggerating their coherence (see, eg, Freeman 2004; Hernes 2018).

[10] Family Directive, Art 7(2).

[11] LTR Directive Art 5(2).

[12] For the full legal analysis, see ch 1.

Howard 2013; Schmid 2021). There are convincing arguments to do so, as from the perspective of TCNs these requirements arguably form equally important or even higher hurdles for access to secure legal status and citizenship. However, strictly legally seen, these other requirements are not *integration* requirements under EU law.[13] And in this book, I will focus on those requirements that are legally seen as integration requirements; these primarily entail language, civic knowledge tests as well as loyalty or naturalisation oaths. I focus on these requirements, because I aim to demonstrate that these requirements interact with and testify to broader public debates and conceptual understandings of the notion of 'integration' in Europe. Within this strategy requirements other than integration requirements as conditions to attain increased rights can also be relevant, so I do occasionally touch upon them, for example in relation to relevant case law. Yet, I will not address the question whether, *all possible types* of requirements considered, requirements for citizenship in Europe have decreased or increased.

Third and lastly, this book will not offer reflections on adjacent real-world problems to immigration and Europe (and beyond), such as the position of undocumented migrants in Europe or what a just resettlement scheme for the 26 million refugees in the world would be (UNHCR 2019).[14] Notwithstanding the importance of these questions, they fall outside of the scope of this book.

III. Preliminary Remarks

Before I begin, I want to make five preliminary remarks to make the scope, aims and limits of this book as clear as possible.

First, it is important to clarify how I approach questions of 'integration'. After all, I discuss different conceptions of the term and, ultimately, defend that integration measures under certain conditions are legitimate. This begs the question of what 'integration' then is. This is a complicated, nuanced and even thorny issue. For some, 'integration' has become a meaningless or illegitimate term, at least in Europe, as it involves a stigmatising double standard for immigrants and their descendants (eg, Schinkel 2017; Wieviorka 2014). It could therefore be argued that it would be better to use less loaded terms, such as immigrant 'inclusion' or 'incorporation' (see Carens 2013: 321, n2). It will become clear that I strongly share this concern, because 'integration' is indeed often interpreted in prejudiced ways (that assume that non-immigrant citizens are always integrated, whereas immigrants are at best seen as conditionally integrated into society). However, at the same

[13] For instance, the 'income requirement' is laid down separately in Art 7 (1)(c) of the Family Directive.

[14] This number is 79.5 million if you also include so-called internationally displaced persons, thus persons who are forced to leave their home because of war or persecution but remain within their country's borders (UNHCR 2019).

time, the term 'integration' is so widespread in both academic work and policy debate (see, eg, MIPEX) that it might be worthwhile to try to 'rescue' the term. Moreover, I do not believe that changing a word automatically solves the problem of the existence of structural societal and institutional biases against certain groups.

Therefore, I decided for now to continue using the term, in the hope that through discussion we can clarify the issues and develop a more adequate use of it. More particularly, in Chapter 4, I will explain how my firewall proposal may lead to a more helpful 'disaggregated' perspective on integration (Freeman 2004). Such an approach assesses (more short-term) policy outcomes of public integration strategies based on their effects on chosen policy goals within certain societal domains, such as the labour market, political realm or welfare state. Within this account, crucially, ideas of both 'integrated societies' and 'integration individuals' disappear. Rather, the term 'integration' is merely used to evaluate certain policies labelled as 'integration policies' applied to newcomers in society that (aim to) affect societal multi-dimensional social processes, in which both persons with and without recent immigrant backgrounds are involved and economic, social and political factors can be taken into account as relevant. That said, the analyses in this book nor the firewall proposal I put forward are particularly attached to the word 'integration'. So, if in the future, integration policies in Europe were to be relabelled as 'incorporation', 'social cohesion' or 'inclusion' policies that would not affect my legal or normative reasonings.

Second, as said, this study engages in 'mid-level' theory and discusses policy trends and societal mechanisms in debates on integration, belonging and equal citizenship in Europe. To be able to do that, I must work with the available empirical and legal scholarship on the shape of integration policies in Europe. However, this scholarship, so far, has remained primarily (though not exclusively) skewed to the initial EU-15. As a result, examples of *Western* European countries may seem overrepresented in my illustrations of what I will describe as 'European' trends. It is my aim to counterbalance this with enough examples of other EU countries, but this is at times a challenge. For instance, regarding certain EU countries, such as most Baltic and Eastern European states, there is some available data on their integration requirements, but this most often entails solely statistical data indicating the number of integration requirements present in different phases in the immigration process (eg, Solano and Huddleston 2020; Goodman 2010a; Pascouau 2014). This is informative but for the research aims of this book, I also need insight into the discourses and political arguments used to implement these requirements, ideally together with their empirical outcomes and other contextual factors. Only then can I adequately scrutinise changes in integration requirements in light of my theoretical lens. To give one example: Malta implemented its first integration requirement in 2020. On that account, statistically seen this country can (still) be qualified as not having a restrictive integration scheme (and as deserving of a low CIVIX score). Nonetheless, the policy has set up an integration trajectory called the 'I Belong programme' and has been presented in a policy document in

2017 with the title 'Integration = Belonging' (Vassalo 2019: 27). This seems vital information, because it suggests that Malta has taken its first step on the path of implementing (what I call) 'individualised' integration strategies in which belonging and rights must be *earned* by newcomers. And if that is indeed the case, the core analysis of this book – criticising individualised integration strategies – would apply to the case of Malta and moreover indicates that it is likely that the Maltese Government will install more integration requirements in the upcoming years. However, there are to my knowledge currently not enough academic reflections on Malta available – for example, discussing changing public attitudes towards (certain groups) of migrants, or political narratives on migration and integration – to fully confirm and convincingly demonstrate this.

As a result, this book will not provide a systematic review of integration requirements in all EU Member States. Instead, it provides an overview of integration requirements in Member States on which more extensive empirical data exists – such as country reports, discourses analyses and public policy evaluations – that together reveal a broader perspective on developments in integration policies in the EU. In certain parts of my examinations, especially in Chapter 1 and Chapter 4, I will take the Netherlands as a paradigmatic example for my argumentation. I do this, because this country has explicitly functioned as 'a model' for other EU governments with pioneering policies in the context of integration requirements connected to the accessibility of rights for TCNs (Joppke 2013: 251; Michalowski 2004) and the CJEU has to date ruled on Dutch integration requirements several times (Groenendijk 2019: 281). Moreover, the Dutch integration trajectory is considered a leading example of a restrictive program within the EU. For this reason, although the Dutch case has been, in the words of Maarten Vink, 'one of the most over-studied cases' by *empirical* researchers working on integration and citizenship (Vink 2007: 337), it offers highly detailed and useful data for analysing the potential effects of integration requirements under current EU law *normatively*. This is also true for the case of Denmark, which I will also regularly discuss. Yet, importantly, the examples of the exclusionary integration requirements I highlight to support my normative reasoning in favour of the firewall solution I present, demonstrate the potentially undesirable outcomes of the latitude that EU directives currently give to *all* EU states to connect integration requirements to obtaining secure residency and citizenship for TCNs. Hence, the countries I discuss are not the result of 'cherry picking' or anecdotal illustrations but show and confirm the *structural risks* of the current legal constellations of integration requirements in EU states. For this reason, the core normative argument of this book is both relevant for Member States that already (excessively) enacted integration requirements connected to rights, as well as to Member States that did not (yet) enact such requirements.

The fourth preliminary remark I want to make is that it will become clear that a significant part of my analysis is based on the observation that it is most often virtually impossible for EU countries to deport or send back TCNs for failing to meet integration requirements, particularly if it comes to refugees and family migrants who are mandated to fulfil integration requirements, because EU and international law prevents and blocks this. On that account, a possible critique on this book might be that I do not explore all possibilities for European states to find legal ways to permanently exclude or deport TCNs (including refugees and family migrants), if they fail to complete integration requirements. For example, one could argue, if European countries leave the EU (as Britain did), it would be theoretically possible for these countries to also opt out of international treaties and install binding integration requirements with ultimate consequences, thereby determining whether immigrants can stay or not. However, I am convinced that it is unlikely that this course of events will actually arise in practice. Moreover, it would be undesirable, based on the very analysis I will outline in this book, in which I raise concerns about the conditions of perpetual precarity and maintaining standards of social equality. If European countries would decide to provide *less* secure rights for TCNs, this cure (more deportations) would be worse than the disease (prolonged legal exclusion). In any event, for Member States to leave the EU and adopt relevant treaties would require and involve major political, legal and geopolitical processes and will not be achieved in the near future. For this reason, the arguments spelled out in this book will apply to EU countries, and hence are relevant for academics and policy makers, for (at least) many years to come.

Fifth and last, I am writing from the context of Europe and the European Union, and this, what Iris Marion Young, calls 'situatedness' (Young 2002: 14) undoubtedly influences the theoretical arguments (eg, in relation to 'individualised integration') made in the following chapters. I do hope, however, that the issues, dilemmas and reflections that I raise are fruitful for those working on the relationship between immigration, integration and liberal-democratic values in other contexts as well and provide stimulus to begin a conversation with many on the potential downsides of installing integration requirements for obtaining residency and citizenship rights.

IV. Outline of the Book

Chapter 1 covers the current legal state of affairs in integration requirements as conditions for TCNs to obtain increased rights in EU states. It discusses EU directives, international treaties, domestic laws and case law in order to provide insights into the formal particularities of these requirements. Moreover, it describes a conceptual shift regarding the notion of 'integration' across Europe that, it asserts, has bolstered the legal proliferation of integration requirements in multiple Member States over the past two decades. The first chapter ends with an enumeration of the most significant (and interconnected) societal and practical ramifications of both the legal and conceptual shift in relation to integration and integration policies.

Chapter 2 discusses several academic bodies of literature that consider integration measures. It begins with discussing the theoretical literature on liberal nationalism, but also delves into social science, political science and legal research on integration requirements targeted at newcomers who are legally residing non-citizens. It argues that we have to rethink our normative examinations of integration requirements connected to obtaining residency and citizenship rights and complement them by paying attention to how these structural risks of these public policies can be (mis)used for exclusionary purposes.

Chapter 3 expounds and builds upon the social equality literature. It starts with a scrutiny of the relevance of this normative body of research for evaluating public policies. In addition, it highlights, through the 'negative methodology' that has been developed in this literature, problematic social hierarchies that integration requirements for newcomers may reinforce between citizens.

Chapter 4 will combine the most important insights and normative arguments of the previous chapters and, based on those, suggest that EU countries should install a firewall between their integration strategies and their laws that regulate residency and citizenship rights. It will demonstrate that installing this firewall would be both normatively desirable and practically helpful.

1

From Societal to Individual Integration

The central aim of this book is to find out how to ensure that EU Member States do not misuse integration requirements for TCNs for exclusionary purposes. In order to do that, I must first explain what is enabling and driving the burgeoning growth of integration requirements in a growing number of EU Member States over the last 25 years. In this first chapter, I will therefore focus on how the proliferation of these public integration policies can be *understood*. What are their formal objectives, legal characteristics and main effects in European societies? To answer these questions, I will, on the one side, expound the legal organisation of (mandatory) integration requirements for family migration, permanent residency and naturalisation in Member States. On the other side, I will describe a wider *conceptual* shift unfolding in Europe[1] on the level of Member States regarding the general notion of 'integration' that, as I see it, intensified and serves to justify the observed *legal* increase of integration requirements as conditions for obtaining residency and citizenship rights for TCNs. To be sure, I do not argue this conceptual shift is the *only* factor that explains the proliferation of legal integration requirements in Member States, but that it does play an important role.[2] This conceptual shift, I argue, has affected and still influences public perception of what 'integration' is and who is responsible for it.

In essence, I analyse that in EU Member States 'integration' is increasingly understood as what I call 'individualised', that is, as solely applicable to individual member of immigrant groups, in particular those with non-EU and non-Western backgrounds (see, eg, Schinkel 2017; Prins 2011). More specifically, the concept of 'integration' is used to assess the *compatibility* of persons with immigrant backgrounds with (idealised) societal standards to determine their *belonging to* 'society'.[3] However, the term 'integration' stems from the functionalist tradition of sociology and was understood as a 'holistic' notion applicable to society as whole and describing its *collective functioning*. In several EU policy and legal documents, it is (still) defined based on this initial conceptualisation, but particularly on the national level in Europe it is increasingly less so.

[1] I do not reflect on whether this shift is *exclusively* European, or that it may have also occurred in similar ways in other parts of the world such as North America and Oceania.

[2] In ch 2, I will reflect on the features of the liberal state that are crucial to understand the (changing) shape of integration and citizenship policies in modern states, from the perspective of political science.

[3] My analysis here leans on the terminology developed by Willem Schinkel. See Schinkel 2010, 2017, 2018.

In this chapter, I concentrate on the ramifications of this broader conceptual shift on the formation and purposes of integration requirements connected to obtaining residency rights and citizenship for TCNs in EU Member States. Ultimately, I hope to demonstrate that one of the most profound effects of the fact that in Europe 'integration' is increasingly understood as a property of individuals with (non-EU, non-Western) immigrant backgrounds, is that the relationship between European states and their newly arrived TCNs is interpreted and discussed in *contractual* terms. The main purpose of integration requirements then becomes to compel TCNs to fulfil their obligation to individually integrate in order to acquire secure residency rights and/or full citizenship delivered by the receiving state. As a result, the focus of integration requirements shifts from their impact on societal goals to judgements of individual merit or deserving. However, if this happens, integration requirements become predisposed to having counterproductive effects on integration, seen from a more long-term, societal and multi-dimensional perspective. Given their focus on measuring who 'deserves to belong' (and, as a corollary, preventing the 'belonging' of newcomers who do not deserve it), these policies are less evaluated based on whether they in fact support or compromise certain desirable policy objectives aimed at broader societal outcomes. Instead, they are constantly amended based on the (arbitrary) benchmark when individual TCNs can be deemed to have integrated 'enough'.

To elucidate this, I will first describe the EU directives that enable Member States to implement integration requirements and examine domestic integration requirements for citizenship. Then, I will describe the conceptual shift in Europe regarding the concept of 'integration', moving from a more 'holistic' to an 'individualised' notion. Following that, I will examine its parallels and connections with the enacted legal integration requirements in various EU Member States. Finally, I will summarise the three most crucial outcomes of these developments on the shape and effects of integration requirements.

Before proceeding, it is important to mention two points of clarification. This chapter might raise the question on the exact causal relationship between the legal and conceptual shift I discuss. Which one reinforces the other; what is the root cause and what is the effect? This concern touches upon the recurring so-called 'structure vs. culture debate' among societal scientist. Do institutions (including public policies and laws) produce a certain culture (including public perceptions and discourses), or is it the other way around? In line with Robert Putnam, I hold that this debate is ultimately 'fruitless' as structures and cultures are not reducible to 'linear causal questions' but constitute a 'mutually reinforcing equilibrium' (Putnam et al 1994: 181). In this regard, also the relationship between the legal and conceptual shifts in Europe relating to integration that I highlight must be seen as intertwined and indeed mutually reinforcing. These shifts are moreover uneven processes across time and space. Looking back historically, we can certainly retrospectively find political debates in which 'integration' was applied solely to individual members of certain (immigrant) groups. Conversely, today we can point out examples of where the term is used as a societal-level property.

Furthermore, the shift from societal to individualised integration has not manifested itself with equal force (yet) in all European countries. Nor do all countries follow exactly the same model. Anita Böcker and Tineke Strik, for example, observe that within political discussions on the national level on sharpening integration requirements, the (what I call) individualised conception of integration has been invoked most explicitly in the Netherlands, Austria and Denmark: 'The desire to limit access to permanent residence to 'well-integrated' immigrants is a rather manifest aim of the [… integration …] tests in all three countries' (Böcker & Strik 2011: 167). However, as will be demonstrated, public discourses of and policy tendencies towards individualised integration are definitely not limited to these countries. Simultaneously, it must be noted that certain European countries such as Sweden have remained, as Lilian Nygren-Junkin puts it, 'test-free zones' as they have, so far, not enacted integration requirements for immigrants as conditions to be met in order to retain secure residency rights or citizenship (Nygren-Junkin 2009: 57; see also Carrera and Vankova 2019: 36). However, 'even' in Sweden the introduction of integration requirements is regularly discussed and in October 2019, the Swedish Government appointed a committee to determine whether a language test would strengthen the status of Swedish citizenship (EMN 2020: 19). This 'Cross-party Committee of Inquiry on Migration' advised in 2020 that 'permanent residence permits should only be granted to aliens who meet the requirements of Swedish-language skills and civic knowledge […]' (SUO 2020: 28). The same is true for Ireland: although to date this country has not installed integration requirements for TCNs as conditions for increased residency or citizenship, in its recent *Migrant Integration Strategy 2017–2020* it examined the desirability of both civic and language tests for those seeking citizenship (ESRI & Department of Justice and Equality 2020).

Second, I do not intend to idealise or support the holistic perspective on integration or suggest that things were better in the past. In fact, in Chapter 4 it will become clear that I neither endorse the 'holistic' nor 'individualised' perspective on integration. As I see it, both do not offer a plausible sociological explanation for the functioning of a society, nor a useful normative metaphor to describe it. That said, this chapter does not take sides but aims to document larger trends in public orientations, pinpointing laws and policies, and identifying some of their results. In Chapter 4, I return to the question of how to approach issues of integration for the purposes of policy debates.

I. The Growth of Integration Requirements in Multiple EU Member States

In this section, I will present the EU directives and national laws that govern the integration requirements in EU Member States for TCNs and summarise, where needed, the relevant case law. This overview does not cover all legal details of the integration trajectories and citizenship schemes in (specific) EU countries. Yet, at the end of this section, the legal structures and constitutional limitations that give EU Member States a measure of discretion to impose (mandatory) integration requirements are clarified. In addition, I will also sketch recent trends in integration requirements for residency rights and naturalisation in European countries.

In relation to integration policies and naturalisation laws for non-EU immigrants residing in Member States, there is no wide-ranging European harmonisation regime in force, but there are several non-binding soft regulatory tools (see, eg, Carrera and Vankova 2019; Arribas Lozano et al 2014: 557). Indeed, although the Treaty of Lisbon foresaw EU responsibility for establishing the means to promote integration policies of Member States, it excluded any harmonisation of these policies. In November 2003, the European Commission did put forward its view on integration policies with the policy paper entitled *Communication on Immigration, Integration and Employment*[4] and in 2004 the Council of Ministers responsible for integration agreed on the document *Common Basic Principles for Integration.*[5] These nonbinding EU documents generally emphasise the importance of integration of TCNs. Amongst other things, the *Common Basic Principles of Integration* states 'integration is a dynamic, long-term and continuous two-way process of mutual accommodation, not a static outcome. It demands the participation not only of immigrants and their descendants but of every resident' (principle 1). In addition, it stresses that enabling immigrants to acquire basic knowledge of the receiving society's language, history and institutions is indispensable (principle 4).

In addition, there are EU directives that pressure Member States to facilitate certain integration outcomes. For instance, the Directive 2011/95/EU of the European Parliament and the Council of 13 December 2011 *on the standards for the qualification of third country nationals or stateless persons for the qualification of third country nationals or stateless persons as beneficiaries of international protection, for a uniform status of refugees or for persons eligible for subsidiary protection, and for the content of the protection granted* (often called 'Qualification Directive') prescribes that Member States have a best-effort obligation to include refugees in their labour market and economic activities under equivalent conditions as their own nationals and give them the same access to education as other TCNs within their territories (see also De Lange et al 2017: 45). For those recognised as refugees, or accorded through some other kind of international protection status, integration policies have also been considered crucial in light of the socio-economic rights enshrined in the 1951 UN Convention relating to the Status of Refugees and its 1967 Protocols, to ensure durable solutions for refugees. However, there is no specific EU integration instrument to monitor these obligations and national approaches

[4] Communication from the Commission to the Council, the European Parliament, the European Economic and Social Committee and the Committee of the Regions on immigration, integration and employment/*COM/2003/0336 final*/.

[5] Council Document 14615/04 of 19 November 2004.

vary greatly (UN Refugee Agency 2013: 8). The two pieces of *binding* supranational legislation that explicitly grant Member States the competence to enact (mandatory) integration requirements and measures are the Council Directive 2003/86/EC of 22 September *on the right to family reunification* ('Family Directive')[6] and the Council Directive 2003/109/EC of 25 November 2003 *concerning the status of third-country nationals who are long-term residents* ('LTR Directive').[7,8] These EU Directives give Member States the option to make respectively family reunification and the acquisition of a long-term resident status for TCNs (after five years of uninterrupted residence) conditional on integration requirements. It is left to individual Member States to decide to implement such requirements. The European Commission and the European Court of Justice ('CJEU') see to it that national policies respect the rules these directives set (Bonjour 2014: 211).

Since the enactment of these Directives at the beginning of this century, there has been a clear trend towards formalised testing of language skills, national civic knowledge and value commitments as prerequisites for family migration, obtaining permanent residency and also for gaining access to naturalisation procedures (see, eg, Goodman 2010a,b; Pascouau 2014; Joppke and Eule 2016). Overall, these measures have been predominately aimed at, and have the strongest obligatory effects on, family migrants and refugees. This results from the fact that there are virtually no legal venues for access to EU countries for non-high-skilled migrants while high-skilled labour migrants are often exempted from mandatory integration measures. Moreover, internal EU immigrants cannot be obliged to undergo integration requirements given their EU citizenship. However, if high-skilled immigrants or internal EU immigrants volitionally seek permanent residency status or the nationality of the EU Member State in which they reside, they must also complete the integration requirements in place to obtain this (see, eg, Permoser 2012: 186; Carrera and Vankova 2019: 23–40).

In response to the Family Directive, the Netherlands, UK, Germany, France and Austria have introduced integration requirements abroad for family migrants. These so-called 'predeparture measures', require family members or spouses of TCNs to pass an integration test and/or a language test in their country of origin at the local embassy of the receiving Member State (Groenendijk 2011; De Vries 2013; Bonjour 2014). In addition, the EU Member States that have obligatory integration requirements for permanent residency are Austria, the Czech Republic, Denmark, Germany, France, Greece, Italy, the Netherlands, Portugal, the UK,

[6] Article 7 (2) OJ L251/12-251/18; 3.10.2003, 2003/86/EC. Some EU countries, such as Denmark, are not bound by the Directive but still have to comply with other international norms, such as the UCHR, that protect the right to family life. See, eg, Guild et al 2009: 14.

[7] Article 5 (2) OJ L16-44; 23. 1. 2004, 2003/109/EC. Denmark is also not bound by this Directive.

[8] The LTR Directive also contains the notion 'integration measures' (Art 15(3)) as part of the provision specifying the conditions for residence of a long-term residence permit holder in a second Member State. This does not apply to TCNs who have been required to comply with integration conditions in order to be granted long-term resident status (Carrera and Vankova 2019: 19).

Cyprus, Croatia, Estonia, Latvia, Lithuania, Malta and Romania (Pascouau 2014: 92; Solano and Huddleston 2020).

In addition, requirements for naturalisation increased across Europe. At first glance, this might only seem to be a slight increase. In 2010, 22 of the current 28 EU countries had implemented such tests; while 20 of the 28 countries already had a language condition in 1998. Yet, on closer comparison, of the 22 countries that used these tests in 2010, 16 had adopted *formalised* language tests, whereas in 1998 only 6 had such formalised tests (Goodman 2010a: 16). In addition, citizenship tests (mostly testing 'knowledge of society') were applied in 6 of the present 28 countries in 1999. In 4 countries, these tests were formalised. By 2010, that number increased to 15, of which 11 were formalised (Goodman 2010a: 16–17). Overall, recent studies determined that today, Austria, Belgium, the Czech Republic, Denmark, Germany, Finland, France, Greece, Hungary, Italy, Luxembourg, the Netherlands, Poland, Portugal, Slovakia, Estonia, the UK, Cyprus, Croatia, Estonia, Latvia, Lithuania, Malta and Romania have at least one integration requirement (either language or civic or both, either formalised or not) as a prerequisite for citizenship (EMN 2020: 19–20; Solano and Huddleston 2020).

That said, as mentioned in the Introduction, in virtually all European countries integration requirements as conditions for attaining increased rights are a remarkable dynamic policy field that is subject to constant changes: national laws on the (number of) requirements, costs, imposed sanctions and time given to complete them are frequently amended (Pascouau 2014: 92). The procedures for TCNs to obtain certain residency and citizenship rights therefore differ between EU nation-states and the differences are also subject to (in some countries almost constant) adjustments.[9] As a result, to obtain permanent residency rights, it may or may not be required to pass language and citizenship tests of varying content and difficulty. Family reunification in some countries is made contingent on integration requirements, while in others it is not.[10] In relation to naturalisation, binding EU standards are wholly absent and integration requirements differ between the Member States. However, no EU country fully blocks the path to naturalisation and the *European Convention on Nationality* signed by multiple EU countries provides that the period of residence for access to naturalisation cannot be more than ten years of lawful and habitual residence.[11] Yet, although this Council of Europe Convention

[9] On that account, the prediction of Yasemin Soysal in her book *Limits of Citizenship* (1994) that the nation-state would become less relevant as the generator of rights due to forms of post-national membership that would secure equal rights irrespective of national citizenship statuses, has not (yet) been fulfilled in relation to residency and citizenship rights. However, EU and human rights law and the Directives discussed in this chapter do unmistakably weaken the position of the nation-state as the sole centre of political decision-making on issues of immigration and the treatment of residing immigrants.

[10] In all Member States, the right to family reunification concentrates on the 'nuclear family': spouses and minor children. Other requirements differ. For example, some countries such as Austria and the Netherlands set a minimum age requirement for spouses of 21 years. And Portugal and the UK allow family reunification of registered partners or unmarried couples who can prove they have a subsisting relationship, but other states only allow it for registered partners.

[11] Article 6(3), Council of Europe, European Convention on Nationality, 6 November 1997, ETS 166.

is the most authoritative European document regarding nationality, it has not been signed and ratified by all EU countries.

In any case, the novelty of the legal circumstances triggered by the Family and LTR Directives is that European states increasingly *oblige* certain TCNs to follow a structured path to secure residency, in which integration is utilised as the formal condition to obtain these. Before the 1990s, most European countries worked with vaguely defined qualifications such as a 'connection to the community' or a 'willingness to integrate' to allocate permanent residency and citizenship rights. These criteria were often based on discretionary decisions by public servants after an informal interview, by completing the relevant paperwork in the language of the host society or merely based on the length of residency. For this reason, it has been argued that the introduction of more formalised citizenship tests has made the conditions under which TCNs can obtain civic inclusion more transparent and limited the state discretion to deny this (Miller 2016: 129). However, in tandem with this tendency to implement a collection of formal instruments to measure an applicant's obligatory integration, the sanctions for non-compliance with integration policies were formalised as well. Increasingly, the integration laws in multiple EU Member States stipulate that the non-fulfilment of mandatory integration requirements for TCNs may lead to fines, revoking, refusal to issue or denied renewal of residency permits and/or having no access to, or loss of, social benefits (eg, Kostakopoulou 2010b: 951; Pascouau 2014: 58; Strik and Pascouau 2012: 341). To provide more insight in the outcomes of these policy changes and formalisations, I will discuss the two EU Directives that enable Member States to install integration requirements and explore the motives behind their implementation. Subsequently, I will briefly discuss integration requirements for naturalisation in EU states.

A. Family Reunification

In response to the Family Reunification Directive, five EU countries thus installed pre-departure integration or 'integration abroad' requirements for family migrants (the Netherlands, Germany, the UK, Austria and France). That said, France repealed this requirement in 2016 and now requires family members to sign a 'Republican Integration Contract' *after* arrival that, amongst other things, requires them to take free language lessons (Solano and Huddleston 2020: France).[12] Be that as it may, integration requirements abroad are prescribed for individuals with a claim to family migration to obtain the relevant paperwork to be allowed to effectively migrate. These integration requirements are hence not open for all individuals interested in migration but are a prerequisite for specifically family

[12] Denmark, that is not bound by the Family Directive, has a similar policy. It grants applicants a shot-time visa of 28 days to pass a language test on Danish territory. For this exam, nationals from the US, Canada, Australia, Israel, Japan, New Zealand, Switzerland and South Korea are exempted. See Strik and Pascouau 2012: 400; Solano and Huddleston 2020: Denmark.

members and spouses whose right to family migration has already been recognised by the receiving state. Mostly, these requirements test minimal levels of language acquisition and/or knowledge of the receiving societies.

The arguments used in political debates on these pre-departure integration requirements and their conditions vary in the various EU countries that installed them and change over time (Scholten et al 2012; Pascouau 2014: 33–50) Nonetheless, during (national) parliamentary debates they have been defended as facilitating the successful integration of those to be included. Particularly migrant (Muslim) women who were relatively often mentioned as the specific target group. The pre-departure tests were expected to ensure that fewer of them would eventually become a burden on the receiving welfare state (Strik et al 2013: 41). The UK and Austria decided to apply their 'integration requirements abroad' to specific countries based on expected (English/German) language proficiency. Germany and the Netherlands based the applicability of their integration requirements abroad on cultural and political-economic grounds (Scholten et al 2012: 26, 89).[13] However, at times, policymakers, legislators and governments also acknowledged that the tests were put in place to deter 'unwanted immigration' (France) (Joppke 2007: 11) or as 'selection criteria' (the Netherlands) (Scholten et al 2012: 12).

However, importantly, from a legal perspective, the integration measures abroad for family migrants allowed by the Family Directive are not supposed to function as a tool for selecting migrants, but to promote family migration (Van Oers 2013: 132). For this reason, in 2008[14] the European Commission was critical of how the Family Directive was implemented by some countries and re-emphasised that the aim of these measures should be to 'facilitate the integration of family members', not to thwart family migration or prevent legal acceptance into the state structures (see Bonjour 2014: 214). Moreover, in 2014, the Commission, again, explained that the Family Directive does not permit integration requirements that are a measure 'that limits the possibility of family reunification'. Instead, these measures should contribute to the success of family reunification. It continued that 'integration measures must be proportionate and applied with the necessary flexibility' and are not meant as 'an absolute condition upon which the right to family reunification is dependent'.[15] The CJEU criticised the Dutch integration requirements abroad in 2015 in its *K and A* judgment. In a nutshell, it ruled that integration requirements should not undermine the objective of the Family Directive, which is to promote family migration.[16] More particularly it stated that: 'integration measures must be aimed not at filtering those persons who will be able to exercise their right

[13] In Denmark (see previous footnote), nationals from the US, Canada, Australia, Israel, Japan, New Zealand, Switzerland and South Korea are exempted. See Strik and Pascouau 2012, 400.

[14] Report from the Commission to the European Parliament and the Council on the Application of Directive 2003/86/EC on the Right to Family Reunification (COM (2008) 610 final).

[15] Communication from the Commission to the European Parliament and the Council on guidance for application of Directive 2003/86/EC on the right to family reunification. (COM (2014) 210 final): 15–16.

[16] Case C-153/14 *Minister van Buitenlandse zaken v K and A*, [51].

to family reunification, but facilitating the integration of such persons within the Member States'.[17] Furthermore, the Court stated that although EU Member States may require TCNs to pass an integration examination prior to family reunification, these requirements can 'be considered legitimate only if they are capable of facilitating [...] integration' and if they ensure that the right to family life remains 'exercisable'. For this reason, exemptions must be made in cases in which applicants cannot take or pass the requirements by taking specific matters into account such as age, illiteracy, educational level, economic situation, and health of the family member.[18] In 2010, the CJEU reflected a similar positive attitude towards family migration in its *Chakroun* ruling. In this case, the Court ruled that the Dutch income requirement of 120 per cent of the minimum wage for family migration, is not permitted by the Family Directive. The Court stated that the Directive should be interpreted in accordance with human rights (in particular, the right to family life in the ECHR and the EU Charter of Fundamental Rights). In addition, it stated Member States should not use their discretion to undercut the objectives of the Directive, which is to allow family migration.[19]

Nevertheless, empirical research indicates that the pre-departure tests of EU states do tend to have exclusionary effects: after their installation, the numbers of granted visas for family reunification have significantly decreased (Groenendijk 2011: 23; Strik et al 2010: 30; Scholten et al 2012: 79–81, see also Human Rights Watch 2008). For example, applications from Turkey and Serbia in Germany, and from Morocco and Ghana in the Netherlands decreased significantly. Moreover, it turns out that these integration requirements are more difficult to meet for women, poorly educated people, certain nationalities and ethnic groups and elderly people (Strik et al 2010: 44). The observed decrease is the result of a combination of, on the one side, people failing to meet the conditions and, on the other side, people refraining from applying for family migration in the first place. The exact number of this latter (indirect) curtailment of family migration is difficult to measure. But given the immediate decline of applicants after the implementation of these mandatory integration requirements, Scholten et al (2012) concluded that we may safely assume that this is the case. Accordingly, they wrote in their review of pre-departure integration measures in Germany, the Netherlands, the UK and Austria that 'their integration effects seem modest at best, [... and their ...] immigration effects more significant' (39). Along the same lines, Huddleston (2011) concludes that integration requirements 'do not significantly help successfully reuniting families to integrate much faster into their new country of residence. On the contrary, they are 'more effective for limiting the number of reuniting families' (1).[20] Also the MIPEX 2015 stated that pre-entry requirements for family

[17] Ibid, [52].

[18] Ibid, [58].

[19] Case C-578/08 *Chakroun v Minister van Buitenlandse Zaken*, [43].

[20] This analysis of Huddleston also applies to high fees, income requirements and age limits for spouses as conditions for family migration.

migration 'do not actually promote integration' but 'are more effective for limiting the number of reuniting families' and 'have a disproportionate impact on the most vulnerable groups: the elderly, young adults, the less educated, people in certain – often unstable – countries and, – to some extent – women' (Huddleston et al 2015; family reunion).

In summary, the 'integration requirements abroad' enacted by EU Member States based on the Family Reunification Directive should de jure not form an impediment on family reunification to Europe, but research suggests that de facto they do reduce the number of family migrants to countries that adopted such legislation. However, formally, integration measures should not form an obstacle to family reunification, but rather facilitate the integration of the applicant.

B. Obtaining Permanent Residency

The LTR Directive gives Member States the discretion to make permanent residency after five years of uninterrupted residence contingent on integration requirements stipulated by national laws. However, in the report of the European Commission to the European Parliament and the Council on the application of the Directive, it is clarified that Member States should ensure that the requirements 'must be in line with the purpose of the Directive' which is 'fostering the integration of long-time residents' and 'must take due account of the general principles of EU law such as the principle of preserving effectiveness ('effet utile') and the proportionality principle' (see also Van Oers 2013: 244).[21] In this context, it is important to also consider a key rule of the Directive that can be found in Article 4, paragraph 1, which provides that 'long-term resident status shall be granted to third-country nationals who have resided legally and continuously within the territory of a Member State for five years immediately prior to the submission of the relevant application'. This implies that these TCNs receive a secure residency status after five years of continuous legal residence and that there are only a limited number of grounds on which this can be withheld or withdrawn (eg, serious threat to public safety, Article 9, paragraph 1(c)). Arguably, based on EU law, it hence seems a disproportional measure to deny TCNs permanent residency based on the sole reason of failing to meet integration requirements (Groenendijk 2006: 224). Nonetheless, as we have seen, after the LTR Directive came into force, a majority of Member States made the acquisition of long-term residency for TCNs strictly dependent on integration requirements, mostly in the form of introduction courses, language and/or civic tests and loyalty oaths (Goodman 2010a: 765;

[21] Report from the Commission to the European Parliament and the Council on the application of Directive 2003/109/EC concerning the status of third-country nationals who are long-term residents. (COM (2011) 585). The CJEU also repeated this consideration in its *Kamberaj* ruling, see Case C-571/10 Servet Kamberaj v Istituto per l'Edilizia Sociale della Provincia autonoma di Bolzano (IPES) and Others.

Pascouau 2014; Carrera and Vankova 2019). In turn, if TCNs fail to meet these conditions, the established sanctions by national laws are the imposition of fines, the lowering or withdrawal of social benefits or the non-renewal or withdrawal of residence permits.

However, if we look at the most far-reaching sanction for failing integration requirements as requisites for obtaining permanent residency a nuanced picture emerges. To examine the legal characteristics and limits of these requirements, it is informative to start with an assessment of these most significant punitive measures. In Austria, the first policy that enabled deportations on grounds of non-fulfilment of integration requirements was enacted in 2003 and stayed in force until the end of 2010. In these seven years, only three persons were threatened with deportation, of which one eventually left the country voluntarily. The other two appealed or managed to successfully complete the mandatory course after receiving a warning (Permoser 2012: 193–198).[22] In the Netherlands, the obtaining of permanent residency was made contingent on integration requirements in 2010 and since 2013 the law states that failing the 'duty to integrate' due to 'negligence' can lead to a non-renewal or the revoking of temporary residency rights after three years (Besselsen and De Hart 2014).[23] However, in 2016 it turned out that not a single TCN who failed to pass all integration requirements was actually forced to leave the Netherlands, nor that this was expected to change (Besselsen and De Hart 2014: 24; Netherlands Court of Audit 2017). Lastly, in Germany, not integrating due to negligence ('wiederholter and gröblicher Verletzung der Plichten') can lead to the non-renewal of residency permits.[24] However, Groenendijk notes that, so far, there are only three of such rulings to be found (in 2007, 2011 and 2012) (2019: 280).

How can these low numbers of actual expulsions be explained? The answer is that the mandatory integration requirements based on the LTR Directive predominately affect family migrants and refugees.[25] However, both family migrants and refugees are strongly protected against deportation by EU laws and international human right norms. Family migrants are admitted and reside based on their right to family life, articulated in inter alia Article 8 of the ECHR (and the Family Directive). The residency rights of refugees are protected by the well-known *non-refoulement* principle enshrined in inter alia Article 33 of the Refugee Convention.

[22] Bundesgesetz über die Ausübung der Fremdenpolizei, die Ausstellung von Dokumenten für Fremde und die Erteilung von Einreisetitel (Fremdenpolizeigesetz 2005 – FPG). BGBl. I Nr. 100/2005 zuletzt geändert durch BGBl. I Nr. 112/2011, §62(2). It must be noted that since 2010 a more restrictive integration regime is implemented, but although the effects are not thoroughly academically researched yet, Permoser (2012) also deems the threat of deportation in this bill, first and foremost, to also be a form of what she calls 'symbolic politics'.

[23] Art 18 (1) sub I, Art 9 Vreemdelingenwet 2000.

[24] See §8(4) Aufenthaltsgesetz.

[25] Other groups, such as TCNs who reside on work visas, are not mandated to pass integration requirements, but if they try to pass them to obtain permanent residency – for example, because they want to secure residency rights independent of their work – and fail they most often do not lose their residency (ie their work visas).

This makes it impossible for European states to 'expel a refugee in any manner whatsoever to the frontiers of territories where her life or freedom would be threatened'. To be sure, *non-refoulement* does not entail that refugees can *never* be sent to their home countries. Yet, this will never depend solely on the fulfilment of integration requirements, but on whether the conditions in their home country sustainably improve and/or sources of persecution or danger disappear. In EU Member States, this possibility for forced return remains open up to five years. After that period, refugees can apply for a permanent residency permit based on the LTR Directive, although gaining this status can thus be made contingent on integration requirements. But if the *non-refoulement* principle applies, the expulsion of a refugee to unsafe territory – for whatever reason – is illegal and would be blocked by (domestic and international) courts.

On that account, the crux (for the purposes of this research) is that Member States such as Austria, the Netherlands and Germany threaten to expulse precisely those TCNs for failing to fulfil integration requirements, who are legally virtually undeportable due to protection of EU laws and international treaties. Put differently, although cases of expulsion occur, these are so rare that it is clear that integration requirements do not function as selective immigration policies determining who is allowed to reside on the territory. Remarkably, academic commentators concur that the governments of EU countries that decided to threaten TCNs with deportation in case of non-fulfilment of integration requirements, have always been aware of these constitutional limitations. Julia Permoser, for example, suggests that Austria mainly installed the integration policy in this way to send 'the restrictive message that the government is controlling and reducing immigration' and not 'to achieve these material effects' (Permoser 2012: 173). She concludes that the seemingly 'tough' integration requirements are forms of 'symbolic politics' to 'keep the myth of sovereignty alive' (197). And indeed, the Austrian Government continues to implement these restrictive measures, even though it must now be aware that international law prevents them from actually deporting TCNs. Furthermore, Elles Besselsen and Betty de Hart observe that in 2011 the responsible Dutch minister of Immigration, Integration and Asylum, while defending the law in the Dutch Senate, in fact reassured that deportations would only occur rarely, if at all, as the affected newcomers were protected from deportation by international and EU law (Besselsen and De Hart 2015: 24).

This outcome is illuminating as it demonstrates that the most drastic result for TCNs who fail to meet mandatory integration requirements in Europe is virtually never expulsion. Rather, as Sarah Goodman and Matthew Wright put it, TCNs are 'not deported' but 'placed in a feedback loop of conditionality' (Goodman and Wright 2015: 1903) This 'feedback loop of conditionality' entails that TCNs that do not complete prescribed integration requirements must reside in provisional legal statuses and with temporary residency rights for longer periods of time. Put differently, integration requirements have the ability to impede residing TCNs to upgrade their temporary residency status to a secure and permanent one. And indeed, for example in Austria, the non-compliance with the Austrian mandatory 'integration contract' for TCNs leads to receiving a one-year residency permit (instead of permanent residency), to be renewed annually. While having this permit, TCNs are however 'excluded from the rights to equal treatment granted to long-term residents, including the right to unrestricted labour market access, social security payments, council (social) housing and education assistance' (Perchining 2010: 60).

To be sure, this is not to imply that integration requirements connected to obtaining permanent residency rights are therefore inconsequential, do not affect residency rights and are not punitive. First, these laws can pose a threat to secure residence under certain specific circumstances. Take for example the situation in which a family migrant's marriage ends before the husband completed his integration trajectory to obtain permanent residency (or naturalisation) successfully. In this situation, it is possible that temporary residency rights that were contingent on the relationship with the spouse are revoked, while 'independent' residency rights are not yet acquired. Moreover, Member States have the discretion based on the Family Directive to make the temporary residency requirement perpetually contingent on the income requirement. As a result, if integration requirements hamper TCNs to acquire permanent residency, they are longer at risk of fully losing their residency rights if they, often unexpectedly and unhoped-for, start to earn less than the prescribed income requirement (Besselsen and De Hart 2015: 21).

Second, currently, it is an open question of what will happen to the residency rights of refugees in the (near) future if the safety conditions of their country of origin improve after, say, nine years, and they have not succeeded in obtaining permanent residency (after five years) due to the non-fulfilment of integration requirements. Will their temporary refugee status then still be terminated, in light of the improved conditions in their country of origin and the failure to obtain a permanent residency permit? It is doubtful whether this outcome would be in line with the EU principle of proportionality. But the current national laws of the Member States that installed integrated requirements for permanent residency do suggest the answer to this question should be affirmative. However, at the same time, we have seen, the LTR Directive also stipulates that after five years of uninterrupted residence TCNs should in principle be able to obtain permanent residency (see also Arcarazo 2015; Stronks 2017: 38–39).

Lastly, if TCNs indeed end up in a 'feedback loop of conditionality', this is punitive as it delays the moment at which secure residency rights can be obtained. Put differently, these policies have the capacity to extend the period of time in which persons reside with a legally precarious position while lacking predictability about the trajectory of their future life. One of the results of the integration requirements allowed by the LTR Directive is therefore that they produce forms of what can be described as 'prolonged legal provisionality' or even 'permanent legal provisionality'. In the academic literature, this is also described as the institutionalised production of 'precarity' through migration status (eg, Goldring et al 2009). This involves a form of generalised insecurity and precarious existence, which is often psychologically burdensome, due to living in a state of unpredictability caused by, in this case, residential insecurity. Future prospects remain perpetually contingent on the (non-)fulfilment of integration requirements. Moreover, the bureaucracy and paperwork that is required to, for example, annually renew residency rights is also often experienced as burdensome and stressful. However, crucially, these forms of precarity barely have effect on the physical composition of the residing population as deportations are blocked by EU and human rights laws. The integration requirements mainly affect the types of legal residency status (often connected to packages of social rights) that parts of the residing population have, but virtually do not change who actually lives within society at large (Lægaard 2010: 459).

That said, the exact legal limitations of integration requirements for permanent residency authorised by the LTR Directive remain to a degree elusive (De Vries 2019). Are all forms of 'legal provisionality' and precarity in breach of the principles of effectiveness and proportionally referred to by the European Commission, or is this to a degree legally permissible? On this question, the CJEU formulated some guidelines, when it ruled in 2015 on the *P and S* case that 'the Directive does not preclude the imposition of the obligation to pass a civic integration examination, provided that the means of implementing that obligation are not liable to jeopardise the achievement of the objectives pursued by the Directive'[26] of which the principal objective is 'the integration of third country nationals who are settled on a long-term basis in the Member State'.[27] To ensure this, it continued, the Member States should take into account 'the level of knowledge required to pass the examination, [...] the accessibility of the courses and material necessary to prepare for that examination, [...] the amount of registration fees, or [...] the consideration of specific individual circumstances, such as age, illiteracy or level of education'.[28] More particularly, the Court gave the instruction to verify if the costs incurred by integration examinations are liable to jeopardise the achievement of the objectives pursued by the Directive and, therefore, deprive it of its effectiveness. More recent case law reaffirms these standards. In its *C&A* ruling, the Court emphasised again that integration requirements 'cannot legitimately go beyond what is necessary to attain the objective of facilitating the integration' of TCNs 'the knowledge required to pass the civic integration examination' should be at 'a basic level' and that 'the condition imposed by national legislation does not lead to an autonomous residence permit not being granted to third country nationals who have demonstrated their willingness to pass the examination and made every effort to achieve that objective'.[29] In its *K* ruling, the Court repeated this once more.[30]

[26] Case 579/13 *P and S v Commissie Sociale Zekerheid Breda, College van Burgermeester en Wethouders van de gemeente Amstelveen*, [66].

[27] Ibid, [44].

[28] Ibid, [81].

[29] Case 257/17, 2018 *C and A v Staatssecretaris van Veiligheid en Justitie*, [63].

[30] Case 484/17, 2018 *K v Staatssecretaris van Veiligheid en Justitie*, [22]–[24]. See also Report from the Commission to the Parliament and the Council on the implementation of Directive 2003/109/EC concerning the status of third-country nationals who are long-term residents: 8.

Ergo, the perspective of the CJEU involves that Member States are legally authorised by the LTR Directive to prescribe integration requirements for TCNs as conditions for permanent residency as these are, in principle, beneficial and support the inclusionary purposes of the Directive. However, as soon as integration requirements become overly demanding or expensive and in fact start to undermine these purposes, they are legally not compliant with the LTR Directive. From a legal perspective, these integration requirements should thus not serve as strict *criteria* for whether TCNs may attain permanent residency in the first place. Instead, they should function as means to facilitate that long-term residents acquire knowledge of the language and society relevant to successfully participate and function in the receiving Member State. Nevertheless, the Court also affirms, most directly in its *C&A* ruling, that EU law does allow Member States to reject an application for an autonomous residence permit if a TCN has not passed civic integration requirements, if (and only if) the detailed rules on the conditions to pass that examination 'do not go beyond what is necessary to attain the objective of facilitating the integration of those third country nationals'.[31]

On that account, the conclusion of some commentators, including Acosta Arcarazo, that the LTR Directive has created a 'post-national form of membership' and a 'subsidiary form of EU Citizenship' (Arcarazo 2015) that limits the control of Member States on matters of legal inclusion possesses a kernel of truth, but is at the same time not nuanced enough. Member States can still, to a certain extent, regulate under which conditions TCNs can obtain permanent residency (or not): TCNs surely do not automatically receive secure residency after five years of residence based on EU laws and certain integration requirements are permitted and even deemed valuable. Yet these conditions captured in national legislation should further integration purposes and not exclude TCNs for reasons beyond their control (eg, age, literacy, sickness, etc). For this reason, if integration requirements lead to situations in which TCNs perpetually fail to obtain permanent residency rights and clearly undermine their participation, these forms of 'permanent legal provisionality' undermine the objectives of the Directive. The legality of integration requirements for TCNs for permanent residency depends on their effectiveness in supporting the wider integration of TCNs. Or phrased differently, if integration requirements prevent, rather than facilitate, the effective integration of TCNs, they violate the Directive.

Against the background of all this information on the Family Directive, LTR Directive, available case law and EU Charter of Fundamental Rights, Sergio Carrera and Zvezda Vankova created a 'toolbox' to determine the legality of integration requirements in a report for the Council of Europe on human rights

[31] Case 257/17, 2018 *C and A v Staatssecretaris van Veiligheid en Justitie*, [72].

aspects of integration policies. The standards they list, that apply to both integration requirements abroad as after arrival, are as follows (Carrera and Vankova 2019: 20–21):

1. Integration policies should aim to facilitate and promote family reunification.
2. They should not constitute an additional restriction to family reunification and thus unlawfully pursue migration-control aiming to filter and limit family reunification. [...]
3. Integration policies should allow for [...] case-by-case assessment in view of specific circumstances, such as 'age, illiteracy, level of education, economic situation or health' [...] In addition, Member states should provide the effective possibility of an exemption, a deferral or other forms of integration measures in cases involving certain specific issues or personal circumstances of the immigrant in question. Specific individual circumstances that may be taken into account are: cognitive abilities, the vulnerability of the person in question, special cases of inaccessibility of teaching or testing facilities, or other situations of exceptional hardship, such as for instance countries of origin, where women and girls have less access to education and might have a lower literacy level than men and boys.
4. Restrictions must be interpreted restrictively and should not make the exercise of the rights guaranteed by the EU migration law too difficult to exercise in practice, especially when they are based on derogations to EU rights and fundamental freedoms of third-country nationals.
5. Integration policies should be proportional, and the proportionality test criteria should cover their accessibility, design and organisation [...].

C. Naturalisation

As noted, there is no overarching set of EU regulations for citizenship that apply to all European Member States. So far, naturalisation remains carefully protected as 'the last bastion of national state sovereignty' for Member States in the EU (Brubaker 1992: 180). As a result, understanding who can become a national within a Member State requires analysis and case studies of specific national laws (see, eg, Bauböck et al 2006; Goodman 2010b; EMN 2020). In some countries, such as Germany, there are also differences between provinces (*Länder*). Nevertheless, the explanatory report of the European Convention on Nationality stresses that its provision stipulating that the permissible period of ten years of lawful and habitual residence before naturalisation, reflects a common European standard, as most European countries already require a period between five and ten years of residence.[32] Additionally, during the last 50 years, EU countries have liberalised parts of their naturalisation schemes, for example by increasingly tolerating dual citizenship and complementing their jus sanguinis citizenship with jus

[32] European Convention on Nationality, Explanatory report, Strasbourg, 6.XI.1997, para 51.

soli citizenship regimes (Joppke 2013: CH2; Schmid 2021; see also EMN 2020).[33] However, for TCNs in EU states it is never obligatory to naturalise, as they can choose to (merely) obtain or retain permanent residency. It is not attractive for persons to naturalise, for example, if they want to retain the citizenship of their country of birth and the receiving state does not tolerate dual citizenship or if (integration) requirements for naturalisation are deemed to be too onerous (see, eg, Bauböck and Goodman 2011 for the requirement of renunciation of previous nationality). Moreover, according to the EMN 'in most Member States, third-country nationals are not actively encouraged to apply for citizenship, and support is limited' (2020: 34). Yet if a TCN naturalises, she obtains equal citizenship and becomes a formal equal member of the state. She loses her lesser legal status of '(permanent) resident' and receives the same package of rights as other citizens, including the right to vote at national elections and to hold a passport. In principle, naturalisation is perceived as irreversible.

Most Member States have applied some sort of language or integration conditions for naturalisation for more than 50 years (Guild et al 2009: 8). Nonetheless, we have seen that in the last quarter of a century more formalised integration requirements were installed because in multiple European countries the perception grew that it had been 'too easy' to naturalise (Strik et al 2010: 307). Access to citizenship should only be possible, it was argued, at the end of a completed integration process. Naturalisation should be seen as 'very special' and the 'first prize' for immigrants in society and something to be 'earned' (Van Oers 2013: 51; Van Houdt et al 2011). For example, in Denmark the minister of Integration insisted that 'citizenship is not just a piece of paper, but a declaration of belonging' and defended the new citizenship test as a means to 'make sure that […] new citizens love Denmark and prefer Denmark' (Mouritsen 2013: 98).

In this context, Ricky van Oers conducted research on the effects of citizenship tests in Germany, the Netherlands and the UK (2013; 2020). She observed that in all these countries the introduction of formalised language and knowledge of society requirements have led to a decrease in the number of naturalisations, both in terms of the absolute number of TCNs that apply for citizenship and the relative number of applicants who successfully pass a citizenship test (Van Oers 2013: 276). On that account, she concludes:

> Despite the difference in the way the tests are shaped and implemented, formalized language and integration tests are destined to lead to lower numbers of citizenship acquisitions. Hence, no matter what context the tests have, what the scope of the rules on exemption is, what possibilities for preparation are provided, and in what way the test is taken, a certain part of the immigrant population was excluded from citizenship

[33] Jus sanguinis (Latin for 'right of blood') is a principle of nationality law by which citizenship is determined by having one or both parents who are parents of the state. Jus Soli (Latin for 'right of the soil') is a principle of nationality by which citizenship is determined by being born within the territory of a state.

> and the accompanying rights the moment formalized language and integration tests were introduced. (277)

Along the same line, Stella Burch Elias observes that while the number of long-term immigrants to Germany, the Netherlands and France has remained relatively constant over the last two decades, the number of naturalisations decreased due to restrictions on naturalisation in the form of integration requirements and citizenship tests. In the UK the number of naturalisation applicants decreased from nearly 37,000 in 2002 to 50 per cent of this number in 2006 (Elias 2016: 2131).

II. Integration: Old and New

In the previous section, we have seen that the legal trends in EU Member States regarding integration requirements have changed significantly over the past two decades. In this section, I describe the conceptual shift that supported these legal changes and that changed the very idea of how integration is understood in public policy, public debate and daily speech. Indeed, the concept of 'integration' is not a new one in European debate – in fact, concerns about integration have been a perennial issue for social scientists and policy makers for over two centuries. However, as we will see, the meaning of integration has changed from being a property of society as a whole to being a condition of particular individuals. In later chapters, I will focus on how we should normatively evaluate policies that impose obligations on those who are already in a precarious legal position (Chapter 2) and their effects on the ambition of liberal-democratic states to uphold a 'community of equals' (Chapter 3). In this section, however, my aim is to introduce these two different conceptions of integration, to be able to show in the next section that the proliferation of legal integration requirements in multiple EU Member States is tied up with the increased visibility and salience of an individualised conception of integration. The contemporary individualised conceptualisation of integration will be elaborated upon more extensively, given its current ramifications on public integration policy.

A. Integration as a Condition of Society

The term and notion of 'integration' traditionally resonated with how the concept was employed in the functionalist tradition in sociology as propagated by scholars such as Émile Durkheim and Talcott Parsons. To be clear, this does not mean that public commentators or policy makers referred to these specific thinkers nor that these thinkers themselves fully agreed on what integration entails. For example, Durkheim searched strongly for shared normative values such as a 'common will to live together' (see Allan 2005: 136), while others, such as Parsons, searched more empirically how subgroups systematically interact in various spheres in society (see, eg, Gerhardt 2016: 33–34). However, the shared characteristics of these conceptualisations of 'integration' is that they discussed the notion as applicable to *collectives*. To be more specific, 'integration' was used to discuss how societies maintain their social cohesion and keep individuals and groups connected in networks of social relations. It rested on the assumption that modern societies form a unity, that is, a collective ensemble pertaining a combination of individuals and subgroups that are in constant reciprocal processes of communal socialisation. Within these processes, the state was often seen as the centre of coordination (Bader 2001: 132).

About this perspective on integration Michel Wieviorka (2014) writes:

> This sociology [...] regards social integration and subscription to shared values and the density of interaction between members of the groups or society as far more important than the analysis of individuals of individuals as such [...] Durkheimian or functionalist sociology [...] aims at the integration of individuals in society and the integration of society as a whole (635).

Theoretically, the term 'integration' was therefore opposed to social distances, group segregations or forms of personal alienation and anomie.[34] Note that this implies that, from this holistic perspective, both groups and individuals would surely be relevant to debates on integration. However, crucially, it discussed them as (potentially) participating in societal systems, in such a way that society is perceived as functioning as an organic holistic entity (Repstad and Furseth 2013: 34). Put differently, from this perspective, integration concerns individuals and subgroups and their position in societal networks, yet not in the sense that only they should be influenced separately (or 'individually integrated'). Rather, integration describes the social mechanisms that keep individuals and groups interacting as a whole, which is always more than the sum of its parts.

Of course, it is debatable whether societies were ever factually reducible to such organic images of societies and it is particularly doubtful whether modern pluralistic societies are driven by only a few general mechanisms of coordination, operating in ways comparable to 'machines' or 'organic entities'. It might be more accurate to describe 'societies' in terms of loosely connected 'patchworks' or even as detached 'heaps of sand' (Bader 2001:133). However, whether accurate or not, for decades this holistic interpretation of integration (and connected interpretations of disintegration) created a fertile academic research agenda and public vocabulary to consider degrees of social cohesion, together with all sorts of societal distances, social exclusions and group segregations that often affected

[34] Durkheim popularised the term 'anomie' in this influential book *Suicide* in 1897 (2018). It occurs if 'society provides little moral guidance to individuals' (Macionis and Gerber 2010: 97), for example, due to the fragmentation of social identity and the rejection of self-regulatory values. Karl Marx described 'alienation' as a form of Entfremdung (estrangement) that is the consequence of being a mechanistic part of a social class and living in a heavily class stratified society. See, inter alia, his Economic and Philosophical Manuscripts (1844).

a variety of vulnerable, marginalised and disadvantaged groups. This research, for instance, highlighted the position of single women, the disabled, the elderly and the young in relation to their access to housing, education or work. Integration concerns hence did not exclusively pertain to immigrants as 'immigrants, much like everyone else, are always excluded and included at the same time, [...] as sectorial players or agents with specific assets and habitual dispositions within specific fields or systems' (Joppke and Morawska 2003: 3).

Within this framework integration was thus something to be achieved at the level of the collective, not at the level of subgroups or individuals. Therefore, the political ideal of 'integration' initially had two crucial elements. First, the notion was applied to and a property of *society as a whole*. Second, the notion entailed a process of *communal socialisation of all its members.*

B. Integration as a Condition of Individuals

These two elements of integration have gradually moved to the background in policy documents, public debates and daily speech. Today, on the one side, 'integration' predominately involves a personal condition that individuals with non-EU and non-Western migrant backgrounds and their descendants should achieve and, on the other side, serves as a criterion for assessing whether these individuals *belong* to the society in which they reside. Christian Joppke has argued that the targeted population of integration discourses and civic integration policies is even more specific, namely mostly Muslim, but this is difficult to substantiate because this is, to my knowledge, not made explicit in policy documents (see, eg, Joppke 2009; see also Prins 2011: 67; FitzGerald et al 2018). In any case, it became uncommon (or even strange) to discuss whether, say, the 'Dutch society' or 'Austrian society' is integrated or not, while it became rather common to discuss the personal integration of, for example, Hussein, Mohammad or Fatima.

It must be noted that it is also common to say that certain immigrant *groups* are not integrated. This is because measurements of immigrant integration are often aggregated at group-level data (Schinkel 2018: 3). On that account, certain individuals are confronted with integration measurements and expectations based on non-individualistic grounds, that is, based on being part of a specific (most often ethnic) immigrant group. However, 'integration' itself is expected to be achieved at the individual level. In particular, if integration is discussed currently, it is most likely that the conversation is about non-Western, non-EU immigrants and/or their descendants and focuses on their individual *compatibility* with (a created image of) 'society' (Schinkel 2017, 2009: 25; Driouichi 2007).

This conceptualisation of integration has manifested itself in public debate, but also affected academic studies. To give an example, sociologist Evelyn Ersanilli and Ruud Koopmans consider Muslim practices as 'eating halal food', 'participating in the Ramadan' and 'wearing a headscarf' as indications of non-integration for Turkish immigrants in Germany, France and the Netherlands (Ersanilli and

Koopmans 2011: 217). To defend this research framework, their analysis states that they 'treat Islamic religiosity as part of cultural retention since Islam is the dominant religion in Turkey but not in any of the host countries'. Again, this is merely one example (focusing on religious practices[35]), but it does show several important aspects of the expanding contemporary perspective on integration and what it expects of whom.

First, integration is fully measured at the individual level and evaluated based on personal characteristics, acts, habits and outlooks. Ersanilli and Koopmans contend that if a person with an (non-EU) immigrant background adheres to certain Islamic traditions, this fact *in itself* provides information about the lesser degree of integration of this person. However, from a societal perspective on integration, compliance with Islamic norms as such, does not tell much about integration outcomes. It would, in this context, be more informative to measure whether (non-EU) newcomers are socially isolated or segregated, individually or at the level of their subgroup, and whether their religious practices have positive or negative effects on this. In other words, from a societal perspective on integration, characteristics of groups and individuals are relevant to the extent that they have an impact on societal mechanisms that keep groups and individuals interacting as a whole that is more than its parts. If we look for example at the measured aspects by Ersanilli and Koopmans (see footnote 35), all these aspects one-sidedly ask personal attitudes and orientations on the side of Turkish immigrants without empirically connecting these to broader societal mechanisms. Rather, Ersanilli and Koopmans are silent on the possible relationships between the personal characteristics they measure and broader social mechanisms. As a result, they also disregard the possibility that adherence to certain Islamic religious traditions may in fact lead to *positive* (societal) integration outcomes, for example by increasing participation in education or the labour market and/or by lessening societal distances between groups. Second, the research of Ersanilli and Koopmans illustrates that the contemporary perspective on integration focuses one-sidedly on the degree of integration of individual immigrants (or citizens with immigrant backgrounds), implying that members of society without immigrant backgrounds are always already integrated. By contrast, advocates of the more societal perspective would stress that for meaningful assessments of integration it is insufficient to solely map the habits, acts and orientations (etc) of immigrants as those of all other groups in society are equally relevant. It is, after all, impossible to describe, understand and evaluate communal processes of socialisation on the basis of data regarding only one part of the whole population. Therefore, seen from the societal perspective on integration, the approach of Ersanilli and Koopmans is impoverished.

[35] In this research, Ersanilli and Koopmans measure four aspects of 'ethnic retention': identification with Turks, Turkish language proficiency, identification of Muslims and observance of religious practices. In addition, they measure four aspects of 'host culture adoption': identification with the host country, host country language proficiency, host country language use and social contacts with host country ethnics. See Ersanilli and Koopmans 2011: 217.

Essentially, their framework rests on the perception that persons with non-EU and non-Western backgrounds (and presumably Muslim), – citizen or not – who engage in Islamic customs do not truly *match with* and *belong to* the European societies they reside in, which are thus presumed to be and remain Islam-free. This last point, Duyvendak et al (2016) describe as the 'culturalisation of citizenship'. I return to this notion in Chapter 3.

On a more abstract level, the concept of 'integration' within contemporary European states became an umbrella term for the idea that (non-EU, non-Western) immigrants and their descendants have 'to be' integrated, perceived as a personal condition, in order to deserve a rightful place 'inside' society. This conceptual shift regarding integration has multiple consequences, varying from, inter alia, the framing of immigration issues in public debate and how the media covers news on multiculturalism, to the self-perception of both native and naturalised citizens. However, in the following, I will focus on three of its (closely interconnected) implications that are most relevant for the purposes of this chapter, that is, to understand the relationship between the redefinition of integration and the proliferation of (mandatory) integration requirements as conditions for obtaining increased rights in an increasing number of Member States. Again, what I describe here is a broader tendency that manifests itself differently across time and space in different EU countries but that is at the same time clearly discernible.

The first implication is that it creates an image of society in which certain persons may be perpetually *physically* present in society, but – even after decades – can nevertheless *symbolically* stand outside of society as non-integrated (Schinkel 2008; 2017) In the terminology of Bridget Anderson, this symbolic exclusion suggests that within society – seen as the mere sum of all residing individuals – a 'moral community' exists of persons who are naturally perceived as 'the protectors of good citizenship', while others are only contingently recognised as equal members of society based on standards of worthiness, selectively applied to them (Anderson 2013: 6). In the context I am concerned with, this entails that citizens *without* (non-EU, non-Western) immigrant backgrounds are seen as automatically belonging to their society and as unconditionally entitled to their citizenship status – their integration is 'granted' as they do not appear on the integration monitor, as Schinkel observes (Schinkel 2018: 4; 2017: 103) – while persons *with* (non-EU, non-Western) immigrant backgrounds are perpetually deemed inside or outside of society based on individualised standards of integration. Within this conceptualisation and discourse of integration, it is not most relevant whether the evaluated persons with non-EU, non-Western origins already have citizenship rights or not: in public discourses, *citizens* with such backgrounds also can be framed in terms of successfully integrated or not, in other words, as standing inside or outside of society. And if these citizens are seen as 'integrated' they are perceived as 'real' citizens that *deserve* the legal citizenship rights they possess. Moreover, the inclusion of (non-EU, non-Western) immigrants into, in the terminology of Anderson, the 'moral community' of 'real citizens' can always still be revoked. If citizens with immigrant backgrounds, for example, develop undemocratic or illiberal political views or (suddenly) engage in undesirable or criminal behaviour, they are perceived as personally non-integrated and no longer belonging to society (for an overview in this context of relevant proliferating denaturalisation policies in Europe, see Chapter 3, section V).

The second implication is that by creating the symbolic possibility that whole groups of individuals with (non-EU, non-Western) immigrant backgrounds can 'stand outside of society' due to their personal lack of integration, an image is created of the 'society' that is harmonious, democratic, secular – or, at least, culturally based on a (secularised) Western strand of Christianity (see, eg, Joppke 2008b: 540; Mouritsen and Olsen 2013: 703) – and reinforced by a list of (supposedly) virtually unchangeable national traditions, values and customs (Schinkel 2008: 58). To put it differently, non-EU, non-Western immigrants and their descendants are considered to be entering a complete, fixed and pre-established society in which they may or may not 'fit'. To recall, in the aforementioned research of Ersallini and Koopmans, it was implied that the pre-established 'real' societies of Europe do not contain individuals with Islamic orientations or customs that are not fully integrated and fully belong to their European society. To be sure, within debates on integration, European receiving countries do acknowledge that they have had their historical struggles regarding the equal treatment of women, LGBT+ persons, ethnic minorities and establishing the separation of church and state within a secular framework. But within integration debates these struggles are presumed to entirely belonging to the past. Modern societies are described as constituting a condition in which all these inequalities have been overcome. This presumption remains empirically unverified however, as citizens without immigrant backgrounds are assumed to be integrated. Questioning, for example, the degree of gender equality of 'non-immigrant citizens' in terms of degrees of integration is simply puzzling. Likewise, general functionalist sociological questions concerning the integration of society, for example the degree of social cohesion or structure of the labour market before and after the arrival of a particular group of immigrants, are raised less when looking through the lens of individual integration.

Additionally, this second implication (that is, the creation of a fixed and complete society into which immigrants potentially can integrate) facilitates a trend in which negative societal outcomes or statistics regarding immigrants and their descendants are qualified as integration issues pertaining exclusively to (subgroups of) individuals rather than societal issues. This is a powerful mechanism that is the result of assessing the belonging of members of (non-EU, non-Western) immigrant groups against an idealised (complete, pre-established, etc) image of the 'real society'. To explain, the contemporary conception of integration thus presumes that if persons with non-EU and non-Western backgrounds are, for instance, unemployed, homophobic, criminal, a school dropout or an (religious) extremist that they are insufficiently integrated and therefore stand outside of the society they reside in. Consequently – although obviously untrue – it is implicitly presupposed that 'inside the real society' no unemployment, no homophobia, no crime, no school dropouts and no or barely no (religious) extremism exists (Schinkel 2017: 107). As a result, due to the *spatial* character of this integration conceptualisation, a standard emerges that does not recognise undesirable statistics, such as a high percentages of crime, undemocratic attitudes or unemployment rates, if among under (non-EU, non-Western) immigrants and their descendants, as *societal* issues that deserve public concern, but as *individual* integration issues pertaining to certain persons who are not 'inside' but 'outside of society' and thus do not belong to it. The qualification of non-integration therefore often leads to *less* rather than *more* public concern to improve the observed negative and undesirable statistics, as the qualification discursively establishes that the involved (non-EU, non-Western) immigrants are alienated from the 'real society'. For example, if in Denmark an immigrant turns out to be not-integrated because he or she is a criminal, this individual simultaneously becomes less Danish, or, as Mikkel Rytter phrases it, 'not-quite-a-real' Dane (Rytter 2013: 116). As a result, the 'real Danish society' is not affected in terms of integration by these statistics, let alone to be held accountable or co-responsible for the social conditions that produced this kind of behaviour. Integration problems concern individuals who stand outside of society, so it cannot be a (shared) problem of 'Us'.

The third implication of perceiving integration as an individualised condition of (non-EU, non-Western) immigrants and their descendants is that it attributes the success or failure of integration one-sidedly to the behaviour, attitudes, efforts or qualities of (non-EU, non-Western) immigrants and their descendants. Given that integration is not a property of society, but a personal condition to be met by (non-Western, non-EU) immigrants, *their* potential successful participation in public and social life demonstrates their personal degree of integration. So, for instance, if an immigrant (or the child, grandchild etc of an immigrant) has many friends that are natives, or has an 'intercultural' marriage, this is perceived and registered as a demonstration of her successful integration, yet *not* of her native friends, native husband or broader society. Or when a child of an immigrant turns out to be a straight-A student, it is perfectly normal to state that she is 'very well integrated' (as if in the 'real society', inhabited by the natives, all children receive only A's in school). But when she drops out of school, this one-sidedly demonstrates her lack of integration and displays her alienation from 'society'.

In contrast, citizens without immigrant backgrounds can *never* fall outside of society in a comparable way. The contemporary interpretation of integration therefore leads to the situation in which citizens without immigrant backgrounds who, for example, are (religious) bigots or commit crimes are condemned as bigots, racists or criminals, but in which non-EU, non-Western immigrants who engage in the same behaviour are not *only* condemned as bigots, racists or criminals but *also* as non-integrated individuals who do not belong and are excluded from 'society'. This can also happen retrospectively (see implication 1). Thus, even those individuals who seemingly are 'well integrated' can suddenly still prove to be excluded in retrospect, due to certain undesirable acts or opinions, such as voicing undemocratic opinions (eg supporting authoritarian leaders abroad), committing a crime or dropping out of school.

Therefore, also the modern conceptual understanding of 'integration' or 'being integrated' contains two crucial aspects. First, it is an *individualised* condition predominately personally applicable to non-EU immigrants with non-Western origins and their descendants. Second, it is used to evaluate and express whether they have *managed to deserve to belong* to the European societies in which they live based on their *compatibility* with idealised societal standards attributed to 'society'.

III. Individualised Integration and Integration Requirements in Europe: Exploring the Links

In the previous section, I described a conceptual shift in Europe regarding the notion of 'integration' from a more societal concept to a more individualised and selectively applied notion. As I see it, this conceptual shift deserves more academic attention than it has received so far. It suggests that in Europe the gap between citizens with and without migrant backgrounds is viewed and discussed in a different light. The full membership of 'Western' citizens to European countries remains unquestioned, while the belonging of citizens with non-Western immigrant backgrounds and non-EU newcomers is increasingly questioned. Their full membership in their European societies is contingently acknowledged and remains vulnerable of being problematised in a discourse of integration that potentially position them as symbolically standing outside of society.

In this section, I focus on the relationship between this changing public perception and discourse of integration as described in section II and the changing mandatory integration requirements in EU countries as discussed in section I of this chapter. Can we see evidence that this new understanding of integration is present within these legal reforms? I will start with the case of the Netherlands, because it is, as mentioned in the Introduction, one of the better-documented EU countries, but also because the Dutch shift to the individualised conception of integration over the last two decades has been particularly clear (Böcker and Strik 2011: 167; Schinkel and Van Houdt 2010). Initially, this country adopted integration measures on the basis of a (holistic) understanding of integration as a societal issue, that is, as a matter of collective responsibility. Later, the introduction of integration requirements progressively transformed public measures to evaluate whether immigrants have individually 'integrated enough' to be entitled to entry, permanent residency and/or naturalisation. After examining the case of the Netherlands, I will highlight developments in other states that also illustrate the relationship between the conceptual and legal shifts on integration in Europe.

The Netherlands was the first European country to implement a mandatory integration program and test with the introduction of the Newcomers Integration Act in 1998.[36] The test was only for educational purposes and part of a mandatory

[36] Wet inburgering nieuwkomers, *Stb.* 1998: 261.

integration course for new immigrants from outside the EU – who were, at that time, chiefly family migrants – who settled in the Netherlands for a non-temporary purpose. The program was provided by the government at no cost and consisted of a 500-hour course of language education and a 100-hour orientation course regarding the labour market and society (Van Oers 2013:14). Non-attendance could lead to a fine. The courses were also open to already residing immigrants that arrived before 1998 ('old comers') but for them it was not mandatory.

This Bill was a response to a report by the Dutch Scientific Council of Government Policy, the WRR,[37] which concluded in 1989 that some form of mandatory education for newcomers should be enacted to stimulate their participation in society, because: 'too many allochtonous live in a marginal position; their participation in society is insufficient. Therefore, it is unacceptable that this situation endures [...] based on reasons of social justice [...] for all residents' (WRR 1989: 10). The relevant policy documents hence recognised that the general welfare and lack of emancipation of immigrants was a public concern based on the broader societal reason of 'social justice for all residents'. As a result, the state-funded courses were offered to newly arrived immigrants and to already 'settled immigrants' including both naturalised immigrants and long-term residents (Regioplan 2005: 6). Moreover, although the integration demands were mandatory, they were not tied to rights of entry, renewals of visas or naturalisation. The integration demands were defended as emancipating and improving the (too long neglected) position of certain immigrant groups in the whole of society.

However, due to a combination of electoral dynamics and the introduction of the EU Directives that legally permitted integration requirements for family migration and permanent residency – I will return to these dynamics in more length in Chapter 2 – the purposes, legal formation and content of the Dutch integration requirements changed rapidly. In 2003, the legal link was established between civic integration requirements and citizenship issues with the introduction of a formalised naturalisation test. In the 'Note of explanation' the Minister of Justice explained that:

> One of the requirements for naturalisation and becoming Dutch is that the applicant can be deemed as integrated in the Dutch [...] society [...] With integration [...] is meant that the applicant has reasonable knowledge of the Dutch language and [...] the Dutch state-structure and society.[38]

Soon after, in 2006 the Newcomers Integration Act and naturalisation test were replaced by a new integration law that prescribed a series of civic integration exams that monitor obtaining or renewing (permanent) residency rights (Pierik 2012).[39]

[37] The WRR ('Wetenschappelijke Raad voor Regeringsbeleid') is an independent advisory body for the Dutch Government and is concerned with the direction of government policy in the longer term.

[38] Besluit naturalisatietoets. Stb. 2002: 297.

[39] Wet Inburgering, Stb. 2006: 625.

These tests were obligatory for non-EU immigrants and had to be completed within three and a half years after arrival – later this would be shortened to three years – on the pain of fines (between €500 and €1,250). With this integration law of 2006, the integration programs were closed off for immigrant citizens, because they could not be compelled to integrate through punitive measures.

During the same period (in 2006), the Dutch Government was also the first to install the 'civic integration exam abroad' for family migrants.[40] Subsequently, in 2013 the Dutch state again heavily revised its integration trajectory.[41] Not only did it stop monitoring and publicly funding integration courses to prepare for the integration exams. It also created the possibility that, in certain instances, not completing the required integration demands would lead to losing residency rights and deportation from the territory (Besselsen and De Hart 2015).[42] In addition, in 2013 the Dutch state decided to, from then onwards, provide virtually all information for TCNs (in letters, online, etc) about integration courses and requirements in Dutch, including details about the sanctions that would follow the non-fulfilment of the prescribed integration requirements (reason: migrants should accept and adapt to fact that in the Netherlands, Dutch is spoken). Additionally, in 2017 the Dutch Government extended the 'duty to integrate' with the signing of an obligatory 'Participation Declaration'. This declaration was defended as a non-optional requirement for newcomers to become familiar with and commit themselves to the core values of the Netherlands, such as freedom, equality and solidarity. Not signing the declaration leads to (additional) fines.

This led to a situation in which, in the Netherlands, all arrived TCNs with an obligation to integrate had to pass four language tests – reading, listening, writing and speaking – a labour market portfolio, a knowledge-of-society test and sign a declaration to obtain permanent residency (or, if desired, naturalisation).[43] To prepare for these requirements, TCNs were expected to find language and integration lessons at private companies and pay for this education and exams themselves. To be able to afford the integration trajectory, TCNs could apply for a social loan up to €10,000. If refugees passed all requirements within the given three years (this was often extended till five years), their debts were cancelled. However, for family migrants, this was never the case: they always had to pay back the integration loan.

During and after the refugee crisis that peaked in 2015 in Europe, some countries, including the Netherlands, altered aspects of their integration programs during (suddenly) highly topical debates on integration strategies. However, individualised integration conceptualisations were not abandoned. For example, on pragmatic grounds, in 2015 the Dutch state translated information about

[40] Wet inburgering in het buitenland, Stb. 2006: 28.
[41] Wijzigingswet Wet inburgering, Stb. 2013: 226.
[42] In 2010, integration requirements already became a condition of *obtaining* permanent residency.
[43] Wijziging van de Wet inburgering en enkele andere wetten in verband met versterking van de eigen verantwoordelijkheid van de inburgeringsplichtige, *Stb*. 2012: 519.

integration requirements and the procedure for obtaining permanent residency and naturalisation in several languages. Furthermore, after the publication of several highly critical research and policy evaluations on the outcomes of the Dutch integration requirements since 2013 (eg, Significant 2018; Nationale ombudsman 2018), the Dutch Parliament in 2020 passed a Bill on a (again) new integration policy that will be implemented 1 January 2022. In the new policy, none of the existing requirements will be abolished and an extra requirement will be added: municipalities will make a 'personal integration plan' with TCNs that they have to fulfil on pain of fines (which created an extra ground for receiving a fine, in addition to not passing all language and civic requirements and not signing the participation declaration). Municipalities will also be given more responsibility for governing the integration and language lessons market and must give special attention to closing down fraudulent schools. The loan-system will be terminated and lessons will be free for refugees (not for family migrants).

Lastly, in the new law, in order to complete the integration requirements and receive permanent residency, the required language level for the language exams will in principle be raised from A2 to B1 level. Under certain circumstances, TCNs can do a more 'practical route' (called the Z-route) to fulfil their integration duty, or still complete the exams on A2 level.[44] Nonetheless, the intention is that the language requirement for naturalisation will be raised to B1 level for all newcomers, with only an exemption for newcomers with severe medical or psychological conditions. This means that in the new system, for example, illiterate or low literate newcomers – after showing enough effort – can complete their integration duty, avoid receiving fines and receive permanent residency, but, if they complete the Z-route or A2 exams, will not have access to naturalisation due to the strict language requirement. In contrast, within the previous Dutch system, after completing the duty to integrate, the TCN could choose between obtaining permanent residency or naturalisation. According to the responsible ministry, this new requirement for Dutch citizenship is required because 'it is something to be proud of and needs to be earned'.[45]

During policy debates on this new integration policy, some earlier narratives on that newcomers should individually adapt and be self-sufficient were at times slightly nuanced, for example regarding sending out all official letters to newcomers in Dutch or the responsibility of refugees to pay for their own integration education and exams. However, this was mostly not the result of principled argument on what 'integration' should entail, but rather a response to the outcomes of the Dutch integration policies since 2013 that turned out to be ineffective and expensive. On balance, despite all critique on the former integration requirements, the possible grounds for sanctions, expected language levels and integration conditions for permanent residency and naturalisation in fact all *increased* again in the 2022 integration law.

[44] *Kamerstukken II* 2019/20, 35483 nr. 2.
[45] Besluit naturalisatietoets 2021 (BNT 2021).

Over the last quarter of a century, the path to permanent residency and naturalisation in the Netherlands has thereby undeniably become more burdensome and conditional. Moreover, the new integration laws were presented with slogans such as 'Make sure you belong!'[46] and 'To stay is to participate'.[47] These slogans, as I see it, neatly convey what became the new narrative behind the Dutch integration trajectory: TCNs must prove their personal integration by fulfilling a series of requirements prescribed by the receiving state, to deserve to belong. Secure residency and full rights are regarded as a privilege for those that can be deemed personally 'well integrated' (Böcker and Strik 2011: 167). However, we have seen, integration trajectories initially started out as being non-punitive and available for both residing members of society and newcomers and were defended as supporting broader societal values and notions such as 'social justice for all residents' and 'equal participation' (WRR 1989: 10).

In the Netherlands the individualised concept of integration hence became highly visible. The eligibility of newcomers to be entitled to full legal membership rights became connected to a concept of individualised integration that must be personally achieved, with as little outside help or public support as possible. The political narrative behind the current integration trajectory has become: *first* demonstrate that you can integrate, that is, that you are compatible with 'Us'– *then* you may belong.

As stated, this Dutch history regarding integration policies does not stand on its own. For example, if we look at Austria, we see similar developments. Though originating from heated[48] political debates, in 2002 the first version of the Integrationsvereinbarung stated that it aimed at offering TCNs sufficient knowledge of the German language 'in order to be able to participate in the social, economic and cultural life in Austria' (Permoser 2012: 185).[49] The first Bill required the attendance of a subsidised (fully, if completed within one-and-a-half years) 100-hour integration course. By 2011, however, Austria had three different language tests and requirements, and today immigrants must pass a pre-departure test, a test after two years of residence and one after five years as a condition for the acquisition of a long-term residence permit. If the immigrant fails to pass the second test within two years after entry, financial sanctions follow and eventually (allegedly) deportation. Moreover, according to this integration law, the government no longer provides for subsidised courses or materials (Permoser 2012: 187).[50]

[46] Integratienota 2007-2011: zorg dat je erbij hoort! (2007).

[47] Rijksoverheid, 2015: Blijven is meedoen [Retrieved from www.rijksoverheid.nl/actueel/nieuws/2015/11/27/kabinet-blijven-is-meedoen].

[48] During these debates, the far-right FPÖ already approached the necessity of integration requirements entirely through the individualised view. Amongst other things, the head of their parliamentary faction stated: 'We want to know within three years who came to Austria after 1998 is at all willing and able to integrate! [...] After three years, we must be able to ask those people who do not want to integrate why they are in this country in the first place. If they cannot answer, then it is clear what shall happen: they will no longer be allowed to stay here!' (Perchining 2010: 12).

[49] Verordnung des Bundesministers für Inneres über die Integrationsvereinbarung (IV-V). BGBl. Nr. 338/2002.

[50] Verordnung der Bundesministerin für Inneres, mit der die Verordnung über die Integrationsvereinbarung verändert wird. BGBl. II Nr.205/2011.

As mentioned in the Introduction, the Maltese Government is enrolling a new integration strategy called the 'I belong programme' to be fully implemented in 2020. They published their plans in a document 'Integration = belonging, an action plan for integration'.[51] The trajectory for permanent residency is quite demanding but it is also relatively supportive – for example, language lessons to reach the expected level are provided by the state.[52] However, the chosen title for the new policy indicates that newcomers must earn their belonging by completing the program (Vassalo 2019). Then in France, in 1998 voluntary half-day classes for certain categories of newcomers (mostly non-Western family migrants) were introduced by the socialist Jospin Government, which were replaced in 2003 by the *Contrats d'accueil et de l'intégration*, entailing 500 hours of French language instruction (Joppke 2007: 2).[53] Today, passing the requirements of this 'integration contract' is obligatory for the renewal of residence permits, including obtaining a 10-year card that establishes permanent residency rights. In political debate, this policy was defended with the argument that a newcomer (particularly if a family migrant) should be obliged to 'insert herself in our society' (Joppke 2007: 9; Goodman 2010a: 760). In signing the contract, migrants commit to completing assigned components, thereby earning certificates to complete the contract. If they fail to do so in time their application to renew their residence permit could be denied (Onasch 2020: 503). In 2019, this integration contract is extended and strengthened by doubling the maximum of state-funded classes from 200 hours to 400 hours and adding a professional component to facilitate the job search (NIEM 2018). Also, academic commentators concur that the process rests on the idea that integration is a personal responsibility and condition for deserving to belong to the French nation (Onasch 2017; see also Hajjat 2012; Hachimi-Alaoui 2016). According to Sarah Mazouz, French citizenship policies have conditioned the admission of migrants into their citizenry on their capacity to be 'élite citizens', showing that they are politically, economically and culturally integrated (2017).

Paolo Cuttitta writes that Italy 'followed the example of other European countries' as well by shifting from 'structural integration of immigrants' to policies concerning their cultural integration including 'the acceptance of purported national and European values' (Cuttitta, 2016: 289–290).[54] Italy now requires residents with temporary residency to sign an 'integration contract' and meet a certain level of integration within a period of two or three years. If TCNs do not succeed, they are (allegedly) sanctioned with expulsion (Cuttitta 2016: 290). In the UK a

[51] Ministry for European Affairs and Equality, 2017. Integration = belonging, migrant Integration Strategy & Action Plan.

[52] This is not the case for the acquisition of citizenship: the new Maltese integration policy does not support TCNs to reach the language requirements for naturalisation, which arguably forms a barrier for full political membership.

[53] Haut Conseil a l'Integration (HCI) (2001). *Les parcours d'intégration.* Paris: La documentation Française.

[54] N.179 14 2011, *Regolamento concernente la disciplina dell'accordo di integrazione tra lo straniero e lo stato.*

comparable series of policy changes can be observed since the 2000s and academic commentators concur that Britain increasingly works with models of 'earned' citizenship for integration (eg, Byrne 2017; Bartram 2018). Monforte et al (2018) for example show that the narratives to describe the 'citizenship process' make distinctions between the 'deserving citizens' and the 'underserving Others'. Furthermore, the growth of civic integration demands in the UK has been clearly contemporaneous with a 'social downturn' (Baldi and Goodman 2015: 4).[55] This means that the number of integration requirements that must be fulfilled to be eligible for social programs and welfare has been gradually increasing since the 1990s. On that account, the message the UK increasingly communicates is that (non-Western) TCNs have to demonstrate a certain degree of integration to deserve unconditional citizenship and are strictly not members of society with entitlements to social benefits before achieving this. In this context, Bridget Byrne observes that integration tests in the UK are, in my terms, evidently underpinned by the individualised conception of integration as they are meant to assess 'a display of the suitability and propriety of potential citizens who have shown a commitment to learning and the potential to integrate' and 'are often regarded in popular discourse as a test for Britishness' (Byrne 2017: 6; see also Turner 2014; Bassel et al 2020).

Anna Simbartlová writes that since 2006 also the integration policies in the Czech Republic put 'more emphasis on the foreigner as an individual and his/or "personal effort and responsibility to [his/her] autonomy, independence and inclusion in society"' (Simbartlová 2019: 82–83).[56] The country changed its laws accordingly in 2006, 2011 and 2016. Although Simbartlová concludes that, overall, the integration policies of the Czech Republic would still, based on the framework developed by Goodman, receive a low CIVIX score, she also notes there is a clear trend towards a 'restrictive character of Czech civic integration policies' (92). For instance, naturalisation now requires that the applicant demonstrates a language mastery at the B1 as well as basic civic knowledge. The exams are state organised, but the costs are borne by the migrant. Moreover, currently the Parliament is debating whether TCNs must pay, attend and pass an integration course in the first year of their stay. In case of non-compliance, the proposed legislation stipulated a fine of approximately €400 (Simbartlová 2019: 85). A similar tendency can be observed in Belgium, traditionally known for its liberal naturalisation process. This country has a federal system, yet both the Flemish and Walloon Region have developed different but both compulsory integration requirements since 2000, which in the academic literature is described as 'representing a substantial shift towards a more interventionist and assimilationist integration policy' (Xhardez 2019: 1; for a study on Flanders, see Debruyne 2019). Moreover, in 2016 the responsible Secretary of State, Theo Francken, proposed that TCNs should sign a 'newcomers declaration' – listing

[55] Such a social downturn is also discernible in other EU countries, such as Belgium, Germany and the Netherlands. (See De Vries 2017: 259).

[56] Ministerstvo vnitra České republiky, Aktualizovaná koncepce 2006: 7.

certain core rights and asking the TCN to promise to put effort into integrating – or are otherwise not welcome and can lose their residency rights.[57] The intended text for the declaration contains, amongst other things, that newcomers have to 'understand and accept that integrating in society' is a prerequisite of keeping their residency status (NWS 2016).[58]

Then in Denmark, integration requirements and the conditions for permanent residency and naturalisation became clearly stricter since 2000 (Howard 2009: 103; Orgad 2019: 527). To be more specific, the Danish language requirements for TCNs have been made more stringent in 2002, 2005, 2008, 2013 and 2018 and have been installed alongside the obligation to sign a declaration of faithfulness and loyalty to Denmark as well as a citizenship test. Remarkably, in 2011 the government revised certain parts of integration requirements as it concluded that some of them had become overly restrictive (Jensen et al 2019: 4). However, at the core, during this period it did not abandon the shift to the individualised perspective of integration, as this government too emphasised it intended to send the signal 'that foreigners [...] whose integration has been successful, can become Danish citizens. The requirements must be high, as Danish citizenship is something special [...]' (Ersbøll 2015: 174). Integration remained something to be assessed solely on the individual level and is described as the standard for TCNs to deserve to belong and be allowed to obtain citizenship. In 2018 the language requirement for naturalisation was raised again to (equivalents of) B1 and B2-level, which makes that, to my knowledge, as Denmark currently has the highest language requirements in Europe (Solano and Huddleston 2020).

That said, in face of the refugee crisis, Denmark passed a law in the spring of 2019 called the 'paradigm shift', that was said to have shifted the focus from *integration* to *return* with respect to refugees. It contains a package of laws and policies, including that refugees will only have their status renewed if not doing so would constitute a clear violation under international law, a reduction of social benefits for people granted international protection or family reunification, and a potential cap on family reunification. To a certain extent, the discourse of 'integration' has therefore been changed into a discourse of 'self-support and return'. Nonetheless, as far as international law applies – which in principle is the case in relation to refugees – the 'paradigm shift' does not replace the Danish integration program, which is still in force and heavily leans on individualised integration conceptions and ideas of 'earned citizenship' (see, eg, EWSI 2020, Denmark).[59]

This list of examples could be extended or described in more detail. And indeed, over the subsequent chapters I will repeatedly return to the different integration

[57] Knack, 2016: Verplichte nieuwkomersverklaring moet integratiedruk verhogen [Retrieved from: www.knack.be/nieuws/belgie/verplichte-nieuwkomersverklaring-moet-integratiedruk-verhogen-niet-zomaar-vrijblijvend-papiertje/article-normal-685615.html].

[58] The declaration is currently 'on hold' and not implemented (yet) by the Regions.

[59] Therefore, if anything, the 'paradigm shift' leads to more precarity and possibly more deportations – but only if conditions in countries of origin of refugees structurally improve.

trajectories and requirements in the above-mentioned Member States and others (particularly in Chapter 3). However, for the purposes of this chapter, I hope that I have clearly demonstrated the legal tendency which played out in various Member States. And if we compare the shift in legal integration policies in Member States as described in section III with the conceptual shift on integration as expounded in section II, we see that the parallel is striking. In a nutshell, the bulk of the changes in integration and citizenship policies in a growing number of European countries increasingly corresponds with the following framework: TCNs after arrival are perceived as non-integrated individuals that are positioned 'outside of society'. However, by their own effort, they may undergo a personal transformation by achieving a degree of individualised integration that can be tested by obliging them to pass examinations that assess their loyalty, behaviour and knowledge of the receiving state's language(s), history, values and political institutions. Indeed, increasingly more, integration requirements monitor, one might say, a *test phase* in which TCNs should invest in and demonstrate their personal integration (ie prove their *compatibility* to a fixed and idealised image of their receiving society). And if they succeed, they have individually managed to become integrated, 'to stand inside society', earn their rights and deserve to belong.

Through this lens of individualised integration, several trends in integration policies of multiple European countries become understandable. Take the tendency in Member States to increasingly threaten TCNs with the loss of residency rights when they fail to fulfil integration conditions. This is a logical result of the political narrative that only those TCNs that personally integrate deserve secure residency and equal rights. After all, if that is the case, the ultimate consequence must be that those TCNs that fail to personally integrate (and are deemed incompatible with society) must leave the territory. Otherwise, if it was openly communicated that the non-integrated eventually can stay as well, the political narrative that only integrated persons deserve belonging makes little sense. At times, legal experts do highlight in public debates that actual expulsion is virtually always blocked by constitutional and EU norms, but this does not strongly affect the symbolism behind these integration policies (Permoser 2012).

Furthermore, the trend to limit the access of TCNs that are in their 'test phase to integrate' to social benefits (see also Hampshire 2013: 113) is also merely a coherent decision for governments operating within the framework, predicated on the presumption that only integrated immigrants belong to society. The rejection of certain Member States such as the Dutch state of public responsibility for offering state-funded integration schemes to prepare for integration tests, or to let TCNs pay for the tests themselves, can also be understood in this context. There is no reason, in the sense of public responsibility (except for charity) to spend public money on or provide social security to TCNs that still have to demonstrate their capacity to 'fit in'. Rather, in fact, any investment in TCNs who might turn out to be unwilling or incapable to integrate is an unnecessary financial risk. It remains to be seen whether they manage to integrate, which is *their* personal condition (and, with that, responsibility). Given that secure residency, citizenship and the right to belong should be earned, there is nothing wrong with asking them to carry this financial burden.

Lastly, integration requirements and education in Member States are increasingly exclusively aimed at non-EU newcomers in society that can be obliged to integrate on pain of punitive measures. From a more holistic perspective, this is not most pragmatic: if already naturalised immigrants (an 'old comer'), or any type of citizen for that matter, might also benefit from language education, there is no reason to limit their access to an integration trajectory. However, if 'integration' is strongly associated with deserving a right to belong, the focus of integration policies automatically shifts to TCNs who have not yet obtained secure residency rights. After all, only they can be compelled to integrate to obtain increased rights or otherwise (supposedly) be sent 'back' to their country of origin.

In a similar vein, individualised integration conceptualisations also affect other public decisions, for example by making it counterintuitive to already enable and support asylum seekers to start with their integration trajectory before the outcomes of their (often lengthy) individual asylum procedures are determined. For example, the French Parliament recently decided not to open up language lessons for asylum seekers, despite recommendations by French civil society to do so (NIEM 2018). But, reasoned from an individualised integration perspective, what if these migrants do not deserve a 'test phase' at all? However, from a broader and more societal perspective, one could argue that even if a certain part of the asylum seekers enrolled in integration programs will eventually be rejected, opening up these programs for them might still benefit broader integration outcomes of those who stay in the long term. I will return to this issue in section IV.

That said, to fully pin down this analysis, I briefly return to the Netherlands as the European forerunner in this field of public policy. In the Dutch case, I believe that the difference between the mandatory integration courses that were enacted in 1998 and the mandatory naturalisation test enacted in 2003 deserves close attention. Most commentators date the rise of the 'about-face' by the Dutch state regarding integration to 1998 – quickly followed by other European countries (Schinkel and Van Houdt 2010; Kostakopoulou 2010b). However, I believe the conception that I highlight, which perceives integration as a personal condition for being entitled to belong to the fixed 'moral community' of 'society' that is 'Us', actually became dominant in and after the 2003 reforms. This reform made passing the naturalisation test a *prerequisite* for legal inclusion and inaugurated a tendency in which individual migrants with non-EU origins must deserve the privilege to be a member of 'society' based on individualised integration standards. 'If you integrate, you may stay' became the central message behind integration requirements, particularly directed at non-EU immigrants from non-Western countries. This was, to be sure, not an implicit or tacit policy change. Rather, it was publicly announced that the perspective on integration became that naturalisation should be seen as 'the 'first prize' (Van Oers 2013: 51) for those who integrated. Furthermore, not long afterwards, in 2006 the Netherlands was also the first country to implement the 'integration requirements abroad' for family migration. In Parliament, the Dutch Government described these requirements, we have seen, explicitly as 'selection criteria' with the purpose not to admit those who fail them, to restrict the immigration of 'non-integratable' (Scholten et al 2012) migrants. This last ambition and formulation, in my view, clearly demonstrates the individualised perception of integration, in which instead of society, individual persons can (and must be) integrated. If one speaks of the degree of the 'integratability' of *persons*, the shift to the individual conception of integration is simply complete. And indeed, since then, virtually all of the changes in integration requirements in the Netherlands – which changed more than ten times since 2007 – have heavily relied on the individualised interpretation of integration. Consider, again, the fact that from 2007 onwards Dutch integration programs were not made available anymore for immigrant citizens (who already possessed secure rights), a tendency that is also present in other Member States. This shows that the focus of integration policies indeed shifted from supporting societal integration towards regulating admission by measuring whether immigrants deserve to belong. Gradually the focus of integration requirements shifted towards the question of: how to assess whether individual immigrants have 'integrated enough' to merit secure residence and/or citizenship?

Finally, it is important to highlight that the individualised perspective on integration also manifests itself in how European states interpret the outcomes of their integration trajectories. To illustrate this, I will discuss the Netherlands and Denmark, both seen as leading examples of restrictive – an in my terms heavily individualised – integration programs in the EU. In the Netherlands, in 2016, research indicated that only 50 per cent of the TCNs that started with their prescribed 'test phase' in 2013 completed all the integration requirements (so within their three-year deadline). Refugees, it turned out, were relatively unsuccessful: of this group only around 30 per cent managed to fulfil their integration duty within the given timeframe (Netherlands Court of Audit 2017). Not soon after, the Dutch liberal party (the largest party in cabinet and also winner of the 2017 parliamentary election) re-emphasised that permanent residency and citizenship should be earned. Moreover, it promised to find legal ways to circumvent existing EU and constitutional laws that prevent deportation and proceed to actually expel TCNs that fail to fulfil the integration conditions, as soon as possible. In addition, it proposed to add another integration requirement to the Dutch integration trajectory: TCNs should also find a job (including the possibility of volunteer work) in order to obtain permanent residency.[60]

In a similar way, in Denmark, in June 2016 it was confirmed that only 31.2 per cent of the newcomers that took the Danish citizenship test passed it.

[60] Integratie Agenda VVD, 2017 [Retrieved from: https://vvd.nl/content/uploads/2017/02/VVD-Integratie-Agenda-Malik-Azmani.pdf].

Not long after, the responsible Danish minister repeated once more that the low passing rate indicates that being Danish is 'very special' and that 'citizenship is something you have to earn'.[61] Indeed, also Jensen et al (2019) conclude that in Denmark politicians welcome the development that 'large groups of potential applicants' are excluded from increased rights due to integration requirements because this would 'optimize the "quality" of nations' citizen pools' as immigrants that fail 'have not tried enough' (15). Hence, here also, low passing rates of integration requirements and citizenship tests were not discussed in terms of societal (collective, functionalist) integration – even though the newcomers that have failed their exams remain physically present in society – but instead as integration problems of TCNs who do not belong, which is laid bare by (in that sense well-constructed) integration policies.

IV. Conclusion

In this chapter, I demonstrated that the recent and ongoing proliferation of mandatory integration requirements for TCNs in Europe testifies to a broader conceptual shift regarding the notion of 'integration' in Europe. First, I described the EU directives and domestic laws relevant for the integration requirements that many European countries adopted. Second, I addressed an underlying conceptual shift in the public understanding of integration in Europe that, I argue, must be taken into account to fully grasp the mechanisms behind the observed growth of legal integration requirements. In closing, let me summarise and review the three main consequences of these developments.

First, a notion of individualised 'integration' became the standard for persons with (non-Western) immigrant backgrounds for determining their *compatibility with* and *belonging to* society. This consequence is implicitly rooted in the idea that personal integration is quantifiable and measurable and can be achieved in a prescribed time period. However, at the same time, the exact traits of a person who may be considered to be an 'integrated individual' compatible with society are often redefined.[62] On occasion, we have seen, it entails not having certain religious orientations or not engaging in certain religious practices. At other moments, it (additionally) entails acquiring certain language levels or demonstrating certain behaviour or adhering to certain (liberal-democratic) convictions.[63] In any event, standards of individual integration are only applied selectively as citizens without immigrant backgrounds are not demanded to meet them in order to be deemed

[61] See Bilefsky in the *New York Times* (www.nytimes.com/2016/07/08/world/europe/denmark-citizenship-test.html) accessed 18 January 2021.

[62] I will return to this point in the next chapter.

[63] I return to this point in ch 3.

as belonging to society. Within this selectivity, there are discriminatory practices discernible (see, eg, Bonjour and Duyvendak 2018). For instance, Germany, Denmark and the Netherlands exempt TCNs from certain (often richer) countries for cultural or political reasons.[64] In general, solely persons with (non-EU, non-Western) immigrant backgrounds are perpetually evaluated as being personally integrated or not-integrated and hence judged as being entitled to legal citizenship or not.

Second, the conceptualisation that 'integration' is a condition of individuals (and not of the society as a whole) facilitates a tendency to interpret the relationship between European states and TCNs as *contractual* (see also Kostakopoulou 2010b; Van Houdt et al 2011; Joppke 2013: 60). It is counterintuitive and unfeasible to expect from individual TCNs to completely guarantee and uphold successful *societal* integration. However, it is imaginable to (contractually) demand the deliverance of individualised integration seen as a personal condition, particularly when the state delivers secure residency and citizenship rights in return. As a result, several European countries including France, Italy and Austria explicitly require arriving TCNs to sign integration contracts that lay down the requirements (oaths, tests, etc) that newcomers must pass to eventually acquire permanent residency and/or citizenship.[65] Also in other EU countries, the notion that 'new immigrants accept the responsibilities that need to be undertaken in order to acquire national citizenship' (Suvarierol and Kirk 2015: 250) has become an important aspect of integration regimes. Citizenship is increasingly seen as a reward or favour that needs to be contractually 'deserved' or 'earned' by TCNs by performing growing series of duties, tasks and investments that prove individual integration.

However, legally seen, the integration requirements for family migration and permanent residency must have inclusionary effects based on EU law. For this reason, the contractual discourses surrounding integration policies that suggest that obtaining increased rights for immigrants becomes more conditional on certain efforts and investments, are increasingly strained, or even at odds, with the stated inclusionary objectives of the Family and LTR Directives, which in fact limited the control of Member States regarding the regulation of family migration or permanent residency rights that TCNs are entitled to (eg, Carrera and Vankova 2019; Permoser 2012: 197).

[64] For example, the Netherlands exempts 'Western countries', meaning non-EU citizens from EEA states, the US, Australia, New Zealand and Japan from their integration requirement abroad (De Vries 2013: Groenendijk 2011).

[65] To be sure, David Miller has developed a 'quasi-contractual approach' to integration in his theoretical work. See, eg, Miller 2008, 373. In his analysis he uses the notion of a 'contract' as exhibiting the same duality as 'integration', in the sense that it can be understood as a 'social contract' that covers all members of society and that enshrines norms of reciprocity. However, this differs from the 'contractualisation' I highlight here, which entails that newcomers have to individually prove that they are deserving to belong and to formally earn secure rights.

Finally, the trend to understand integration as an individualised condition that can be demanded and instrumentalised within immigration and citizenship policies, creates disorientation and confusion about how to *evaluate* the quality of integration policies. If integration requirements are built on a more collective perspective on integration, they are enacted to further broader emancipatory societal goals – such as reducing social distances, enhancing language levels in society or stimulating equal participation. Therefore, the method to assess the quality of such policies is quite straightforward: if one is concerned with fostering certain social mechanisms, it follows that integration policies should be evaluated based on careful empirical research exploring whether they in fact promote or jeopardise these specified mechanisms. So, if, for example, it turns out that certain integration requirements clearly hamper the inclusion of TCNs into the labour market, or that much better outcomes could be achieved through alternative public integration strategies, the policies should be assessed as counterproductive and altered.

However, the new integration policies in European countries are based on individualised conceptions of integration and focus on something else, namely on whether individual TCNs deserve to belong, and so measure success or aim to prevent undeserved access to belonging. But the pursuit of this goal – limiting belonging to those who earn it – can (paradoxically) conflict with broader societal integration goals, for instance when integration requirements become burdensome and exclusionary. Nonetheless, since European states shifted to an individualised perspective of integration, governments tend to respond to disappointing outcomes of integration policies through individualised integration rhetoric. Yet at the same time, it takes little common sense to see that counterproductive integration requirements – or requirements that evidently do not enhance societal policy objective outcomes as effectively as other institutional configurations would – are a missed opportunity for receiving states to facilitate the successful incorporation of immigrants into their societies. Put differently, it will only be a matter of time before the alleged personal integration problems of TCNs who do not deserve to belong, will result in broader societal problems, not in the least because the TCNs that fail to integrate are not actually deported but will remain members of society, albeit with precarious legal rights (and possibly debts due to financial sanctions). Nevertheless, by shifting to personal integration standards, Member States have lost their method to effectively and straightforwardly adjust their integration requirements based on their factual impact on societal goals. Rather, they now constantly modify their integration policies based on the question: have TCNs *integrated enough* to deserve to belong?

Having described both the legal and conceptual trends regarding integration and integration policies in EU Member States and their most salient outcomes, the task for the remainder of this book is to engage in a normative evaluation of these trends. Do they pursue legitimate aims, using legitimate means? What do they imply for liberal-democratic values such as equality? Are they (too) open to abuse? To help answer these questions, I will look at several bodies of academic literature theory, each of which has addressed (if only in passing) or is able to address integration policies. In particular, I will discuss the liberal nationalism literature; social science literature; and the social equality literature. As we will see, each offers valuable insights into the normative dimensions of these policies, but I will argue that none offers a complete and satisfactory account of how to ensure that EU States do not misuse integration measures for TCNs for exclusionary purposes.

2

Structural Risks of Integration Requirements

In the previous chapter, I clarified the legal frameworks of integration requirements as conditions for attaining increased rights for TCNs in a growing number of Member States. In addition, I discussed a conceptual shift in Europe regarding the notion of 'integration'. This shift involves integration becoming increasingly understood as an individualised condition that (non-EU, non-Western) immigrants and their descendants must personally achieve to deserve to belong to their societies, instead of a broader notion pertaining to society as a whole. I argued that this conceptual shift has fortified and continues to fuel the observed increase of (mandatory) integration requirements for TCNs in EU states.

My next aim is to find appropriate moral vocabularies and theoretical concepts to analyse how to ensure that integration requirements do not become exclusionary in EU Member States. In this chapter, I will begin with discussing three academic perspectives on integration requirements that I believe are useful for this endeavour. First, I will turn to the scholarship on liberal nationalism that focuses on liberal forms of nation building and the boundaries of a liberal national identity (eg. Tamir 1995; Kymlicka 1995; Miller 1995). This normative body of literature has not extensively engaged with integration requirements for residency and citizenship, with the exception of a few noteworthy points. Its focus has been to explore whether such requirements can be justified *in principle* based on liberal accounts of nation building. In the end however, I find this research approach to be insufficient. To substantiate this claim, I will also – and this is the second academic perspective I discuss – examine the social science scholarship that has emerged on the integration requirements in Europe, conducted by empirical scientists such as comparative legal scholars, sociologists and political scientists. This literature is equally relevant as, although it consists of empirical research, it (implicitly) operates within a similar theoretical framework as liberal nationalists (eg, Joppke 2007; Kiwan 2008; Cooke 2009; Guild et al 2009; Peucker 2008; Van Oers 2013; Goodman 2010a; Goodman and Howard 2013; Borevi et al 2017; Howard 2009). Most often, it maps and categorises the different integration laws across European states and places them on a continuum from 'prohibitive' to 'enabling' (or similar terms, such as 'liberal' to 'restrictive'). However, the main goal of this chapter is to demonstrate that this approach – indicating when integration requirements are permissible and not – should be supplemented with a normative analysis.

Thus, acknowledging that a solution should be found for the most prominent risk of integration requirements, which is that they are prone to exploit the inherent power imbalance between receiving states and legal immigrants that are not equal members yet of the political community and legal order. In other words, I argue that if we want to evaluate the normative quality of integration requirements as conditions for attaining increased rights such as secure residency and full citizenship, we should not only search for possible *defences* of the legitimacy of these policies. Instead, we should also be attentive to the *actual risks* of such integration requirements and think through how to provide safeguards against their susceptibility to be used for exclusionary purposes. The current academic scholarship, notwithstanding that both liberal nationalist theory and the social science scholarship are critical of overly restrictive or illiberal integration requirements, lack analyses on how to avert the risk of growth of overly prohibitive requirements as conditions of access to social programs, permanent residency, citizenship and so forth in Europe today.

On that account, in the first half of this chapter, I will deduce that both liberal nationalists and social scientists working on integration requirements provide helpful information about the potential justifiability of integration requirements, but do not deliver us comprehensive responses, let alone solutions for, the intensified use of (mandatory) integration requirements for TCNs as described in Chapter 1. Interestingly, the underlying reason why they are unsuccessful in delivering such comprehensive responses reveals indispensable information about the supplementary normative approach that is required for assessing these requirements.

Moving from this discussion, in the second half of this chapter, I address a third academic perspective on integration requirements. More particularly, I will explore the work of James Hampshire and Linda Bosniak to understand the legal and political dynamics behind the integration requirements in Europe. I conclude that the weak spot of these policies involves a normative focal point, highlighting that these measures are applied to non-citizens who have no secure residency, no full constitutional protection and no strong political voice (yet) in the liberal-democratic state that receives them. *This* aspect makes the integration requirements for TCNs in EU Member States vulnerable (from a normative viewpoint), particularly when anti-immigrant attitudes are on the rise and politically mobilised. Therefore, I argue, academic debates on integration requirements need normative analyses that focus, in particular, on this weak spot. Otherwise, the risks of granting states the discretion to contractually impose 'integration' obligations that demand efforts and costs on legal immigrants who are in a precarious position remain underestimated.

To explain this, the structure of this chapter is the following. First, I will summarise the main arguments of liberal nationalists regarding integration requirements for citizenship and expound the main approach of the social science literature on integration requirements in EU Member States. Second, I will explain the limitations of the normative approaches of these bodies of literature. After that, I will revisit the political and legal mechanisms that shape integration policies, through the work of James Hampshire and Linda Bosniak. Third, I return to the main findings of Chapter 1 to illustrate that we should indeed not only evaluate integration requirements based on whether they can be defended as legitimate in principle, but also evaluate if they are likely to be justifiable in practice.

I. Liberal Nationalism and the Social Sciences on Integration Requirements

In political theory 'liberal nationalists' such as Will Kymlicka, Yael Tamir and David Miller describe the bandwidth for fostering national identity in the context of liberal democracies. On the one hand, they seek to understand the neutrality of the liberal-democratic state and, on the other hand, they explore the merits (or necessity) of upholding a national identity that motivates citizens to recognise each other as belonging to the same historical and intergenerational society. In a nutshell, defenders of liberal nationalism argue that states are permitted to foster forms of nationhood in order to secure solidarity and stability, as long as the promoted national identity is 'thin' (Kymlicka 2002: 265) and underpinned by the principles of liberal democracy. This thinness involves that it is inclusive towards people from different (ethnic, cultural, religious, etc) backgrounds and that it does not limit the capacity of individual citizens to choose or revise their personal conceptions of the good. In other words, according to liberal nationalists, it is from the perspective of liberal democracy not per se troublesome if states employ strategies of nation building and promote a national identity. They observe that, just as other nations, liberal-democratic states are 'imagined communities' of groups of people that share a territory, historical community and future (Anderson 1983). Nonetheless, crucially, liberal democracies are distinguishable from illiberal and undemocratic states based on the inclusive type of nationhood they promote.

On a more fundamental level, liberal nationalists acknowledge and assert that the norms and skills of democratic citizenship are not innate, but must be learned, socialised and practiced. The state is therefore permitted to create an 'ethical community' (Miller 1995: 23) with an official language, national symbols and common institutions. Under these conditions, it is then thought, people are most likely to fulfil their obligations of justice towards each other and will be able to participate as equals in democratic deliberations and societal life. An open question for liberal nationalists is why the nation-state would be the best – or perhaps only – political unit to achieve such an 'ethical community'. In relation to this debate, most liberal nationalists argue that this cannot be philosophically proven but that the nation-state has historically emerged as the political forum with which citizens most strongly identify (but that this in principle could change through time, for example regarding the EU). That said, liberal nationalists thus argue that liberalism and nationalism are not only described as reconcilable but in fact as potentially complementary and that strengthen each other. Or as Yael Tamir puts it: 'No individual can be context-free, but … all can be free within a context' (Tamir 1995: 14).

In this body of literature, the use of integration requirements is discussed, but only in relation to monitoring the *political* inclusion (ie naturalisation) of newcomers – not in relation to obtaining other rights, such as a visa to migrate for family migrants or obtaining permanent residency. In general, liberal nationalists hold that to install some language or civic pre-naturalisation demands for newcomers should be perceived as a standard political practice. More specifically, the enactment of integration requirements for citizenship is regularly listed as one possible example of a public tool that may be employed by the state to promote its national identity, official language(s) and to stimulate democratic socialisation. Will Kymlicka, for example, holds that permanent immigrants should have: 'relatively easy access to citizenship after, say, three or five years of residency, with minimal tests of national integration, including knowledge of the national language, knowledge of national history and institutions, and an oath of loyalty to the country and its constitution' (Kymlicka 2001: 36–37). Along the same line, David Miller writes that permanent immigrants 'should be admitted on the basis that they are citizens in the making'. This implies they should be 'granted a wide range of rights straight away, and the rest will follow as soon as they have fulfilled whatever residence requirements and citizenship tests the state imposes' (Miller 2008: 375). In short, liberal nationalists conclude that integration policies for increased rights can in principle serve legitimate liberal nation building goals. Simultaneously, they acknowledge that it would be illiberal and illegitimate if these policies involved unduly 'thick' conceptions of national identity that interfere with an inclusive attitude towards diversity in personal matters (such as religion, culture, personal views on the good life, etc), impose overly burdensome requirements, or imply that assimilation into the majority culture is required to become a full citizen.

To grasp that this research approach for increased rights for legal immigrants is informative but requires to be supplemented if we want to evaluate the proliferating integration requirements in EU countries, I think it is interesting to also look at the social science literature that emerged over the last two decades on these policies. This social science literature (implicitly) builds on the liberal nationalist position to the extent that it distinguishes 'liberal' and 'enabling' forms of integration policies from the more 'illiberal' or 'prohibitive' forms (eg, Goodman 2010a; Howard 2009). Accordingly, social scientists most often accept that integration requirements can be employed as reasonable tools of communication that lay out the responsibilities, knowledge and civic virtues required to be a citizen (eg, Orgad 2009; Hansen 2009; Hampshire 2011). Nevertheless, they also emphasise that these requirements provide policy makers with 'instruments to use positive, politically acceptable language of integration and inclusion to achieve potentially objectionable and discriminatory outcomes of exclusion' (Goodman 2011: 235; see also Van Oers 2013, 2020). Therefore, although social scientists clearly offer more context-sensitive and also more critical analysis of the integration demands for TCNs in Member States than liberal nationalists, they essentially mirror the political theory on liberal nation building. It is assumed that integration requirements as conditions for increased rights can be benign, but it also identifies forms of integration policies that are exclusionary and illiberal. This research perspective therefore in principle also accepts the legitimacy of such policies and then highlights when integration requirements are inclusionary or exclusionary – *not* how to best prevent them being misused for exclusionary effects.

For example, when integration requirements emerged in the UK, Dina Kiwan argued that the enactment of these requirements in the form of language standards were not a restrictive measure but 'more an entitlement than a hurdle, providing new citizens with the opportunity to actively participate – socially, economically and politically – within their new society' (Kiwan 2008: 73). Yet, Melanie Cooke fiercely criticised Kiwan's research and was of the opinion that the integration and citizenship laws she defended, though justified by politicians and their advisors as 'empowering', are in fact 'highly illiberal legislation which seeks to limit the rights of asylum seekers, spouses wishing to join their families and migration from outside the EU'. Additionally, Cooke wrote that the language requirements in the UK are 'a powerful linguistic gate-keeping mechanism which disproportionally affects low-paid workers and vulnerable members of society' (Cooke 2009: 76).

The influential CIVIX of Sarah Wallace Goodman categorises the (mandatory) integration requirements for residency rights and political inclusion in several EU countries. She develops categories of these requirements based on the underlying citizenship strategies of these countries (eg, Goodman 2010a; 2011; 2012). In 2010, for example, she discerned that Austria, Denmark and Germany had 'prohibitive' citizenship strategies and had installed high barriers towards full citizenship. In contrast, Belgium, Finland and Ireland opted for 'enabling' citizenship strategies. This shows that Goodman's analysis rests on the (tacit) assumption that the use of integration requirements as conditions of residency rights or political inclusion is not necessarily problematic.[1] This is also illustrated by an argumentation she co-authored with Marc Howard, in which it was observed that Belgium had, at a later date, also enacted integration requirements for naturalisation that asked for demonstrations of integration and knowledge of one of the national languages. However, instead of assessing Belgium's citizenship strategy as more 'prohibitive', Goodman and Howard (2013) concluded that it had 'normalized' (130). After all, they concluded, Belgium's citizenship scheme was initially remarkably liberal compared to other EU Member States. So, also here, Goodman and Howard assume that integration requirements as conditions of residency or citizenship are not inherently problematic. Rather, for a country to have a small number of integration requirements that structure the path to permanent residency and

[1] Marc Morjé Howard developed a similar Citizenship Policy Index (2009) that distinguishes 'restrictive', 'medium' or 'liberal' countries. Additionally, also Koopmans (2005) has developed an Index of Citizenship Rights for Immigrants, which measures the restrictiveness of nationality acquisition and cultural rights attribution. The argument I present in this chapter in response to the social science literature including the work of Goodman applies equally to these indexes.

citizenship (compared to having virtually no requirements) is qualified as the *normal* situation.

Additionally, in the social science literature, comparisons are often made between different countries to signify that integration schemes for increased rights in different countries can serve different purposes, even if they, prima facie, appear similar. Mario Peucker (2008), for example, compares citizenship tests in the US, Canada, the Netherlands and the UK. He concludes that integration requirements can only be understood within a specific political framework to grasp their actual functioning and that their outcomes largely depend on the national context (241; for similar approaches see also Bloemraad 2006: 675; Paquet 2012). From that perspective, he discerns that the citizenship tests in the US and Canada are designed to 'strengthen the prospective citizens' commitment and loyalty to their new country', whereas the Dutch test is designed as a 'test to single out applicants who are not sufficiently integrated' and the British test is employed as an instrument to 'increase the significance of becoming a British citizen' (Peucker 2008: 257–258).

As a result, to my knowledge, no empirical country report or legal comparative study on the latest European mandatory integration requirements concludes that integration requirements as a condition for obtaining increased rights *as such* are too susceptibly for abuse. The task at hand for academic commentators is taken to be pointing out those requirements that fall safely within the boundaries of the permissible and those that do not, based on wider empirical explorations that connect to their (official or unofficial) purposes, preparation costs and content, timing and (intended or unintended) outcomes.

II. Integration Policies in Principle or in Reality

Both liberal nationalists and social scientists thus oscillate in their assessments of integration requirements as a condition to gain a more secure legal status, between highlighting the merit of nation-building and the risks of exclusionary or discriminatory outcomes. However, in my opinion, the recent developments in Europe as described in Chapter 1 require us to revisit the nature of the involved risks and to sharpen the underlying and most relevant questions. To start with – without fundamentally challenging the tenets of liberal nationalism or the importance of integration – we should focus on the question: is it fair and legitimate *as such* to apply (mandatory) integration demands on legally admitted immigrants as conditions for gaining access to more secure residency rights as EU law now permits? Surprisingly, this narrower question has rarely been explicitly raised in academic debates, although it opens up a whole new perspective on the issue of the integration requirements applied to TCNs to regulate their legal incorporation. In the same vein, scarcely any academic energy has been spent on the question of how to *prevent* the growth of exclusionary requirements – though an increase of such legally impermissible requirements has been repeatedly observed and disapproved of by social scientists, the European Commission and the CJEU. In the academic literature, analysis usually stops after it has been established that integration requirements should solely be used to promote the national identity, further language levels and encourage participation while ensuring that these integration requirements do not function as insurmountable and discriminating barriers for legal immigrants to obtain certain rights.

Why is it that the question is not explicitly raised: how we can make sure that integration requirements will not be exploited to further politics of exclusion? The answer to this question is partly, I contend, a methodological one: most academic assessments of integration policies focus primarily on if, in principle, justifications for integration requirements can be found, instead of scrutinising the actual political dynamics and electoral mechanisms that shape these requirements. This is most strongly the case for liberal nationalists working on this topic. Nonetheless, social scientists also choose comparable approaches for their empirical research (perhaps because the conceptual backgrounds they work with are influenced by the normative frameworks put forward by liberal nationalists). They limit their reflections to listing examples of integration requirements for residential inclusion and/or citizenship that are inclusionary or not, while barely presenting additional guidance on how to respond to the institutional risks of these policies and how to remedy the tendencies to enact increasingly impermissible requirements.

To be more specific, we have seen that representatives of liberal nationalism such as Miller and Kymlicka typically do not problematise integration requirements applied to legal immigrants as pre-naturalisation demands at all. In technical terms, I believe this is the result of the fact that academic political philosophy typically engages in so-called 'ideal theory' that aims to sketch whether certain public policies can be defended in situations in which all relevant agents (receiving states, citizenries, etc) are sincerely committed to upholding (liberal) principles of justice (see, eg, Valentini 2012: 655; Rawls 1971: 4–6).[2] In their reflections of integration requirements, the only question liberal nationalists therefore answer is: could states and citizens, that are truly motivated to act upon liberal-democratic values, have legitimate reasons to authorise integration requirements as a condition for accessing citizenship?

From such an idealised point of view, linking integration measures to political inclusion is obviously unproblematic. When it is already *assumed* that receiving states comply with the demands of liberal-democratic justice, they will only implement such measures to benignly encourage language acquisition and societal know-how of 'citizens-in-the-making'. In other words, in an ideal world,

[2] Several versions of the distinction between ideal and non-ideal theory exist, but I will not unpack the intricate academic debates on this topic. For the purposes of my research questions, it is enough to establish that liberal nationalists chiefly look to see if a principled justification for (integration) policies can be construed and, as a corollary, do not focus on the actual politics behind, and institutional weaknesses at play in implementing such policies.

integration requirements for legal immigrants to obtain increased rights seemingly only have functional benefits. It offers countries opportunities to add symbolical and ceremonial aspects to the 'path to citizenship'. This has beneficial didactical effects and can stimulate feelings of belonging. However, due to the assumptions underlying this ideal methodology, liberal nationalists are unable to reflect on the most relevant questions surrounding the rise of integration requirements in the EU. As a result, they pay too little attention to the non-ideal possibility that integration requirements can take advantage of the weak legal position of immigrants and may be motivated by exclusionary agendas such as indirectly reducing immigration, discrimination or stigmatisation. Indeed, a thorough analysis of the precarious position of legally residing immigrants without secure residency or equal democratic rights is not to be found. Nor are there concrete institutional proposals for forms of checks and balances, as ways to suggest how to provide institutional counterbalance for the real-world possibility that states may very well enforce integration policies in illegitimate ways. As a result, I believe (idealised) theories of liberal nationalism disregard crucial normative questions about the current requirements in EU Member States.

Admittedly, this analysis does not directly apply to the work of social scientists on integration requirements. Given the empirical nature of their work, social scientists surely do not engage in 'ideal theory', nor would they recognise themselves as engaging in it. It is more probable that they (often implicitly) address the permissibility of integration requirements within the current legal framework as clarified by the CJEU. And as we have seen in Chapter 1, the CJEU also deems integration requirements as conditions to attain increased rights in principle valuable but warns that they can become overly demanding and tools of exclusion. Moreover, the social science literature, in contrast to the liberal nationalist literature, is replete with efforts to distinguish integration requirements that enable successful inclusion of TCNs from those that hamper access to the territory, secure residency or full membership.

However, and this is the crucial point, the social science literature rarely emphasises that, due to the vulnerable position of the legal non-citizen, even supposedly enabling integration policies carry serious risks of being used for exclusionary purposes sooner or later. Furthermore, given that these risks are never specifically identified and discussed, no social science study explores how this development could be addressed, neutralised or prevented. On that account, the gap in the academic literature that social scientists leave open is comparable to that of the liberal nationalist: the analysis ceases after it is established that ideal states would only make granting secure rights for TCNs conditional on completing certain inclusionary integration requirements to facilitate purposes of nation building, integration or education for 'citizens-to-be'.

In addition, it seems that social scientists at times are inclined to take official justifications of the current integration requirements in Europe (too much) at face value. If we look, for instance, again at Kiwan, we saw that her positive conclusions about the British integration requirements (cited by, eg,

Peucker (2008)) were immediately questioned by Cook. Moreover, since the publication of Kiwan's research, the number of commentators highlighting the increasingly exclusionary outcomes of the British integration and naturalisation schemes has only piled up (see, eg, Van Houdt et al 2011; Byrne 2017; Bartram 2018; Monforte et al 2019; Bassel et al 2020). In addition, Goodman's research also shows us that when empirical researchers qualify the integration regime of a particular country as 'enabling', this is often premature. It may only take little time and slight shifts in ruling political parties, before the same country implements a more or even overly 'prohibitive' integration and citizenship regime. And indeed, not long after the research by Goodman and Howard was published in which they established that Belgium had 'normalized' its integration trajectory, the country has rapidly intensified its integration requirements. In fact, as we have seen in Belgium, integration requirements for permanent residency and naturalisation have multiplied and the country now belongs to the stricter countries in the EU (Xhardez 2019; Waerniers and Hustinx 2019; Solano and Huddleston 2020). On that account, it will be interesting to monitor the developments in Ireland and Sweden in the upcoming decade as it is, as mentioned in the previous chapter, novel that these countries now also consider implementing mandatory integration requirements as conditions to attain increased rights.

In summary, the reflections of both liberal nationalists and social scientists provide us with valuable information about circumstances under which integration requirements are permissible, but also leave important questions unsolved. On the one side, theories of liberal nationalists should be supplemented by ('non-ideal') reflections on integration requirements for increased rights for migrants in a precarious legal position, considering the possibility that receiving states and their citizenries are not truly motivated by liberal democratic values and might act partly or outright unjustly. On the other side, social scientists could broaden up the scope of their research. It would be helpful if they would explore under which circumstances integration requirements are prone to be exploited for exclusionary goals and if there may be feasible solutions for preventing this. In any event, our evaluations of integration requirements for residential and citizenship rights to date can be complemented by assessments of the potential motivations and electoral mechanisms as the driving forces behind the integration requirements, together with examinations of the legal and political position of TCNs who are obliged to complete these requirements. Second, we should look for remedies to counteract the risks of these policies. I will focus on the former in the next section and turn to the latter in Chapter 4.

III. The Politics of Integration Requirements

If we look at social psychological research (see, eg, Verkuyten 2013) to explore the motivations behind integration requirements for residential inclusion and also naturalisation, we see that there is in fact little reason to *presume* – as ideal theory does – that receiving states and their citizenry are always willing to accept and include newcomers such as refugees and migrants (and minority groups in general) on equal terms. Human beings habitually perceive themselves as parts of many groups and, furthermore, understand many situations in terms of group memberships. In fact, humans are predisposed to think in opposing dichotomies, such as 'foreign/indigenous', 'established/outsider' or even 'friend/enemy'. Accordingly, if the social conditions to counteract these innate responses to 'others' are not in place, this regrettably leads to strong so-called 'in-group orientations' and 'out-group rejections' (racism, prejudice, etc) (Verkuyten 2013: Ch 3).

Furthermore, public opinion polls and studies on societal attitudes structurally demonstrate that across all liberal democracies and across time, substantial segments of society hold negative (or at least strong) opinions about immigration and immigrants. In 2017, for example, an *Ipsos* survey of adults world-wide on 'global views on immigration and the refugee crisis' found that 44 per cent on average say that immigration is causing their country to change in a way that they do not like (Ipsos 2017). Amongst other things, this research demonstrated that, when asked, high percentages of people in North America, Australia and Europe believe that there are too many immigrants living in their country and say they would prefer more restrictive immigration policies to be implemented. If we look closer at EU countries, we see that the Eurobarometer of 2019 indicated that Europeans consider immigration as the most important issue facing the EU (Eurobarometer 2019). Moreover, in 2018, the Eurobarometer focused on immigrant integration and indicated that a majority of EU citizens (69 per cent) consider third-country immigration problematic and over a third (29 per cent) believe that their government is not doing enough to foster immigrant integration (Eurobarometer 2018). The exact opinions and trends in attitudes vary across states, but even in EU countries with relatively positive views on migration such as Germany, Sweden and the Netherlands, at least half of the population for example think that Muslim immigrants do not want to integrate into society at large (Pew Research Center 2016). In addition, high percentages in most EU states hold that refugees are a burden on the country as they take people's jobs and receive social benefits (Pew Research Center 2016).[3]

However, for the purposes of this chapter, most relevant is whether, and to what extent, such public attitudes have the potential to influence the formation of integration policies within liberal democracies including EU Member States. To answer that question, I will expound the insightful analytical framework presented by James Hampshire in the book *The Politics of Immigration* (2013).

[3] In general, the research by the Pew Research Center indicates that older people and less-educated citizens are more negative about immigration, refugees and Muslims. Yet, in most countries the largest divide in opinions tends to be political. For example, in France 57% of the supporters of the National Front hold negative opinions on Muslims while of the Socialist party 25% does. In the UK a similar split exists between supporters of UKIP and Labour (respectively 54% and 22%).

This framework maps both the exclusionary and inclusionary dynamics that shape the immigration, integration and citizenship policies of liberal-democratic states.

When confronted with immigration, Hampshire writes: 'the institutional response of liberal-democratic states originates from an interaction between four "constitutive features" of the liberal state.' These features, he explains, are not meant as an exhaustive definition of 'the liberal state', but function in his work rather as 'empirically observable commonalities of the major immigrant destination states that are widely labelled as liberal' (13). These four constitutive features are *representative democracy*, *constitutionalism*, *capitalism* and (a liberal form of) *nationhood*. The crux of Hampshire's analysis is that these features often impose contradicting demands on the state in relation to public policies regarding immigrants, but never fully overthrow or neutralise each other. These features therefore do not provide a 'theory to predict outcomes' but a valuable 'framework of analysis' as they often clash and lead to paradoxical outcomes (13). On that account, he states it is essential for understanding 'why effective and coherent immigration policies are so elusive' and to grasp that the contested nature of immigration and integration policies is rooted in the general institutions of the liberal-democratic state itself (2).

In particular, Hampshire argues that 'representative democracy' and 'nationhood' are the two features that are prone to lead to more restrictive dynamics in politics of immigration and integration, whereas 'constitutionalism' and 'capitalism' can be associated with openness. So, to oversimplify these dynamics for the moment: if through democratic processes anti-immigrant attitudes become mobilised or calls for the protection of the national identity and values become politicised, this generates pressure on the state to adopt more restrictive policies for immigrants, including more restrictive integration requirements. However, appeals to constitutionalism and human rights norms put pressure on legislation to develop more open policies, and business lobby (in a globalised world) for immigrant labour has a similar tendency. For the purposes of this chapter, I would argue that the tensions between representative democracy, nationhood and constitutionalism are most crucial and illuminating for the shape and the growth of integration requirements for TCNs in Europe, but I will also briefly discuss the influence of capitalism.

The feature of *representative democracy* is relevant as public opinion of the electorate influence the policies that politicians propose and the prominence that is given to a certain issue. This is simply how democracy works, but it is particularly true in relation to sensitive and salient political topics such as immigration and immigrant integration. Of course, there is a chicken-and-egg question here as political parties do not only simply react to public opinion and the tone of public discourse on immigrants, but also shape it. However, although there is no strong academic consensus on why political controversy on migration and integration has intensified in Europe, this process appears to be 'top-down' (Van der Brug et al 2015) and often with a special role for political party competition (eg, Grande et al 2019). The fear of losing votes puts ongoing pressure on politicians to never be seen to be 'out of touch' with public opinion or reality (Hampshire 2013: 6). For this reason, European politicians must deal with research that suggests that, between 1980 and the present time, majorities of their populations became progressively more attached to their nationality and that immigration is (not solely but) increasingly perceived as a threat. Hampshire therefore asserts that outcomes of public opinion polls such as the aforementioned by Eurobarometer, Ipsos and the Pew Research Center do have the power to affect the formation of integration policies. In this context, Christian Joppke, shows that 'leftist' governments are typically in favour of increasing citizenship rights of immigrants (which Joppke coins as processes of 'de-ethnization' of citizenship), in contrast to right-of-centre governments that tend to resist this while expanding the country's connections to those who have emigrated (processes of 're-ethnization' of citizenship) (Joppke and Morawska 2003). Moreover, Vilde Hernes also concludes, based on a dataset on the ministerial structure of immigrant integration in 16 Western European countries during 1997 and 2017, that 'right-oriented governments are more inclined to couple integration with immigration' (that is, making integration a condition of obtaining increased residency and civic rights) than left-oriented governments are (Hernes 2020). However, Marc Morje Howard explains that having a leftist government is for liberal-democratic countries indeed a 'necessary' yet not 'a sufficient' condition for citizenship liberalisation (Howard 2010: 744). The other condition is that anti-immigrant sentiments do not become 'activated'. This activation can occur due to a variety of causes, for instance 'a successful far right party, a popular movement or a referendum of some kind on the issue of immigration or citizenship' (Howard 2010: 744, see also Grande et al 2019) In any event, it is clear that domestic politics trigger change or continuity in the policy field of integration requirements. More specifically, Howard concludes, if immigration becomes politicised, the growth of integration requirements for increased rights is *likely* and a decrease *improbable* (see also Howard 2009; Goodman and Howard 2013).

In my view, the proliferation of *integration* requirements in the circumstance that the issue of *immigration* becomes politicised is in European Member States particularly likely, because EU and human rights law have limited the discretion of Member States to decide upon immigration policies, particularly in the context of family migration and asylum. Put differently, given that Member States cannot fully reject family migration or expulse arrived refugees easily, national politicians have installing integration requirements for full residential and civic inclusion as a 'second best' option. Indeed, Bridget Byrne observes that the integration and citizenship tests in the UK should be seen as 'an attempt to reassure […] public anxieties about immigration' (Byrne 2017: 3). Also, in Germany, the government sent the political message that obtaining permanent residency was not possible for refugees who do not integrate well, when it changed its integration requirements in 2016 after admitting over a million refugees (Chemin and Nagel 2020: 15). Accordingly, Goodman and Wright conclude in their assessment of the outcomes of the integration requirements in EU Member States that it may be that they are 'simply designed to signal to voters that the government is "doing something" about immigration' (Goodman and Wright 2015: 1891).

Nonetheless, Hampshire writes, given its divisive nature, mainstream political parties generally aim to keep the issue of migration depoliticised. But, if this strategy fails or becomes impossible – for one reason or the other – they often opt for, either, not directly rebutting anti-immigrant discourses and policy proposals, or endorsing them. Centre-left parties then habitually take the stance that the national workforce has to be protected from immigrants, while centre-right parties argue that the national culture has to be preserved (Hampshire 2013: 30). Moreover, it is certainly not uncommon that mainstream political parties start to support or copy anti-immigrant parties in order to win or retain votes (eg, Adam and Jacobs 2014; Van Spanje 2010). In this context, Tjitske Akkerman found that in EU countries the ideological differences between centre-right parties and the far right have diminished on issues of immigration and integration since the 1990s and that over the last two decades centre-right cabinets have installed most of the novel restrictive integration and citizenship laws in Europe (Akkerman 2012). For example, the former French interior minister, Nicolas Sarkozy, of the political party UMP (now Les Républicains) publicly announced his intention to carry back 'one by one' the voters of Le Pen's anti-immigrant political party, the National Front, into 'the Republican Family' by enacting new laws on immigration and integration (Joppke 2007: 11). Indeed, a growing body of research indicates that mainstream parties are particularly sensitive to the actions of other parties when it comes to the issue of immigration and often adapt their immigration policy positions in response to the rise of anti-immigrant parties (eg, Green-Pedersen and Mortensen 2015; Abou-Chadi 2016; Meijers 2017). Interestingly, recent research on sub-national level integration policies in Germany, Italy and Spain demonstrates as well that the implementation of more restrictive immigrant integration policies is most often triggered by 'minority nationalism and the strength of anti-immigrant parties' (Zuber 2019).

That said, in the context of the feature of representative democracy, it is also relevant to note that immigrants who are affected by the integration requirements that monitor their residential and political inclusion are themselves inherently structurally underrepresented in the political community that receives them. Non-citizens (such as TCNs) cannot make themselves heard through most of the political forums of their receiving country, most obviously because they lack citizenship: this excludes them from voting (and also from standing for public office).[4] Furthermore, because they do not belong to the electorate, politicians have little incentive to pro-actively consider them as a group whose interests must be taken into account. Also, the political exclusion of non-citizens is commonly strengthened by the fact that they are confronted with language barriers, relatively weak socio-economic status, discrimination and often also the lack of social,

[4] In some EU countries, long-term immigrants do have voting rights on the level of municipalities.

political and professional networks. For all these reasons, it is simply unlikely that the political representation of legal non-citizens in a representative democracy is forceful enough to influence the formation of integration requirements, whereas anti-immigrant attitudes fostered by citizens in fact do wield influence on these policies. At best, the political voices of immigrants are indirectly represented in public debate through investigative journalism, academic research, NGOs and social movements that support the interests of immigrants and minorities. On that account, Hampshire even concludes that there are strong reasons to doubt whether a representative democracy will *ever* generate demand for enabling integration policies 'given the inherently exclusionary tendency in populations towards newcomers' (Hampshire 2013: 60–61).

Considering these exclusionary perspectives on migration in representative democracies, the question rises why countries do not (at least periodically) simply deny all immigrants entry to their countries and political communities. If there are inherent exclusionary tendencies towards immigrants, it seems more rational and coherent to close the border rather than to install integration trajectories for newcomers. The explanation lies in *constitutionalism*, as the second relevant constitutive feature of the liberal-democratic state. In its thinnest form, the constitutional state (or *Rechtsstaat*, or 'rule of law') is a 'state of laws' in which the authority of the government is derived from and limited by law. For EU Member States, these laws are founded upon the core liberal principles of individual freedom and equality that are enshrined in an international human rights regime. These norms, Hampshire states, 'are the essence of liberalism and they act as a kind of moral baseline: equal treatment is the default setting and divergence requires special justification, otherwise a state loses its liberal credentials' (Hampshire 2013: 8). For Member States, the exercise of their state power is therefore 'self-limited' (Joppke 1998: 268) meaning that they uphold their laws in their treatment of individuals, importantly, not only if citizens are involved but also in important respects in relation to non-citizens. To be sure, this does not mean that liberal-democratic states do not engage in illegitimate or illegal practices of coercion towards citizens or immigrants –unfortunately, they do so often enough – but that the values that underpin constitutional states provide a resource to challenge and legally contest this coercion. And this self-limitation explains why Member States, though admittedly at times with great reluctance, continue to accept immigrants, and in particular family migrants and refugees – even if they are unwanted in the popular political arena.[5] The constitutionalism of liberal states thus warrants that the potential presence of strong anti-immigrant mobilisation (representative democracy) cannot entirely subsume certain core humanitarian

[5] It must surely be noted that the power of constitutionalism is vastly weaker if family migrants and refugees are outside the territorial domain of the receiving state. Indeed, even in relation to the mandatory integration requirements abroad (as discussed in ch 1, s I.A) there are legal avenues available to challenge European Member States that perpetually obstruct the right to family migration, but these are admittedly time-consuming and often difficult to access.

norms (constitutionalism). Consequently, 'accepting unwanted immigrants is inherent in the liberalness of liberal states' (Joppke 1998: 292).

The power of constitutionalism has already been illustrated in this study by the CJEU cases referred to in Chapter 1: the CJEU repeatedly held that integration requirements based on the Family Directive and LTR Directive must facilitate the integration processes of newcomers, not form barriers or result in exclusionary or blatantly discriminating outcomes. Another illustration in this regard is the *Biao v Denmark* case in which the Grand Chamber of the European Court of Human Rights ('ECtHR') issued a decision in May 2016.[6] In that case, the so-called '28-year rule' was challenged, which entailed that if a Danish national with an immigrant background – so Danish-born citizens were exempted from this attachment requirement – was married to a non-EU citizen she or he had to prove, to enjoy the 'privilege' of family reunification, that the residing spouse had stronger ties with Denmark than with any other country. The threshold for establishing whether such ties to Denmark were sufficiently strong was that the spouse had to have resided in Denmark for at least 28 consecutive years. The Grand Chamber of the ECtHR ruled that these laws constituted indirect discrimination on the basis of ethnic origin as it 'places a disadvantage or has a disproportionately prejudicial effect on persons who acquired Danish nationality later in life and who were of ethnic origins other than Danish'.[7] As a result, the Danish authorities, committed to the rule of law, amended their Aliens Act and abolished the 28-year rule. To be sure, this is merely one example of the power of constitutionalism.

The next constitutive feature Hampshire lists is *nationhood*. The first section of this chapter described how liberal nationalists theoretically delineate the boundaries of a liberal national identity and how they see the limits of permissible nation-building policies. From a more empirical perspective, Hampshire observes that Western liberal-democratic states are indeed committed (and recently increasingly explicitly dedicated) to upholding and promoting their national identity. Moreover, Hampshire holds, appeals to nationhood are presupposed to be exclusionary and prone to being utilised to, for example, substantiate the frames that newcomers are a threat to the cultural characteristics of the nation or (presumably) hold illiberal views (Hampshire 2013: 32–35). However, Irene Bloemraad in her review of Hampshire's book responds, with all due respect to Hampshire, that receiving states do not *necessarily* promote an exclusionary national identity and henceforth install restrictive integration requirements. For instance, she writes, most academic commentators who evaluate the integration and naturalisation regimes of North American countries concur that the US and Canada do not foster exclusionary national identities or pursue restrictive agendas through integration requirements, in the same way as European regimes (Bloemraad 2016: 2–3, see also Peucker 2008).

[6] *Biao v Denmark* (Grand Chamber), App no 38590/10, Council of Europe: European Court of Human Rights, 24 May 2016.

[7] Ibid, [138].

Nonetheless, it is undeniable that national identities – through history and today – are all too often invoked for exclusionary purposes. For example, in Chapter 3, I will refer to an Austrian politician who stated after a new integration law had been installed that with: 'this law we can make one thing clear, Austria is not an immigrant country and it will never be one. We will make sure of that!' (Permoser 2012: 185). In other words, here a version of nationhood was promoted through the enactment of integration policies that conveyed a national self-definition based on alterity: *one of our main characteristics is that we are not like you/them*. More generally, it is often asserted that there are fundamental differences between the national identities of European and North American countries, as the latter see themselves as 'nations of immigrants' while European states have populations with deeper historical roots and are more used to understanding their identity in terms of ethnicity and religious composition.

In my view, however, the relevance of these differences between Europe and North America is easily overstated in relation to the risks of potential exclusionary policy making. Of course, the (immigration) histories of countries are different – and so are their national identities. But all European countries are also characterised by histories of migration and diversity and all Western countries – including North America – periodically perceive(d) immigration as a threat to their national identity. For example, in the first half of the twentieth century, both Canada and the US explicitly prohibited (allegedly undesirable) Asian immigrants from entering their countries based on the concern that the national identity would erode (see, eg, Backhouse 1996). And today, in the US there is a debate about Latino immigration that would divide the American nation into two cultures, creating a 'crisis of national identity' (Huntington 2005: 3). Moreover, the Trump administration in fact implemented a new naturalisation test in December 2020 that is complex and much harder to pass.[8] Lastly, it is argued that Europe is now going through a 'nativist backlash', which implies that its national identities used to be more inclusive, which was the case, one could argue, during the initial decades following the Second World War (Hampshire 2013: 18).

In any event, Hampshire writes that when a nation thinks its national identity is under threat, exclusionary tendencies, in the field of policy making and beyond, are most likely to prove persistent. If, for example, people collectively think that immigration forms a threat to 'their way of life', this 'perception is difficult to contest because, unlike, say, a belief that immigration depresses wages, a belief that immigration threatens national identity is not easily disproven' (Hampshire 2013: 32). Therefore, in all liberal-democratic countries, ideas about national identity can profoundly shape discussions about integration policies. It matters how the national identity is imagined – in particular, if immigration and immigrant citizens are perceived as part of the national narratives, or as eroding them.

[8] US Citizenship and Immigration Services 2020: The 2020 Version of the Civic Test [Retrieved from:.www.uscis.gov/citizenship/2020test].

Finally, Hampshire writes that all contemporary liberal states are *capitalist* states and he agrees with Gary Freeman who wrote that migrant labour is 'not merely a temporary convenience or necessity, but a structural requirement for advanced capitalism' (Freeman 1979: 3). So even when immigration is unpopular with voters (in a representative democracy), liberal-democratic states must often respond to demands of employers for immigrant labour, particularly in relation to so-called '3D jobs' (dirty, dangerous and degrading) that non-immigrant majorities are often reluctant to do (Hampshire 2013: 32). If we relate this feature of capitalism to integration requirements for TCNs in EU countries, we indeed see that during the last century such requirements were virtually absent to expedite the migration and desired inclusion into the labour market of actively recruited 'guest workers' from countries as Turkey and Morocco for such '3D jobs'. However, a few decades later, when it turned out these guest workers would not return 'home' but instead turned out to be 'guests who stayed' (Castles 1985), Member States tried to hamper the inclusion of their (ill-educated) family members by enacting integration requirements as 'criteria' for migration (see, eg, Lucassen and Lucassen 2011: 118–140; Joppke 2007: 11).

Moreover, currently, the strategies of Western states to monitor the rights of different types of immigrants (for example family migrants, exchange students, refugees or highly skilled immigrants) seem increasingly conditioned based on economic considerations. Particularly high-skilled immigrants are wanted and attracted with attractive packages of rights, and such targeted groups are often exempted from mandatory integration hurdles (Hampshire 2013: 133). According to Lydia Morris, this 'monitoring and control of migration management' reveals which immigrants are deemed useful and which ones are not (Morris 2002: 9). On that account, it seems that Hampshire's claim that capitalism always pressures liberal countries to enable immigration as it 'cannot afford – literally as well metaphorically – not to solicit immigrants' (12) should be nuanced. Capitalist liberal states tend to opt for open immigrant policies towards those migrant workers whom they think can fill vacancies and address labour shortages across the labour market of their economies.

Hampshire's framework brings us closer to a better understanding of the dynamics of inclusion and exclusion, in the actual motivations and electoral mechanisms that shape the integration and citizenship laws in liberal democracies. It also provides helpful insights about the distinctive legal and political circumstances created by the integration requirements for TCNs in EU Member States discussed in this study. These (obligatory) integration conditions, we have seen, are predominantly targeted at legal immigrants who have a right to residency and often enjoy relatively strong protection against expulsion according to EU and international laws, if necessary, enforced by national and institutional courts ('constitutionalism'). These integration policies are legally and thus explicitly not meant to function as immigration policies. Nonetheless, the potentially restrictive number and the content of the integration trajectories they stipulate for TCNs to obtain full residential security and potential citizenship, strongly depend on prevalent public perceptions in relation to immigration and integration ('representative democracy') and the extent to which the image of the national identity welcomes immigrant citizens or is more 'nativist' ('nationhood').

However, before turning to analysing the normative implications of this analytical framework for the legitimacy of European integration requirements as conditions for attaining increased rights, I believe it is valuable and enriching to extend it. To be more precise, I think it is essential to deepen the analysis of the feature of 'constitutionalism' as highlighted by Hampshire by supplementing it with the work of Linda Bosniak on the position of non-citizens and the 'Janus-face of citizenship' (Bosniak 2008: 99). In particular, if we assess the integration requirements for TCNs in Europe, we should both understand the potency and limits of constitutionalism for protecting legally residing non-citizens (such as TCNs in EU Member States) in liberal democracies. Bosniak writes that within liberal-democratic political communities, citizenship stands for inclusion, equality and universalism. But for those outside of the political community, citizenship means exclusion. This 'Janus-face' of citizenship, Bosniak observes, does not only affect foreigners who are physically excluded from the territory, but also – and this is what she focuses on in her work – immigrants who are legally residing on the territory of a receiving state, yet without national citizenship. Legal immigrants remain 'outsiders' in a significant sense, even though they spatially share the same territory as 'insiders' who operate on the basis of equal citizenship (2008: 4). This legal inequality enables, amongst other things, the relatively limited packages of social benefits and political rights that non-citizens may enjoy compared to citizens.

If such social rights would be unequally distributed between citizens, or if groups of citizens were required to meet certain standards in order to gain access to them, this would be considered as an unacceptable infringement of constitutional equality norms. Nonetheless, in relation to legally residing immigrants such as TCNs, the unequal distribution of such rights is not unconstitutional per se: individuals in a territory with a different legal status are treated differently on (supposedly) objective legal grounds. The Janus-face of citizenship thus allows states to institutionally treat legally residing non-citizens in the territory in ways that would be discarded as discriminatory public policies in relation to citizens. For this reason, Bosniak concludes that the concept of citizenship in modern liberal democratic countries is 'soft-on-the-inside' but 'hard-on-the-outside', also for citizens and non-citizens that live side-by-side (Bosniak 2008: 4). 'Alienage matters,' she writes 'not merely at the border but for the allocation of rights and benefits in the interior as well' (48).

It has been argued that the distinction between citizens and 'denizens' (a term used in academic debates to describe legal migrants residing in the territory) is not most relevant anymore, because progressively constitutional, civil and social rights are decoupled from citizenship (see, eg, Jacobson 1996; Arcarazo 2015). For instance, in most liberal democracies denizens have full due process rights in criminal proceedings, expressive and religious freedom rights, voting rights in local (municipal) elections, protection of state labour and employment laws and access to certain social benefits, based on both human rights law and more local constitutional norms. Nonetheless, I think this analysis is not correct. Although the legal protection of denizens under the rule of law has improved over the past centuries (particularly since the rise of an international human rights regime), to state the distinction is not relevant anymore is simply unsustainable. In the world of today, it is (still) empirically the case that residing immigrants always enjoy less political rights, less social rights and sometimes even less civil rights. In fact, in Europe, since the 2000's, the gap between citizens and denizens has increased again. For example: Member States have placed restrictions on non-contributory social programs, such as housing benefits and income support (see, eg, Howard 2006: 445). On that account, to be fully released from concerns of precarity, the *communis opinio* in the citizenship scholarship to date remains that in our current-day world for all types of immigrants 'citizenship still matters' (Bosniak 2008; Hansen 2009; Stronks 2022).

On that account, Hampshire is right when he contends that 'constitutionalism' produces strong inclusionary dynamics on the formation of integration requirements: it secures the human rights and a number of domestic constitutional and civil rights of legal non-citizens, including their residency rights and protection against expulsion. Nevertheless, it must be noted as well that this does not mean that *TCNs are recognised as full equals under the law*. On the contrary, the integration requirements for residency rights and citizenship discussed in this book are in fact a case in point of the type of unequal legal treatment the Janus-face of citizenship can produce: since TCNs are still non-citizens and reside with a precarious legal status, Member States have the power to ask them to demonstrate certain efforts and achievements before they obtain a more secure or equal legal status. Indeed, in its *Alo and Osso* ruling in 2016, the CJEU affirmed that TCNs can be treated unequally compared to citizens in terms of access to the welfare state as long as they have not completed their integration requirements (see De Vries 2019).[9]

If we combine the analyses of Hampshire and Bosniak, we hence see that the integration requirements in European countries create a unique set of circumstances for liberal democracies. While liberal-democratic states are strictly bound to stipulations of equal treatment towards their citizens when implementing public policy, these stipulations do not prevent states from imposing additional obligations for legal and residential security on TCNs since they are not (yet) full members of the legal order (the 'limits of constitutionalism'). Yet, at the same time, TCNs often cannot be legally deported due to humanitarian law and EU law that prescribes that they should in principle obtain permanent residency after a given number of years of residency (the 'potency of constitutionalism'). Nonetheless, calling for extra integrational demands for TCNs is, more often than not, in

[9] Joined Cases C-443/13 *Kreis Warendorf v Ibrahim Alo* and C-444/14 *Amira Osso v Region Hannover*.

the interests of politicians, while TCNs themselves can hardly make themselves politically heard ('representative democracy'). Therefore, (almost always latently) present anti-immigrant political dynamics are structurally predisposed to, if the issue of immigration politicises, take advantage of the precarious legal position of TCNs. And if this happens, integration requirements are often not primarily enacted to benignly facilitate the successful societal incorporation of TCNs with public policies that have proven to be effective. Rather, they convey the political message towards the electorate that the government is 'taking care of migration' and/or the national and culture is protected ('nationhood') (Permoser 2012: 10). Interestingly, recent research indicates that if this cycle starts – that is, politicians implementing integration requirements to signal that 'something is done' about immigration – this is bound to continue. Hannah M Alarian and Micheal Neureiter (2019) found that although mandatory integration requirements are (partly) implemented to affect public attitudes on immigration, eventually 'neither mandatory integration requirements nor civic integration requirements appear to meaningfully affect public support for immigration' (1). In other words, if the feature of represented democracy calls for more restrictive immigration policies and this is translated by politicians into proposals for more restrictive integration requirements, actually installing these requirements does not neutralise the politicisation of immigration because their implementation 'appears to do little in terms of reducing widespread anti-immigrant sentiment' (1).

Moreover, the feature of constitutionalism will also not counterbalance the proliferation of integration requirements because installing them is not necessarily in breach with the rule of law, as citizens and non-citizens can be treated unequally (again, 'limit of constitutionalism'). Integration requirements can always be defended through the explanation that they do not *deny* TCNs the possibility to obtain increased rights: they only make the accessibility to these rights contingent on an *extra* requirement, as is broadly permitted by the Family and LTR Directives and/or the discretion of Member States to enact integration requirements for naturalisation.

Based on this analysis, it must be concluded that integration requirements as conditions for obtaining increased rights in Member States carry the structural risk to take advantage of the inherent power-imbalance between receiving EU states and their legal immigrants who are not yet equal members of the political community and legal order. Despite the power asymmetry between the state and the TCN, these requirements namely grant the *strong* party in this relationship (the state) the power to (constantly re-)define a set of performances, achievements, efforts and costs that the *weak* party (the TCN) as legal non-citizen (without secure residency and political voice), must demonstrate and fulfil to obtain a more secure legal status and to be (fully) released from residential unpredictability. Moreover, the TCN is not only in a precarious legal position, but also (often) politically belongs to a relatively unpopular group in society. Therefore, if immigration and integration become hotly debated political issues, the integration requirements as conditions for increased rights provide politicians and governments with a political tool to assure voters that immigrants are not easily included or to even scapegoat newcomers.

Lastly, as soon as the proliferation of integration requirements starts, this can trigger an ongoing cycle because implementing these requirements is in fact not effective in assuring that immigration is taken care of. Nevertheless, in EU countries, there are currently no strong institutional precautionary measures in place to counteract the possible growth of exclusionary and stigmatising integration policies or to countervail the precarious position of TCNs, who are not full members of the legal order or the political community yet.

IV. Individualised and Contractualised Integration

So far, the analysis in this chapter indicates that if we limit our normative reflections on integration requirements in Member States to evaluating whether states in principle might have legitimate reasons to install them (such as liberal nationalists do, for example), we do not give enough attention to that the legal design of such policies are structurally susceptible to take advantage of the vulnerable legal and political position of TCNs, given the power imbalances at play and the influence of political interests. In this section, I will fortify this conclusion by zooming in on the main consequences of the recent history regarding both the notion and policies of 'integration' in Member States as described in Chapter 1. This will illustrate that the current integration requirements in Member States do not only hypothetically carry certain structural risks as sketched in the previous section, but that these risks actually already manifest themselves in existing integration policies in Europe. Second, it will also illustrate that we should indeed also understand and normatively analyse integration requirements as state policies dominated by profound power imbalances, due to their current legal configuration.

In Chapter 1, I established that in multiple Member States two (closely-connected) tendencies can be observed: (1) to understand the notion of integration as *individualised*; and (2) to discuss the relationship between arriving TCNs and their receiving states as *contractual*. As such, I concluded that the raison d'être of integration requirements in Europe increasingly became to monitor a contractually laid down 'test phase' in which TCNs must demonstrate their personal integration to (legally) belong. Furthermore, I observed that the integration trajectories that have resulted from these developments, often do not support desirable broader societal outcomes, or do not support them as well as other integration trajectories would. I will now discuss these developments, in light of the findings of this chapter.

A. Individualised Integration

To recall, I determined that individualised integration involves the idea that TCNs – most often with non-EU and/or non-Western immigration backgrounds – must personally integrate to be deemed as 'standing inside of society' and to merit secure residency rights or citizenship. In Chapter 1, I highlighted that this leads to unfairness as citizens without immigrant backgrounds are exempted from meeting personal integration standards to obtain, or to be deemed as entitled to, their citizenship. I will return to potential normative consequences of this double standard in the next chapter. In the following, I will scrutinise these individualised integration requirements considering the frameworks and analyses of Hampshire and Bosniak, that is, against the background of the severe power inequality between TCNs and their receiving states. In particular, this perspective I contend, makes visible that the integration requirements in EU countries for TCNs are (even more) problematic because they make the legal condition to regulate the allocation of rights to TCNs principally *arbitrary.*

In essence, the fact that that no one can exactly pin down who exactly would be an 'integrated person' that is 'compatible' with society, makes the content of integration requirements arbitrary as soon as governments underpin them with individualised conceptualisations of integration (as currently is the case in a growing majority of European Member States). To explain this further: it is not uncontroversial to observe that all European countries are characterised by heterogeneous citizenries in terms of individual differences, such as education levels, careers, family lives, ethnic backgrounds, religious outlooks, political orientations, socio-economic positions, etc. All these types of diversity are present, particularly within what Saskia Sassen calls 'global cities' (Sassen 2004–2005). This does not mean that it is impossible to observe that countries (or cities) have certain common characteristics. For example, in France people do relatively eat a lot of baguettes, in the Netherlands a relatively high percentage of citizens support gay rights, etc. However, notwithstanding that regional statistical differences exist, it remains impossible to create a specific list of qualities and efforts that an individual can meet that would demonstrate her personal compatibility with the 'real society' of a particular country – and, with that, her entitlement to deserving secure rights, citizenship and belonging. For example, some French citizens do not eat bread and homophobia is also pervasive amongst Dutch citizens and has been so for centuries. In fact, from the perspective of liberal and democratic principles, forming such a list would even be an unjust and inappropriate ideal (I will return to this point in the next chapter.)

In the same vein, it is also simply not true that all citizens of European Member States share certain degrees of knowledge about the national history, language and income levels, moral outlooks, democratic views and so forth. Still all of them are citizens. Accordingly, it is incorrect to suggest that certain characteristics would make individuals 'real citizens', meriting their citizenship and equal protection under the law in these countries. As a result, as soon as integration requirements start evaluating whether *individuals* are personally 'sufficiently integrated' to deserve to belong, this standard of integration has no natural ending point and it, as Lubomira Radoilska (2014) puts it, structurally 'exposes immigrant groups to arbitrary critique for being insufficiently integrated' (111).

Take, for example, a public letter that the Dutch Prime Minister Mark Rutte wrote to 'All Dutch' in 2017, which illustrates how the notion of 'integration' is evolving in the Netherlands.[10] Rutte advised Dutch citizens with immigrant backgrounds to 'act normal or leave', instead of 'not adapting and reviling our customs and values'. In his explanation, he gave insight into what he saw as un-Dutch like behaviour that would make immigrant citizens unwelcome. He mentioned: 'Those who scorn homosexuals, harass women in short skirts or call normal Dutch people racists.' In addition, he clarified that 'acting normal' in the Netherlands means:

> shaking hands and treating each other equally [...] That you show respect to teachers and that you do not tease people with online *vlogs*. It is normal that you work for your money and make the best of life. Help each other if things are difficult and embrace each other in dark times. It is normal that you are committed and do not walk away from problems. That you listen to each other carefully, instead of shouting each other down if you disagree with something.

Thus, indeed, it seems that 'Being Dutch' and 'being integrated' can be attributed to nearly anything – from 'not making certain vlogs' to 'giving hugs' or 'not calling people racists' – and that failing to exhibit 'normal' Dutch behaviour could influence the entitlement of persons with immigrant backgrounds to belong. Of course, standards of 'personal integration' mostly tend to involve a package of desirable behaviour or competencies, but, at the same time, it essentially remains an open-ended term. In this context, in a research on the relationships between non-Western immigrant groups and the non-immigrant majority in the Netherlands, a respondent (with a non-Western immigrant background) stated: 'You can simply never be Dutch *enough*' (SCP 2015: 166).

Another example is the *Funda Yilmaz* case in Switzerland. Although Switzerland is not part of the EU, this example does illustrate the open-endedness of the requirement of 'integration' for the attainment of increased rights. Yilmaz was deemed not sufficiently integrated for naturalisation, even though she was born in Switzerland, spoke fluent Swiss-German and received a perfect score on a written citizenship test (100 out of 100 points). However, based on an additional interview her integration was deemed as unsatisfactory. For instance, she could not name *Hornussen* and *Schwingen* as typical Swiss sports (although she did mention skiing) and she could not specify local cinemas and museums. For these reasons, she was not integrated, because she was deemed to be not Swiss *enough* (Orgad 2019: 526).

On that account, if we assess the integration requirements in Member States as conditions to attain increased rights based on the core analysis of this chapter, that is, based on their possible predispositions to be misused (in addition to whether states might have legitimate reasons to install them), we see the following. Asking TCNs to fulfil certain conditions to attain increased rights for legal security

[10] VVD, 2017: Brief aan alle Nederlanders [Retrieved from: www.vvd.nl/nieuws/lees-hier-de-brief-van-mark/].

as such is, normatively seen, a vulnerable legal set-up, given their legal and political position and the involved power imbalances between receiving states and their legal migrants. Yet, on top of that, making the condition that TCNs must fulfil within this legal set-up (individualised) 'integration' makes it even worse, as it is an ill-suited notion to serve as a requirement for obtaining (residential, political or other) rights. Given its open-ended nature, it namely gives – already very powerful – receiving states the opportunity to constantly redefine requirements for inclusion (upwards). Amongst other things, states can demand arrays of standards that would indicate 'good', 'national' or 'cultural' behaviour or customs; very specific knowledge of historical facts that are unknown to most (non-immigrant) citizens; series of oaths promising active citizenship; levels of language proficiency that exceed the level of (some) groups of citizens; having a stable job; acts of civic responsibility such as taking up volunteer work; the presentation of portfolios to demonstrate (labour market) participation; and so forth.

In summary, in the first part of this chapter I established that the vulnerable position of the TCN, without political voice and secure rights, is normatively relevant for assessing requirements for TCNs in Europe. In this section, I moreover demonstrated that this vulnerable position is even *amplified* in that receiving states can ask TCNs to (personally) 'integrate'. In relation to deserving citizenship, this term inherently lacks a clear definition and therefore creates too much leeway for receiving states to unilaterally define 'integration' and expand on what 'integrating' would entail.

B. The Contractualisation of Secure Residency and Citizenship

In Chapter 1, I also observed that many Member States explicitly expect TCNs to sign 'integration contracts' and virtually all of them discuss and defend their integration trajectory using contractual discourses. In this contract, TCNs are then expected to deliver their personal integration, upon which states will deliver them more secure or equal rights. However, if we focus on the vast power inequality between TCNs and their receiving Member States, we see that the observed discoursal contractualisation of their relationship clouds the importance of acknowledging, and where possible neutralising, the unequal power-relationship between the receiving state and TCN. In order to show this, it is of importance to separately discuss: (1) the mandatory integration for family migration; (2) potentially mandatory integration requirements for permanent residency; and (3) optional integration requirements for naturalisation. To be sure, contractual discourses are invoked in relation to all these types of integration requirements, but their legal particularities are unalike and therefore also their normative characteristics.

One of the key legal differences between these requirements, as we have seen, is that integration requirements abroad, if installed, are mandatory for family migrants; that integration requirements for permanent residency are mandatory for TCNs that are family migrants or refugees and optional for other TCNs (such as non-EU economic migrants, who after five years of residence volitionally seek permanent residency independent of their work visa); and that integration requirements for citizenship are never mandatory as there is no obligation to naturalise.

If integration requirements abroad or those for permanent residency are made mandatory for family migrants and refugees, the legal delicacy of these requirements is that they are compulsory yet inclusionary conditions that monitor the prescribed access of these TCNs to increased rights, who are entitled to their residency rights based on EU and human rights law and virtually cannot be expulsed from the territory. In contrast, this is not the case for potential additional integration requirements for permanent residency for other groups of TCNs or for full citizenship. TCNs that consider completing these can always opt out of doing so – for whatever reason – as they can decide not to obtain permanent residency or merely obtain a permanent residency status.

I will begin with the integration requirements for family migration and permanent residency that can be made mandatory (predominately for family migrants and refugees) under EU law. If we assess these based on their structural susceptibility to be used for exclusionary purposes, it is clear that the position of TCNs who are compelled to complete them is troublesome. Given the provisional legal positions of these TCNs, their humanitarian or family related motivations for migrating and the punitive measures connected to the non-fulfilment of integration requirements (in addition to, most often, their lack of political and social networks and language barriers), they simply have no other choice than to submit to all possible integration requirements, irrespective of their content, cost or the political discourses that surround them. Accordingly, these TCNs shall enter into any 'integration contract' installed by their receiving state, whatever the terms – also if the state frames 'integration' as individualised and fully *their* responsibility in terms of efforts, qualities, behaviour and costs. In the same vein, if the results of integration policies turn out to be disappointing, this can easily be one-sidedly framed as *their* failure to fulfil their side of an agreed upon integration contract instead of, at least partly, the result of deficient state policies.

On that account, if state-promoted discourses in European countries suggest that the relationship between the state and the involved TCNs is *contractual* – implying, amongst other things, that the terms under which increased rights can be obtained is based on some sort of a mutual agreement between them – this clearly misrepresents the situation, and, with that, obscures the vulnerable legal and political position of these TCNs, as described in the first part of this chapter. As in fact, given the vast power imbalance between receiving EU states and TCNs who can be mandated to integrate, integration requirements that demand certain performances on the side of TCNs are never the result of an exchange between equals, but always of a coercive proposal between radically unequal parties. These TCNs do not possess a legal position that enables any negotiation on the terms of their residential inclusion, even not if integration requirements become unfeasible, counterproductive, outright silly or stigmatising.

Along the same lines, Kostakopoulou also argues that a contract is not the right legal or normative metaphor to understand the relationship between receiving states and TCNs who are mandated to integrate (see, eg, 2010b). In her analysis, she additionally highlights that a major imbalance exists between the two parties of this 'contract' in relation to the consequences for not complying with the integration contract (951). Whereas it is explicitly specified that the TCNs under this contract are vulnerable to heavy consequences such as fines, the loss of social benefits or denied (residency) rights, it is unclear what direct sanctions would follow for the state if it does not perform – for instance, by not providing the required information, supervision or education or if it would unilaterally change the conditions of the contract. For this reason, she contends, it is also not helpful and even misleading to understand the relationship between TCNs and their states as contractual.

Against her and my analyses, a possible reply might be that these TCNs do in fact have a choice as they can decide to settle elsewhere in the world. For example, refugees can seek asylum in another state, and family migrants and their families can decide to settle in another country (for instance, the country of origin of the joining family member or partner). The underlying argument then is that these migrants implicitly do (tacitly) sign a contract by deciding upon residence in a particular country. And if they cannot agree with the mandatory integration requirements of this particular state (that will in principle receive them based on humanitarian and EU law), why not live somewhere else? Seen this way, it could be argued that the position of TCNs is not overly precarious and there is actually some form of a negotiated contract between these TCNs and states, based on a form of mutual consent.

In an ideal world, there may be a kernel of truth in this argumentation. But in our current non-ideal world it is for most refugees and family migrants not so easy to 'pick' a European Member State to reside in, as they most often flee from violence or political persecution, or at least arrive from less stable countries and/or want to join their spouses or close family members. On that account, for the lion's share of these TCNs objecting to integration requirements of their receiving state that would grant them a right to residential inclusion would result in losing a life-defining interest and all connected opportunities, without a feasible alternative. Deciding not to undergo all stipulated requirements for secure rights (and a secure future), is a decision that is virtually impossible to expect. Moreover, the argument that these TCNs can always move elsewhere also more practically fails, because at the point that TCNs are obliged to integrate, they already passed important immigration 'hoops' and already gained partial rights in a particular state.

For this reason, I contend that normative reflections on these integration requirements applied to them should recognise that virtually all these TCNs lack a genuine bargaining position and have no real exit-option. On that account, to suggest that these integration requirements are part of contracts between state and TCNs, blurs the normatively relevant fact that the position of these TCNs is characterised by severe precarity.

If we then turn to optional integration requirements for permanent residency (for example for non-EU labour migrants) or for naturalisation, we see that the legal and political situations are different. Nonetheless, important normative issues with asking TCNs who want to complete (non-mandatory) integration requirements because they seek increased rights are clouded, especially if the relationship between states and the involved TCNs is presented as contractual. First of all, there are vast differences between the political and personal circumstances of TCNs residing on non-humanitarian statuses in terms of how developed and safe their states of origins are, so to simply assume that there is less at stake when they attempt to acquire permanent rights in Europe is unwarranted. Moreover, most of the political and legal dynamics and risks as expounded by Hampshire and Bosniak also apply to integration requirements for these groups of TCNs. They are politically structurally underrepresented, as they are a numerical minority in society and lack full active and passive political rights (Hampshire 2013: 31). Moreover, the liberal or restrictive nature of the integration regimes they are confronted with are responsive to public attitudes and democratic dynamics, and politicians, particularly in times that migration becomes politicised, have an interest in increasing integration requirements for permanent residency and naturalisation to, for instance, convey the message that the privilege of national citizenship is not easily given to immigrants.

Nevertheless, it must be noted that there are also, normatively seen, relevant differences between groups of TCNs, in terms of national background, citizenship arrangements, legal position and humanitarian need. For instance, high percentages of the highly-skilled labour migrants that reside in Europe are often not from unstable or unsafe countries. Therefore, their fundamental rights would not be severely harmed if they did not eventually obtain permanent residency and, at some point, would even lose their residency rights in a Member State. Moreover, constitutionally seen, economic TCNs are not to a significant degree non-deportable as family migrants and refugees are, because they do not reside on migrant status protected by humanitarian laws. For this reason, subjecting these groups of TCNs to contractual integration requirements for increased rights is arguably less normatively troublesome and also pragmatically less counterproductive. It is less likely they will perpetually remain in society in a situation of 'prolonged legal provisionality' as described in Chapter 1. Rather, they will usually be able to (safely) move back to their country of origin in due course.

Moreover, and perhaps most importantly, migrants such as labour migrants, have been initially selected as 'visitors' and not to eventually reside permanently, so selective intentions and effects of (contractual) integration requirements for increased residency rights applied to them are more defendable. Otherwise, decisions of states to admit temporary migration would (very often) in effect entail admitting permanent migration, which is normatively counterintuitive but would potentially also pragmatically limit the motivation of receiving states to allow any migrant to enter their territories for shorter periods of time.

However, in my view, albeit in different degrees, the issue of precarity is normatively relevant in the context of all groups of TCNs. I acknowledge that reasonable disagreement may exist regarding whether applying (contractual) integration requirements to different groups of TCNs as conditions to obtain access to increased rights is permissible. Nonetheless, if we engage in the normative strategy to evaluate integration requirements based on their institutional risks to exploit power imbalances, it must be concluded that it leads to normative tensions in relation to all TCNs, if receiving EU states contractualise their integration trajectories, given the inherent involved precarity at the side of TCNs. Based on the developed methodology in this chapter, I therefore conclude that it is worthwhile to explore alternatives for describing and legally regulating integration strategies for all TCNs that go beyond metaphors and (legal) discourses of contractualisation. These alternatives should recognise that: (1) 'integration' is not a commodity that individuals can deliver (see previous paragraph); (2) the circumstances under which TCNs (may) receive full legal inclusion is governed by stark power asymmetries between receiving state and TCNs; and (3) that this power asymmetry ideally should be counterbalanced instead of amplified (for instance by contractual discourses).

V. Conclusion

So, taking stock, in this chapter I established that normative reflections on integration requirements for legal immigrants as conditions of attaining increased rights should be attentive to the fact that these policies carry great risks of being used for exclusionary purposes. I reviewed the work of liberal nationalists and the social sciences on the recent increase of integration requirements in EU Member States and concluded that their research approaches are helpful, yet incomplete. They tend to give too little normative attention to the weakest point of these policies. For in practice, integration requirements are imposed on legally residing immigrants who do not yet have a secure and equal position in the legal order and political community.

Furthermore, based on the work of Hampshire and Bosniak, I deduced that in liberal democracies the mobilisation of anti-immigrant attitudes that demand restrictive policies is not an exception to the rule, but rather an ever-present lurking possibility. Due to the combination of structural anxiety about migration and immigrant integration, party politics and democratic election dynamics, the issues of migration and national identity can easily become politicised. And if this scenario unfolds, a vicious circle is established that puts pressure on all political parties on the ideological spectrum to propose, or at least not explicitly refute, exclusionary integration policy proposals, reflecting anti-immigrant sentiments.

Through this lens, I scrutinised the legal and political situation in which TCNs are placed if they must fulfil integration demands to obtain secure residency and citizenship. I observed that this situation creates a unique set of circumstances and, with that, creates a normative challenge for general liberal-democratic practice.

It demands efforts from individuals who are to a high degree subject to the discretionary powers of the state, while empirical research indicates that this power-imbalance is predisposed to be exploited when the political issue of migration becomes politicised (as integration requirements can be employed to create popular impressions, such as that foreigners who are incompatible with 'society' are rejected, or other messages that scapegoat migrants).

Finally, I applied these conclusions to my findings in Chapter 1. I found that these further illustrate that the normative fragility and problem of the integration laws in EU countries is indeed that they grant states discretion to impose (increasingly more) requirements on individuals who are already in a vulnerable legal and political position and not in the position to be able to object. To be more specific, I observed that in the context of contemporary Europe, the utilisation of 'individualised integration' conceptualisations within immigration and citizenship laws and the growing prevalence of a contractual perspective on immigrant integration, both blurs the precarious position of TCNs as legal non-citizens (even more). This contributes to the fact that receiving EU Member States are currently in the position to demand all kinds of possible integration requirements for TCNs in order to secure their rights.

Nonetheless, there are no strong institutional or legal checks and balances in place to counteract the possible growth of unreasonable, stigmatising or counterproductive integration requirements for TCNs, who possess precarious residency rights and lack a political voice. Nor have I encountered academic or political debates on how to potentially counterbalance such illegitimate integration requirements in the future.

For this reason, the task at hand is to propose an institutional strategy that would remedy the risks of the current integration requirements for TCNs in EU Member States. In Chapter 4, I will pick up this challenge. But before that I will first, in Chapter 3, explore another effect of the current integration requirements in Member States, reflecting on their potential stigmatising societal implications and how these might affect the ambition of European countries to uphold the liberal democratic value of maintaining 'communities of equals'.

3

Integration within a Community of Equals

Thus far, I have argued in this book that academic attention should be given to searching for institutional possibilities for preventing integration requirements in EU Member States, as described in Chapter 1, being misused to further politics of exclusion. Indeed, in Chapter 2, I explored several academic bodies of literature that discuss the permissibility of integration requirements to monitor territorial and civic inclusion. In particular, liberal nationalism literature and social science literature on integration and citizenship. I observed that they largely leave undiscussed possible normative responses to states having the discretion to impose additional integration obligations on legally residing immigrants who are already in a precarious position due to lacking secure residency rights or citizenship. Moreover, I concluded that our evaluation of the normative quality of integration requirements should be attentive to how well they are equipped to neutralise their proclivity to be used for exclusionary purposes.

Before turning to proposing an institutional possibility that would counterbalance the risk of integration requirements being put to the wrong use in Chapter 4, I will first add a theoretical 'social equality' perspective to our normative discussions on the integration requirements for residential and civic inclusion in EU states. In short, I will scrutinise the potential ramifications of integration requirements for newcomers by examining their impact on relationships between citizens *with* and *without* immigrant backgrounds, as such policies can result in reinforcing difference between these groups in terms of their status as *equal citizens*.

This perspective offers a contribution to academic scholarship, as it brings to light that there are additional reasons to be concerned about the relatively novel integration requirements for TCNs in contemporary Europe, *supplementing* their impact on TCNs who are not (yet) citizens. I will thus make clear that these integration requirements provoke a process of precarity and a process of stigmatisation – that are two distinctive types of harm. I contend that both are at work in Europe today and both are problematic, but for different reasons. Indeed, a person can have a precarious legal status without being subject to stigmatisation and, conversely, naturalised immigrants may no longer legally be in a precarious position but may still be stigmatised. The institutional solution that I propose in the next chapter, I believe addresses these two processes at the same time.

In this chapter I will hence not assess European practices of integration from the view of those *excluded* from the territory and political community (as I did in the previous chapter), but from the perspective of the *included*, that is, the citizens of the receiving country. This might sound puzzling because the integration requirements in EU countries are not targeted at citizens, but at newcomers without equal citizenship rights. Nevertheless, if we examine the political messages these policies express (in general connected to the conceptual shift towards individualised integration, as described in Chapter 1) and their broader societal implications, we can enhance our understanding of the normative significance of these integration demands by also taking an insider's perspective into account (for a similar strategy, see Lægaard 2012).

In particular, I believe it is important to examine their societal 'spill-over effects' on how (non-EU, non-Western) immigrant citizens and their descendants and non-immigrant citizens perceive each other. In EU Member States, integration requirements are increasingly used to produce narratives about national identity and, in that context, to convey political messages that symbolically express varying degrees of belonging, between, on the one side, citizens without immigrant backgrounds and, on the other side, citizens with (non-EU, non-Western) immigrant backgrounds. On that account, even though integration requirements for new immigrants in Member States do not affect citizens with migration backgrounds *legally*, some do contribute to their social marginalisation in terms of their status as equal citizens. In particular, these requirements, to varying degrees, emphasise that certain types of immigrant citizens are unwanted or only conditionally accepted as equal citizens. Such implicit messages inculcate societal double standards, expecting citizens with immigrant backgrounds to perpetually demonstrate efforts, attitudes and/or cultural characteristics in order to remain as being perceived entitled to their national citizenship (which are never expected from citizens without immigrant backgrounds).

On that account, I agree with commentators who have noted that the changes in integration policies in Member States must (also) be understood as an 'ideological turn' (Mouritsen et al 2019: 6), or as 'symbolic politics' (Permoser 2012) that valorise 'the self-representation of the national majority and defining certain migrants against it' (Larin 2020: 9). However, I also note that, thus far, no commentator has defined *in detail* which integration requirements are normatively problematic from this perspective. As a first step to fill this gap in the normative scholarship, my ambition is to explain in this chapter when such integration requirements are problematic from the perspective of justice. I will argue that the liberal state has a distinctive responsibility to promote equal citizenship wherever it can, and to create a political community in which citizens see each other as equal co-citizens. For this reason, I will evaluate the integration requirements in Member States for TCNs that monitor the access to increased rights through the following question: which immigration requirements symbolically suggest that the receiving society is no community of equals, that is, a political community in which no objectionable social hierarchies and social divisions of superiority and inferiority exist between citizens in terms of their status of equal citizens?

It will become clear that the analysis in this chapter will build upon (and add to) the fairly recently developed literature on 'relational' or 'social' conceptions of liberal egalitarianism, often defined in opposition to (more mainstream) conceptions of egalitarianism that adopt a 'distributive' approach (I will discuss the main differences between the two below). In my view, the analytical outcomes of the academic discussions that try to envision what a 'community of equals' in which norms of 'social equality' operate would look like, can sharpen our normative assessments of migration, integration and naturalisation policies (De Waal 2020). They provide a moral vocabulary to highlight potentially problematic social effects of certain public policies that are not easily made visible with distributive theories of justice. In turn, I believe that this chapter may also contribute to the social equality literature, by shedding light on what the ideal of 'social equality' involves in relation to equal citizenship. The case of migration brings out neglected challenges for theories of justice and social equality that all too often ignore the effects of increased mobility, border-crossing and immigration. Such theories implicitly assume that who is or should be a member of the 'community of equals' (they aspire to uphold) is already pre-determined. For this reason, most theories of social equality provide no guidelines for how to ensure that the practices by which people become members of a community of equals do not leave some citizens stigmatised or disadvantaged.

This chapter is divided into four parts. First, I will reflect on the notion of social equality and elucidate its usefulness for normative evaluations of public policies. Second, I will highlight the challenges that migration, integration and equal citizenship pose for theories of social equality. Third, I will highlight two trends in the formation of, and political rhetoric around, integration requirements as conditions for increased rights in multiple European states, which I believe are objectionable from a social equality perspective. In this analysis, I will give extra attention to so-called 'culturalised' accounts of integration and citizenship, implying that immigrants have to embody the majority culture of their receiving country to have access to the (universal) values that underpin it. Lastly, I will briefly discuss the rise of denaturalisation policies in EU countries that testify to the prevalence of the trend of regarding immigrant citizens as merely possessing a conditional form of citizenship.

I. Social Equality and Justice

Within contemporary academic discussions on political justice there is a growing sympathy for the idea that 'social equality' is an indispensable part of a just society, that is, a 'community of equals' (eg, Fourie et al 2015; Anderson 1999; Scheffler 2003; Wolff 1998; Fourie 2012; Kernohan 1998; Fraser 2001; Young 1990). The motivation behind this body of literature is, as I see it, fuelled by the insights that theories of justice need to provide more than blueprints of ideal political institutions and formal distributions, and that securing justice requires more than citizens who simply abide by legal rules. Constitutional rights and freedoms require a far-reaching commitment on behalf of citizens in order to be effective. For example, if it comes to minority oppression or gender inequality it is incontestable that the effective implementation of liberal-democratic and constitutional laws relies heavily on attitudes of citizens – a realm that cannot be directly legislated and enforced. The law will fail to protect equality and equal citizenship in the broadest sense of the word, if citizens discriminate in the informal institutions of civil society and in daily interactions. For example, it is one thing to have legal protections against discrimination, it is quite another to ensure that no discrimination actually occurs. Therefore, social equality theorists observe, formal equality (eg, equal rights) is only a starting point for equality in a more meaningful sense. Liberal democracies need citizens that, in principle, treat all fellow citizens as equals, refrain from discrimination in hiring and education, deny and, if needed, refute supremacist moral theories based on gender, ethnicity, and so on.

To be sure, in the liberal political philosophy tradition social equality concerns can be found in different forms. For example, John Stuart Mill (1859) who observed that informal sanctions of public opinion that impose expectations on minorities to behave in certain ways, can amount to 'social tyranny' (13). Along similar lines, Alexis de Tocqueville (1838) famously wrote about 'informal tyrannies of the majority' (252). Moreover, the issue is also clearly covered in the well-known literature on *recognition* and justice in which Axel Honneth, amongst others, writes about normative problems produced by 'unjustified relations of recognition' (Fraser and Honneth 2003: 14; see also Taylor 1994).

That said, social equality theorists aim to develop specific normative frameworks to assess public institutions, taking into account that the way liberal democratic societies function in practice strongly depends on the dispositions, attitudes and behaviour of those who live within them. Justice is not merely about erasing formal hierarchies, but also about structurally upholding a societal set of conditions in which all citizens ('native' and naturalised, female and male, white and people of colour, etc) unite in the ideal of a 'single status community' (Waldron 2011: 1). Accordingly, Elizabeth Anderson (1999), a forceful advocate of social equality, holds that formal equality is even 'a sham' without social equality as:

> Political equality […] cannot be realized without a democratic culture pervading civil society. This is not a matter of legal equality, but habits and sentiments of association on terms of equality (93).

Therefore, liberal theories of justice, and states that adhere to them, should both be concerned with the quality of the vertical relationships that citizens have with their state as well as the horizontal relationships that citizens have with other citizens (Lægaard 2012: 453). As such, social equality theorists fully agree with the well-known (feminist) slogan 'the personal is political' (see, eg, Cohen 1997: 3). Justice theories are expected to provide analyses in which the principles and duties of justice do not solely apply to the official institutional context, but apply as well, at least to a certain extent, to the institutions of civil society and individual personal choice.

I write 'at least to a certain extent' as the implications of this social perspective are not always straightforward and clear. For example, the state obviously has no complete control over the attitudes of its citizens. So, if, for example, racism, bigotry, homophobia or sexism is prevalent in society, or particularly present under a certain group of citizens, this may not be attributable to state influences. Moreover, there are limits to how intrusively the liberal state can intervene within the personal sphere, especially in relation to private values. As a result, even if we recognise that for liberal-democratic states the prevalence of social equality norms in society are unequivocally a prerequisite for justice, the state should not adopt policies – for instance to further values such as individual freedom and equality – that might amount to indoctrination.

Nonetheless, until now, social equality theorists have not provided detailed perspectives on the boundaries and obligations of the state in the context of different societal circumstances and phenomena (including migration). Instead, most academic debates on social equality have concentrated on clarifying the contrast between theories of justice that operate through 'distributive' and 'social' accounts of equality. In addition, much attention is given to the question of whether the former should entirely be replaced by the latter – and often it is argued that the answer to that question should be affirmative (see, eg, Anderson 1999; Wolff 1998; Scheffler 2003).

The main difference between these two theoretical approaches is that those defending 'distributive' theories of justice start with the assumption that within a society of equals 'there is something of which justice requires people to have *equal amounts of*' (Cohen 1997: 907). In this view, which has dominated political philosophy over the last four decades, citizens in a just society hence have a certain *equalisandum* (which can be 'primary goods', 'capabilities', rights, political power, opportunities, resources, and so on[1]) in equal measure.[2] Theorists that advocate the social equality approach, conversely, argue that those defending distributive justice are misguided, as they put the cart before the horse by merely focusing on patterns of distributions instead of creating the right types of relationships between people. The central point of social equality theorists is that the highest priority of justice is to avoid certain hierarchal evils in society, such as oppression, exploitation, domination, servility and structural snobbery (Wolff 2015: 213). Or to phrase it differently, the prime concern of a just society should not be maintaining a certain allocation that provides people with an equal amount of X

[1] See, eg, Rawls 1971 on primary goods as an example of the (primary goods and) resourcist approach, and Dworkin 1981 for a defence of recourcism and criticism of welfarism. See Sen 1980, Nussbaum 2001 on capabilities and Arneson 1989 for his defence of 'equal opportunity for welfare' as the currency of justice, and criticism of the capabilities approach.

[2] These debates on forms of distributive justice tend to centre around two topics. First, the discussion on the 'currency of justice' or in other words: what kind of equalisandum is most important. The second is on the 'patterns of distribution' or in other words, whether strict equality is required or whether justice will be served through sufficiency (providing 'enough'), or by prioritising resources for the worst off.

(for instance, Rawls' primary goods), but instead enabling people *to interact as equals* in the political sphere, civil society and on a daily basis. The ambition to realise such relationships probably has drastic implications for questions of distribution (eg, wealth or income), but, crucially, the value of equality is then focused on realising non-hierarchical relationships and not on realising certain distributions, which are then only instrumentally valuable in terms of how well they reflect or help to achieve equal relationships.

In the remainder of this chapter however, I will presuppose that the aim of the debate on social equality should not be to replace distributional accounts of justice. To me, the assumption that we must choose between either a distributive or social conception of equality seems misguided. I do not see why valid concerns for social equality should be interpreted as grounds to altogether abandon theories of justice that are built on more distributive notions. First of all, one could question whether social equality concerns have actually been ignored by distributive theories of justice, or rather meagrely or less explored. For example, in his distributive approach, John Rawls does mention that people are entitled to equal access to what he calls 'the social bases of self-respect', roughly defined as the social infrastructure that gives people confidence in the value of their lives and pursuits. Nonetheless, he does not develop the notion much further, even though he does mention that it is 'perhaps the most important primary good' of all (Rawls 1971: 386). In addition, also convincingly, Nancy Fraser (2001) argues that recognition (captured in her status-model) should not be desired for its own sake, but as strongly connected to underlying issues of redistribution of power and resources in society.

For this reason, I see no contradiction in recognising that theories of distribution and theories of social equality may supplement each other. There might be distributive injustices that are not reducible to violations of social equality. Vice versa, there may be forms of societal hierarchies that profoundly shape people's opportunities in life that are better captured by identifying certain societal inequalities than by reducing them (to metrics of) a certain equalisandum. Seen this way, theories of distribution and theories of social equality are not competing but rather reinforcing each other. They are two sides of the same coin: establishing a just society, in which equal opportunities for welfare for its members are secured (see again Fraser 2001). On that account, I am convinced that the main ambitions of the social equality literature should be to clarify what 'social equality' entails and, moreover, what states are permitted to do (or precluded from doing) to promote it.

Be that as it may, the key drawback of the social equality literature immediately becomes visible, if we turn our research approach towards concerns of social equality: it lacks a satisfactory definition of what a genuine egalitarian relationship would look like, or a fully developed positive account of what it means to be treated or interact 'as equals' (Fourie et al 2015). Most conceptions of social equality boil down to generic propositions, such as that it is 'a moral ideal in which people have equal standing' (Scheffler 2003: 21) or that 'we have to create a community in which people stand in relations of equality to others' (Anderson 1999: 289).

Another example is the 'society of misters' as described by Michael Walzer, who captures the 'social' component of equality with the image that people 'greet' each other on equal terms. More specifically, he contends that in such a society people address each other as 'Mr' or 'Ms' rather than addressing upper-class people as 'sir' or 'madam' and lower-class people as 'Jones' (Walzer 1983: 252). Generally, the ideal can be described as supporting a 'classless' society, not in the Marxist sense of abolishing wage labour, but in the sense that class positions or social status (based on heritage, gender, wealth, skin colour, and so on) should never determine one's' social relationships. Arguably, in most countries, such barriers of class still exist between woman and men, people of colour and whites, old people and younger people, children of working-class parents and children of middle-class people and so on. And yet much remains unclear. Social equality theorists provide no specific criteria to assess if 'a community of equals' has been realised, or when people are 'treated as equals' or 'feel and interact as equals' in the appropriate way.

This is prima facie a severe limitation. Even if we are willing to agree that it is most likely that certain forms of structural social inequalities (eg, racism, sexism, homophobia) are detrimental for a society to operate justly, we clearly need a more profound theoretical analysis. For example, citizens are *physically* never equal, nor are their opinions, talents and relationships. As a result, certain social hierarchies will always exist, for instance when persons receive recognition for intellectual achievements, bravery, sports competitions or beauty pageants. Are these social inequalities relevant to matters of justice? Is it still allowed to (collectively) praise or scorn people, by virtue of hierarchical frameworks? To my knowledge, social equality theorists assure that, in principle, this is the case (Fourie 2012). But this does beg the question: what (stratified) social inequalities, institutional routines and undesirable class relations then do fall within the scope of justice, and how should we understand the role and responsibilities of the state if these occur? In reply to this question, the social equality literature broadly responds in the words of David Miller: 'It is possible to elucidate the ideal of social equality in various ways, but difficult to give a sharp definition … [I]t is a matter of how people regard one another, and how they conduct their social relations' (Miller 1997: 233). However, how then to operationalise and implement a (claimed fundamental) prerequisite of justice without being able to pin it down? A potent and convincing theory of social equality must make transparent *when* relationships are equal *in the relevant sense* in order to uphold a community of equals, and when social inequalities between individuals 'are neutral comparisons of amounts of variables between entities that are irrelevant for justice' (Young 2001: 2).

As a way forward, Jonathan Wolff argues that social equality theorists should utilise a 'negative' methodology while researching social equality. He observes that, although social egalitarians indeed lack positive definitions of 'equal relations' or 'being equal', they tend to do have forceful ideas on the types of unequal relationships they reject and consider illegitimate (Young 1990). In this context, he refers to the research approach proposed by Amartya Sen in his book *The Idea of Justice* (2009). Wolff observes that Sen argues 'that the task for political philosophers is to identify manifest injustice and to work out how those injustices can be overcome' (Wolff 2015: 215). In a similar vein, Iris Marion Young wrote that careful normative reflections on democratic practice and inequalities should be 'looking for possibilities glimmering in it which we nevertheless feel lacking' (Young 2011: 10).

To some, this may sound as analytical backpedalling. Instead of addressing the theoretical deficit that a positive account of 'social equality' is needed, the escape route is chosen to focus on 'social inequalities'. However, if we follow Sen and Wolff, this is not a strategic move, in lieu of an alternative. Quite the opposite, according to their view, this method is the only correct interpretation of the task political theorists should engage in: to point out evident injustices and propose remedies for them. For this reason, having no full positive account of 'social equality' is not a theoretical dead end. All a theory of social equality needs is a clear vision of which arrangements of asymmetric social relations should evidently be *avoided*.[3] In this train of thought, the predominant task of political theorists is to point out a number of societal ills and find ways to circumvent them.

II. Migration, Equal Citizenship and Social Inequalities

It is worthwhile, I would argue, to think through the merits of this approach for the case of migration and equal citizenship. As mentioned, social equality theorists so far have not explicitly reflected on the effects of migration, nor on the fact that in modern liberal democracies not all individuals who reside in society are in fact equal citizens. In fact, most theories of justice – distributive or social – traditionally have given relatively little attention to the phenomena of international migration, if compared to the attention given to the relationship between the state and its citizens and its internal societal affairs. In well-known classical texts by for instance Thomas Hobbes (*Leviathan* in 1651) or John Stuart Mill (*Considerations on Representative Government* in 1861), issues related to immigration receive no mention at all. And if we move forward in time, also Rawls decided in his books to conceive society 'for the time being' as a 'closed system isolated from other societies [...] of which the members only enter by birth and leave by death' (Rawls 1971: 12). As a result, most of Western political philosophy is explicitly or implicitly grounded in the presupposition that those who form the citizenry of a political community is already established and fixed.[4]

[3] Interestingly, this implies that a variety of communities can achieve conditions of 'social equality' while having very little in common than *lacking* problematic unequal societal hierarchies. Wolff refers as examples to Quaker Society, a Kibbutz and a 1960s Californian Hippy community as possible (small-scale) communities of equals, yet very different from each other (Wolff 2015: 221).

[4] Some theorists in history did reflect on immigration. Most famously, Immanuel Kant discussed in his essay the principle of 'cosmopolitan right' that requires those who arrive on the territory of a foreign state to be received without hostility. But also others in the historical scholarship on natural law, such as Vitoria and Grotius, discussed migration (see, eg, Cavallar 2017). For example, in 1615 Grotius defended that it would be barbaric and 'unnatural' to repulse foreigners (see, eg, De Wilde 2017, 2019).

Nonetheless, even if we leave aside the normative question of who should be permitted to immigrate in the first place (yet see Carens 2013; Abizadeh 2008; Walzer 1983), justice and social equality theorists must acknowledge that all liberal democracies in the world have borders that are 'porous' (Benhabib 2004: 88) and no state bestows full citizenship automatically upon all those who enter its territory. For most, this is just a part of life and politics, as there simply is a great deal of movement across borders. Not all foreigners within the territory should be entitled to citizenship and, moreover, not all immigrants are interested in citizenship. However, the reality of migration does pose important normative problems for countries that aim to uphold a community of equals and for theories that aim to describe what this ideal should entail. More specifically, it creates the challenge of how to regulate, accommodate and neutralise the possible side-effects of the unequal treatment of citizens and non-citizens residing within the territory, considering the ambition to uphold a 'one class-society', in which there are no problematic relationships of 'superior' and 'inferior' members based on, for example, lines of heritage, nationality or cultural backgrounds. On that account, if a community of equals admits immigrants, reflections are needed on the shape of the conditions under which newcomers receive access to equal rights.

It could be argued that we stumble upon a deep-rooted problem here, as there is an inherent difference between (so-called) 'native' citizens who gained their equal citizenship 'effortlessly' at birth, and citizens with migrant backgrounds who belong to groups of persons who had to 'gain' citizenship at a certain point. For native citizens, their citizenship is thus an unearned status and an entitlement, while citizens with migration backgrounds had to obtain it. Is true social equality between all citizens hence ever possible at all, since different groups differ in 'where they are originally from'?

As described by the liberal nationalists referred to in Chapter 2, liberal-democratic states are, in principle, built on the assumption that this (potential) hurdle can be overcome as they are founded on the belief that citizens with all sorts of backgrounds can view each other as 'one of us' (in terms of citizenship). In fact, what distinguishes liberal democracies from illiberal states is that they do not ground their national identities in things such as a common ethnic descent or cultural-historic backgrounds, rather promoting a version of national identity that advocates that profoundly diverse citizens can belong (or can develop to belong) as equal citizens to one 'ethical community' (Kymlicka 2002: 267; Miller 1995; 23; see also Modood 2019). Liberal-democratic countries therefore have no in-built reasons to object to the inclusion of newcomers into their political communities and democratic activities. On the contrary, according to the tenets of their political regimes, it is even perfectly possible that immigrants, also those with different cultural or religious backgrounds, become included into their 'community of equals'. In relation to naturalisation, the idea is that citizens can indeed obtain citizenship in different ways, but that this process can be shaped in such ways that there are different possible routes to the same equal status, instead of that the outcome is inherently hierarchical.

Empirically, nonetheless, this liberal aspiration might be hampered by various reasons. Arguably, each nation has, one could say, a cultural shading to its public sphere. This implies that immigrants always, to a certain degree, have to culturally and ideologically adjust themselves, in order to participate successfully in their new country with a particular (political) history and customs. Moreover, since newcomers are often confronted with language barriers, discrimination and a relatively weak socio-economic status, this regularly puts them in a disadvantageous position in various spheres of society such as employment and education. Crucially, however, all these *empirical* considerations leave the *normative* challenge for liberal-democratic states untouched, as they must strive to adopt an inclusive self-perception and public policies that enable both 'native citizens' and 'citizens with immigrant origin' to see themselves and each other as full and equal members of the community. So, even though degrees of social equality are *factually* never fully in the hands of the state, social equality theory suggests that the liberal-democratic state only legitimately governs 'a people' and a territory if it takes up the normative duty to promote the value that all citizens should treat each other as equals. In this line, Joseph Carens writes: 'it is not morally acceptable if citizens from the non-immigrant majority think that the "real" members of the nation must have several generations of ancestors who were also member of the nation. Equal membership is incompatible with that sort of hierarchy' (Carens 2013: 68).

As I see it, if communities of equals indeed must strive to avoid stratified social inequalities between members of the community, they should, in face of immigration, address (at least) two challenges. The first pertains to the responsibility to encourage naturalisation and the second to make sure that the public policies that regulate migration, integration and the obtaining of citizenship support social equality norms instead of compromising them. In the following, I will briefly discuss both concerns.

A. Importance of Naturalisation

Given that it is obviously unjust if in a community of equals permanent members of society are perpetually granted unequal packages of rights, social equality theory indicates that liberal-democratic states should favour relatively easy access to citizenship for settled immigrants. This argument is in line with the influential argument on naturalisation developed in the ethics of migration literature, that is, the field of normative academic research that focuses on the legitimacy of territorial and civic borders (mentioned in the Introduction of this book). Indeed, although between migration theorists considerable disagreement exists on permissible forms of *immigration* control, a remarkable consensus (for political theory standards) exists on how to legally treat immigrants that are present in the territory. This consensus entails that residing immigrants should not structurally remain excluded from full membership and should have the option to naturalise sooner or later. The stipulation that is generally made is that this argument only applies to long-term immigrants, so those who are – or eventually (have) become – 'permanent settlers' and reside within a territory for an extended period of time, not to those who are obviously guests, such as tourists.

Different versions of this argument can be found in established scholarship.[5] However, the heart of the argument is that liberal democracies, based on their own inner moral logic, should treat all permanent members of society that are continuously subject to the laws of the state as equals with rights and include them in political decision-making procedures. Or conversely, it is argued that for a liberal democracy to allow a group of permanent members in society that is subject to the political and coercive powers of the state but unable to participate in determining the political authority or processes of law making, is to create a caste system that undermines the credentials of the state (eg, Carens 2013; Walzer 1983; Rubio-Marín 2000; Dahl 2000; Kostakopoulou 2008; De Schutter and Ypi 2015).

At first glance, this line of reasoning seems to put restrictions on the sovereignty of the democratic state to decide, for example by a majority vote, whom of those residing on its territory can become citizens. According to Robert Dahl (1989), however, the 'full inclusion' of 'all persons subject to the laws of the state' is in fact the very basis of democratic sovereignty (78). Indeed, he holds that this principle is the key feature that makes democracy a form of government distinguishable from other forms such as aristocracy or oligarchy in which small groups of people perpetually hold all political power. It is impermissible, he explains, for a democracy that a self-defined group of 'political insiders' monopolises the power to determine which 'political outsiders' are allowed to join the political community, because that gives this confined group of insiders all political power (potentially forever). Take women suffrage. If in a political community only male members are granted political rights and the right to vote, this male group could in principle democratically decide to permit women to vote – but could also enduringly decide not to. This is an unacceptable outcome for a democracy, Dahl reasons, because it enables the possibility of a permanent democratic deficit. If the male part of society keeps rejecting women suffrage, the women in that society, although continuously subject to the state and its laws, will never obtain full and equal political membership rights. For this reason, within a democracy, the procedures that uphold universal suffrage cannot depend on citizenship rights being granted by a particular group but should be assured entitlements for all who continually reside on the territory and are present in society. Phrased more radically, the creation of 'the people' of a democracy should follow social reality, which makes the democratic state continuously dutiful to a 'pre-existing demos' (Rubio-Marín 2000: 26).

As stated, to my knowledge, the foundations of the argument that those residing in the territory should eventually be allowed to naturalise are virtually not

[5] For example, the 'stakeholders doctrine' (Bauböck 2009); the *jus nexi* membership allocation (Shachar 2009); 'social membership theory' (Carens 2013). For a legal account, see Ballin 2014.

refuted in the literature of (liberal-democratic) political and legal theory. Views do vary on *when* and *how* naturalisation should be possible, but not on *whether* it should be obtainable at some point. Indeed, more communitarian thinkers such as Michael Walzer, advocating restrictive border controls, argue that admitting immigrants to the territory without offering them an assured path to naturalisation amounts to an 'enduring rule of citizens over non-citizens' which is a form of 'political tyranny' (Walzer 1983: 52–61).

There is, however, disagreement on one issue. This entails the question of whether permanent immigrants should be able to (easily) apply for citizenship, or whether citizenship should be mandatorily bestowed upon them. Rainer Bauböck and David Miller, for example, argue that long-term immigrants have a right to receive citizenship if they choose to apply for it (Bauböck 1994; Miller 2016). In contrast, Ruth Rubio-Marín for instance defends mandatory citizenship for immigrants. In her view, possessing the national citizenship of the country in which you reside should not be voluntary for anyone: not for native-born citizens and not for permanent immigrants, as that would result in an unjustifiable asymmetry.

I believe that social equality theories generally indicate that commentators who defend mandatory citizenship for immigrants are right, because social theorists emphasise a particular version of the argument that long-term immigrants should be included in the political community. Indeed, from the perspective of social equality, members of a community of equals cannot *justify to themselves* to perpetually exclude members of society from full legal equality. On this ground, for instance Lea Ypi and Helder de Schutter (2015) defend their case of obligatory citizenship for immigrants by (also) stressing the importance of social equality:

> If we accept laws that should not discriminate on grounds of race, gender or social class, we should be prepared to accept that introducing different standards for citizens and immigrants corrupts the democratic ethos of host societies. It implicitly legitimizes laws that do not treat everyone as equal and threatens to absolve the apartheid- like condition of those who are not offered an equal say in the making of laws to which they are subjected (16).

To be sure, arguments in favour of mandatory citizenship remain controversial, as they remove the option for immigrants to opt out of citizenship. However, I do not think that the claim that naturalisation is important for social equality stands or falls on whether it should be mandatory. The crux is that the social equality arguments in favour of (easily accessible or mandatory) naturalisation do not normatively depend on that it would be beneficial for *excluded* immigrants to have full citizenship. Rather, they depend on the insight that citizens *who are already included* have an interest in protecting their community of equals, which is jeopardised by (endured formal) differential treatment. To illustrate the difference, De Schutter and Ypi make an analogy with slavery. Slavery is wrong, they explain, as it conflicts with the interest of the slave but also because it is an unjust and unequal institution. For this reason, the immorality of slavery and the reasons for forbidding it cannot be fully contingent on the interests of those who are enslaved (or their personal opinion of being enslaved), as it is also in the interests of a just state – considering its self-imposed principles – to uphold a society in which there are no slaves. Based on the same reasoning, Owen Fiss writes that models of bounded solidarity which apply exclusively to citizens but not to immigrants in the territory are problematic as 'we ought not to subjugate immigrants, [...] to preserve our community of equals' (Fiss 1999: 16).

For this reason, a social equality perspective (minimally) suggests that states must actively promote the importance of naturalisation and communicate that the state wants immigrants in their territories to do so. Accordingly, integration requirements that delay the moment that newcomers naturalise or de-motivate them to apply for it are undesirable. In European countries, however, this will require a shift in mentality towards how important it is that immigrants obtain full citizenship. For example, Bauböck et al (2006) observed, after scrutinising the nationality laws in 15 Member States, that it is 'astonishing to see how little effort they put into encouraging their potential citizens to naturalize and informing them how to do so' (2006: 16). In a more recent study, EMN also concluded that 'in most Member States, third-country nationals are not actively encouraged to apply for citizenship, and support is limited' (EMN 2019: 4).

In this context, from a stringent social equality viewpoint, internal EU immigrants also pose a threat to the minimum standards of a society of equals because they lack equal political rights. It could be argued that the possession of a shared EU citizenship – that protects extensive packages of rights and enables all EU citizens to vote during elections for the European Parliament – secures acceptable social equality standards in EU states (even though internal EU immigrants have no voting rights during national elections outside of the state in which they hold citizenship).

In any event, in times of migration, the first normative guiding principle that the social equality literature provides in relation to migration is that it should evidently be avoided that in a community of equals, (groups of) members of the community perpetually possess unequal rights. Structural unequal treatment does not reinforce a social ethos characterised by the value of equality. Receiving liberal democracies should try to ensure that the percentage of residing immigrants that acquire full citizenship is as high as possible. I will return to this point in the next chapter.

B. Stigmatising (Those Who Become) Citizens

Another consequence of the fact that theories of social equality and most justice theories tacitly operate through an assumption of pre-established bounded societies, is that they do not provide reflections on the processes by which people join and become members of the community of equals. However, the ambition to uphold a 'community of equals' is clearly not the same as the ambition to uphold a 'globe of equals' based on (something like) the equal worth of persons. For this reason, the second challenge for social equality theory is to explore the possible links between processes of residential and civic inclusion and the realisation of a community of equals.

From this point forward, I believe that the social equality approach genuinely starts to supplement more distributive theories on the topic of integration policies, such as the ethics of migration literature, as this literature mostly focuses on under which circumstances immigrants should obtain certain *rights*. It illuminates (better) that justice requires considerably more than only the equal distribution of legal rights to residing immigrants after a certain number of years of residency. Rather, based on the principles of liberal democracy, social equality demands that the state should also be concerned with how all citizens (new and old) fare on a more general note, as a community of equals. This entails that it should be committed to facilitating that public and social institutions enable all citizens to participate on an equal footing with others and can belong to society in equal degrees. That implies that the state should, inter alia, to the best of its ability facilitate equal opportunity for all citizens in various spheres (employment, education, and so on); stimulate the emancipation of those who are in a disadvantaged position; and monitor how well different citizen groups do according to various indications of well-being in social and political life (Miller 2008: 375).

On that account, it is, first of all, clear that the liberal-democratic states should constantly promote equal citizenship directly and explicitly. For instance, the state and the government can take up the role of emancipator through statements of political leaders, forms of civic education and integration courses, public policies that stimulate emancipation, having public memorial days to treasure an inclusive national identity and/or funding certain initiatives in civil society that promote equal citizenship (see, eg, Gutmann 1995; Brettschneider 2016). Second, liberal-democratic states must be perpetually vigilant not to, intentionally or unintentionally, contribute to problematic social hierarchies between citizens, by carrying out public schemes, policies or statements that happen to have the (side-)effect of furthering societal stigmas, social exclusion and forms of discrimination that jeopardise the ideal of equal citizenship. This might, at times, be a complicated task as (oppressing) societal dynamics often spring from nuanced and complex sets of relationships between public assumptions, expectations, stereotypes, institutional policies, individual actions and the collective outcomes of all of these together (Young 2001: 10). However, for liberal-democratic states, a pragmatic normative guideline should be that as soon as it becomes apparent that public policies, deliberately or accidentally, instigate or bolster social hierarchies in terms of first-class and second-class citizens, principles of justice would demand that such policies are either replaced or improved.[6]

[6] Elizabeth Anderson and Jonathan Wolff's well-known criticisms of distributive accounts of justice essentially amount to this form of normative reasoning. Both Anderson and Wolff hold that distributive forms of liberal egalitarianism focus on deserved and undeserved inequalities between people (by taking into account things such as 'the lack of natural talents' or 'an underprivileged childhood

If we apply this line of reasoning to the integration requirements for TCNs in Europe (for family migration, permanent residency and naturalisation) I think these policies, given their direct links to the admittance and incorporation of immigrants, deserve special attention from the perspective of social equality as they possess strong symbolic potential (Larin 2020). On that account, if EU states decide to install integration requirements as a condition for obtaining increased rights, they should carefully assess which political messages and public perceptions these integration requirements might communicate, and whether they might instil social inequalities between citizens, especially regarding their *status as equal citizens*. Consequently, another challenge that the social equality literature reveals in relation to immigration and integration is that the state should strive to avoid that policies regulating the incorporation of newcomers stigmatise citizens with immigrant backgrounds. Most likely, this stigmatisation might affect immigrant citizens even after they are naturalised and citizens with the same ethnic, cultural, national or religious background as newcomers who are obliged to integrate. In the following section, I will scrutinise the integration requirements in multiple European countries more closely based on this conclusion.

III. Integration Requirements: To Deserve to be One of 'Us'

The recent changes of integration and citizenship laws in multiple European states are too diverse to draw a single conclusion in relation to their outcomes for social equality. First, (only) five Member States have adopted an integration requirement for incoming family migrants that are still abroad (and France eventually repealed it). Second, although a majority of Member States have now enacted at least one integration requirement for obtaining permanent residency, the requirements differ per country and are frequently adjusted. Lastly, naturalisation is not a matter of European law, and the exact requirements for it also differ between Member States.

However, overall, I observe two trends within the general increase of integration requirements for TCNs in Europe that deserve normative scrutiny from a social equality stance. The first concerns integration policies that communicate

upbringing'), in order to reach just distributions. However, this practice of the state – although it might be fair on an abstract level – promotes a skewed ethos in society, as it views disadvantaged citizens as 'potential cheaters' that must engage in 'shameful revelation' to prove that they are indeed in a disadvantaged position (Wolff), or leads to disrespectful pity to the 'deserving' poor and paternalistic menacing of the 'undeserving' poor (Anderson). In other words, both Anderson and Wolff envision that if strict rules of distribution are implemented in this way, the result will be that bonds of solidarity, respect and mutual concern will (unintentionally) erode between citizens. In other terms, strict equality in a formal sense demands a process that undermines the relationships between people that make them care for justice and each other's well-being in the first place. See Wolff 1998; Anderson 1999.

that the arrival and naturalisation of certain immigrants is plainly *unwanted*. The second concerns integration requirements that nurture the public perception that persons with non-EU and non-Western backgrounds have to *deserve* their citizenship (and to belong). This leads to a social hierarchy between, on the one side, citizens without immigrant backgrounds who are unconditional citizens of the political community and, on the other side, citizens with (non-EU, non-Western) immigrant backgrounds who are perceived as, at best, obtaining a conditional form of citizenship. I will discuss both social inequalities respectively.

A. Unwanted Citizens

The first trend involves integration requirements that convey that certain immigrants or forms of diversity are outright undesirable. To date, there are only a few specific examples of this trend. A prime example is the statement of the FPÖ politician Peter Westenhaler who introduced a more restrictive integration and citizenship scheme with the words: 'With this law we can make one thing clear: Austria is not an immigrant country and it will never be one. We will make sure of that!' (Permoser 2012: 185) Another example is how certain European countries implemented their 'integration requirements abroad'. The exclusionary purposes behind these integration conditions are not nearly as unambiguous as the statement by Westenhaler, since these policies were often also defended as furthering integration and inclusion (Strik et al 2013: 41). For example, in Germany, limiting migration was explicitly rejected as a policy aim of their integration requirement abroad, which was said to promote integration and to prevent forced marriages (Scholten et al 2012: 5). However, in France, former interior minister Nicolas Sarkozy explained that the government purposely inconvenienced the path of 'low-skilled family migrants' to bend the influx of immigrants to Europe from 'unwanted' to 'chosen' (Joppke 2007: 11).[7] And in the Netherlands, we have seen, the purpose of the integration requirements abroad has been explained as restricting the immigration of 'non-integratable' migrants from particularly 'non-Western countries'. During the parliamentary debates, it was explained that these migrants after all mostly become 'housewives, unemployed or unfit for labour' (Scholten et al 2012: 10–11). Moreover, in the Netherlands, after it turned out that the initial exam implemented in 2006 was passed by almost 90 per cent of those who had to take it, the government decided to raise the level and length of the test explicitly because the average passing rate – and with that, the number non-Western family migrants – was too high (Groenendijk 2011: 13).

These statements are remarkable because, as we have seen in Chapter 1, integration requirements that function as immigration laws and permanently

[7] Family migrants are not 'chosen' according to Sarkozy, because they are not selected by France based on merit but included based on humanitarian laws.

exclude certain family members are inconsistent with the EU directives that permit them. In addition, such statements and policies affect the relationships between included citizens in several ways. If integration requirements are made stricter or are installed solely to further forms of exclusion – also if the exclusionary effects remain largely symbolic – this leads to a state backed social hierarchy between 'wanted citizens' and 'unwanted citizens'. In part, this analysis resonates with the normative approach of Michael Blake on racist immigration criteria. He reflects, for example, on the 'White Australia' immigration policies that operated from 1901 until 1957 and barred entry of immigrants of Asian origin. He concludes that these policies were impermissible because they (also) discriminated against insiders. 'Seeking to eliminate the presence of a given group from your society by selective immigration,' Blake writes, 'is insulting to that group already present' (Blake 2005: 232–3). In other words, if a country tries to exclude immigrants based on specific origins or characteristics, this is an affront to all citizens with the same origins or characteristics who are thereby treated as unwelcome and, with that, second-class citizens.

It could be argued that if integration requirements to obtain access to residency and citizenship rights problematically stigmatise immigrant citizens, they could still be normatively permissible in light of further considerations that also have moral weight. For example, Wellman argues, in response to Blake, that racist immigration policies might be morally regrettable but cannot fully outweigh the right of states to control their borders (Wellman 2008). However, as I see it, the analysis on integration policies presented here sidesteps this possible critique as it does not affect the right of states to enforce border controls, but pressures Member States to treat already admitted TCNs with non-stigmatising integration requirements. This is a far less demanding normative outcome.

On that account, statements as made by the FPÖ do stigmatise 'insiders' by describing immigrant citizens as unappreciated citizens. After all, by stating that 'Austria will never be an immigration country', the message was sent out that immigrant citizens already present and prospective immigrant citizens are not, and can never become, a true part of the national identity. To be more precise, obviously, the 'we' in this statement that 'makes sure of that' does not include citizens with immigrant backgrounds into the political community that protects itself. Citizens without immigrant backgrounds are therefore publicly endorsed as having more 'entitlement' to the state and its identity.

If we focus on the family reunification policies, we see, first, that immigrant citizens with the same national or cultural background as the prospective family migrants who are described as 'unwanted' or 'unintegratable' receive the affront that Blake warns of. Second, the 'immigrant spouse' that joins his or her partner will obtain territorial inclusion together with the message that they are unwelcome. In addition, the citizens of the receiving country will receive the state-endorsed message that there is no need to give family migrants a warm reception upon arrival. Rather, it is publicly legitimised to perceive them as an unwanted influx of newcomers that managed to slip through a restrictive path to entry. The desirability of the presence of these new immigrant members and the citizens with the same immigrant backgrounds can hence be openly questioned. That being so, Member States evidently contribute to impermissible social inequalities in society if they suggest there is a distinction between 'wanted' and 'unwanted' citizens and/or suggest that certain groups of citizens are not (and never will be) truly be part of the national identity.

B. Conditional Belonging

The second trend deserving attention strengthens the public perception and societal standard that the entitlement to citizenship of persons with (non-Western and non-EU) immigrant backgrounds is contingent on certain competences, characteristics and efforts. In his book, Sune Lægaard coined this phenomenon as the 'desert paradigm of naturalization' that symbolically makes citizenship a right for some and a reward for others (Lægaard 2012). As elaborated on in Chapter 1, I identify this as a prominent trend in Europe. It manifests itself in several forms, but at its core lies the individualised conception of integration: (non-EU, non-Western) TCNs, immigrant citizens and their descendants need to demonstrate that they deserve secure residency and equal citizenship by being 'personally integrated' and hence 'compatible with society'. This is seen as a condition an individual can embody, for example by having a job or being liberal-minded. In this model, integration policies are increasingly framed in contractual terms and compel immigrants to integrate in order to acquire secure residency and citizenship rights. Moreover, citizens with immigrant backgrounds are not principally regarded as being entitled to their equal citizenship irrespective of their behaviour and orientations, while non-immigrant citizens are.

If we look at integration requirements from this perspective, the first question to be addressed is whether not *all* integration requirements (language courses, citizenship tests, oaths, etc) as conditions of increased residency rights and citizenship for TCNs feed the public perception that the possession of citizenship is an earned right for only integrated immigrants. Along this line, some commentators such as Kostakopoulou argue that all migration and integration requirements are indeed tools of stigmatisation (Kostakopoulou 2008, 2010b). This question does not concern whether states may enact integration strategies *as such*. Even if we accept that receiving states have legitimate interests to enact integration strategies to monitor and stimulate the integration of newcomers, we can still call into question if they should have the discretion to *connect* these integration strategies to controlling when TCNs can 'earn' more secure and equal rights. I will return to this line of reasoning in Chapter 4. There, I argue that if integration strategies are fully *decoupled* from laws that regulate the access to increased legal statuses or citizenship of migrants, this will indeed help to diminish the symbolic difference between the social status attributed to the citizenship of those with and without immigrant backgrounds.

However, a less rigorous approach would start by highlighting those integration requirements that have been explicitly defended with the argument that obtaining residency rights and citizenship should not be a *right* for TCNs, but a *privilege* based on certain efforts or attitudes. Illustrations of such requirements have been discussed in Chapter 1, when examples were given of (Dutch, Danish, Austrian, French, Czech, Belgian, etc) politicians in power and policy documents that stated that legal security and citizenship is something special to be *earned* (see also Van Oers 2013; Van Houdt et al 2011; Böcker and Strik 2011; Schinkel 2017). Furthermore, another well-known example is that the UK proposed to create 'probationary citizenship' in 2009. The idea behind this policy proposal was that immigrants had to prove to be deserving of their conditional citizenship status by, amongst other things, demonstrating 'active citizenship' and additional efforts such as 'civic activities' (eg, volunteer work). At the last moment, the UK Government abandoned most of the specifics of this plan, as it would be too much of a bureaucratic burden. Nevertheless, it did retain the decision to increasingly work with models of 'earned citizenship' (Byrne 2017: 6; Monforte et al 2019).

However, in Italy a form of probationary citizenship has actually been implemented. There, part of the 'integration contract' that the state has with TCNs involves a point-based system in which 30 credits or more should be obtained over two years. Once the agreement has been signed, the temporary residency permit of the TCN is made contingent on the number of credits gained or lost and 'losing all credits results in the withdrawal of the permit of stay and in the expulsion of the foreigner' (Cuttitta 2016: 292). Upon the signature of the agreement, every TCN is awarded 16 credits.

> Credits can be reduced if the TCN commits a crime, an administrative or fiscal offence or is detained. Credits can be gained by attending school, university or professional training courses, by obtaining degrees, by being granted awards of civil merit, by carrying out certain professional or voluntary work activities, by choosing a family doctor, by buying and renting a flat, by learning Italian and acquiring cultural knowledge (Cuttita 2016: 294).

In other words, for TCNs in Italy, impeccable citizenship became the condition for obtaining permanent residency and citizenship.

In her research on (mandatory) citizenship ceremonies in the UK and Germany, Elisabeth Badenhoop has found a distinctive version of conditional belonging. In her words, these ceremonies communicate that naturalised citizens are expected to become 'supercitizens' in the sense that they must become a political, economic and cultural *asset* to the nation-state (Badenhoop 2017: 410). Interestingly, these type of, prima facie, more positive discourses on immigration, integration and citizenship also 'reinforces a hierarchy of "deservingness" and merit' (419). For example, during British and German citizenship ceremonies it is suggested that new citizens must personally enrich the cultural diversity of society, stimulate the economy and at times also, particularly in Germany, adapt a form of 'new nationalism' to 'set an example' to 'Neo-Nazis' and form an 'antidote against […] racism and xenophobia' (420–421). For this reason, Badenhoop concludes, it is suggested that naturalised citizens are expected to live up to a variety of individual responsibilities and duties, in contrast to those with a form of citizenship defined by birth right membership (422).

Similar expectations are also communicated through the declarations and oaths that newcomers have to sign in an increasing number of Member States. Most countries that have such a declaration – for instance, the Netherlands has its 'participation declaration' and Belgium its proposed 'newcomers declaration' – do make sure these do not insinuate that newcomers have to promise to (personally) endorse liberal-democratic principles and human rights in an illiberal fashion, but do demand them to declare that they will 'respect' or 'abide by' them (Orgad 2009). However, these declarations do most often contain the phrase that newcomers must promise that they will 'participate actively in' or 'contribute to society' (Oomen and Leenders 2019; NWS 2016), while it is never asked from 'born citizens' to explicitly promise that.

To briefly take stock, from a social equality perspective, the problem with such integration requirements is *not* that they generally encourage active citizenship or a commitment to liberal democratic values. On the contrary, social equality theorists emphasise that all liberal democracies rely on active and committed citizens, and instruments to encourage this are welcome. However, the problem is that virtuous behaviour, talents, personal outlooks and deeds for non-Western and non-EU immigrants are promoted as *prerequisites* for deserving legal citizenship. This stands in sharp contrast with the tacit understanding of the citizenship of people without immigrant backgrounds. They are, of course, expected, supported and encouraged to be familiar with the law, to abide by the law or demonstrate certain behaviour or deeds. But they are never deemed to engage in civic activities, to have exceptional merits or asked to sign to agree with liberal-democratic values to be deemed *to become or remain entitled to their national citizenship*. Indeed, the citizenship of non-immigrant citizens remains intrinsically and fundamentally unquestioned, *even if* they were to adopt illiberal and undemocratic ideologies and never participate in community service. On that ground, Joppke described integration requirements creating forms of probationary citizenship statuses as 'the most drastic invasion of democracy (to choose a friendly term) into the citizenship domain' (Joppke 2010: 58) as idealised standards of behaviour and characteristics that start to affect matters of citizenship.

Put differently, from a social equality perspective, it is unacceptable if integration measures that in a narrow legal sense require of TCNs to be integrated and 'ready' (Byrne 2017: 12) to earn secure legal residence or citizenship, (also) nurture and exacerbate *broader societal hierarchies* towards citizens with non-EU, non-Western backgrounds, implying that they should (perpetually) demonstrate their personal integration to 'deserve' to belong. Instead, the liberal-democratic state should consistently promote equal citizenship and be vigilant not to convey the message that immigrant citizens must do well in various societal spheres before they may be deemed as true co-citizens. Otherwise, the state contributes to the establishment of an evidently problematically ranked society in which there is a hierarchy of citizens. More particularly, it contributes to a social ethos in which only immigrant citizens who are personally successful – or, in Badenhoop terms, 'supercitizens' – are deemed as deserving their citizenship, while this is not the case for non-immigrant citizens. And in turn, if non-immigrant and immigrant citizens turn out to be less successful, this only has a negative impact on the position in the fabric of belonging to the national community for the immigrant citizen. A possible result may be that, for example, in situations that immigrant citizens are unemployed, illiberal or criminals, they are looked upon as undeserving of their citizenship, and condemned for unjustifiably burdening 'our' national welfare state. It is potentially suggested that they could better 'return to their own country'. However, citizens without immigrant backgrounds who are unemployed or engage in criminal behaviour may be regarded as a nuisance, unlucky, malignant or lazy – but, crucially, never as less of a *citizen* for being so.

IV. Universal Values and Equal Citizenship

To fully understand this conditional belonging-trend that perceives the citizenship of certain immigrants as something that needs to be deserved, I believe it is valuable to concentrate on the peculiar roles of the notions of 'national culture' and 'universal values' in European debates on policies monitoring integration. The implementation of integration requirements is often not only defended as stimulating increased language levels and participation, but also as *securing* the 'universal values' that underpin the cultures of receiving European states. In the academic literature, it is argued that the risk of stigmatisation is not applicable to such nationally anonymous universal values, such as human rights, non-discrimination, toleration, rule of law and so forth (see, eg, Joppke 2008a: 538; Orgad 2009). However, as it happens, actual discourses of universal values in Member States are frequently framed in exclusionary ways – that is, as part of a *culture* that immigrants do not (yet) belong to. As a result, the importance of universal values is often invoked in such a manner that it inculcates a social inequality that damages equal democratic deliberation between all citizens.

Indeed, if integration policies and citizenship are discussed in Member States, the image is increasingly created that the universal values that characterise European liberal democracies are fully intertwined with the specific culture and (religious or cultural) history of the state. In its most extreme form, this amounts to what Triadafilopoulos (2011) has coined as 'Schmittian liberalism', which calls for the full exclusion of (supposedly) illiberal immigrants, as the protection of universal values requires, paradoxically, levels of cultural homogeneity (867). In more moderate forms, within such statements, universal values are presented and described as *so* intertwined with the national culture that (often non-EU and non-Western) immigrants have to personally embody the nation's majority culture before they are perceived as equal citizens (Rostbøll 2010: 406). In other words, it is suggested that to be taken seriously in the political realm and to discuss public issues, it requires *being* Dutch, French or Belgian (and so on) in a majority cultural sense.

In the terminology I used in Chapter 1, this can be described as one particular manifestation of the broader European shift towards individualised integration, in which it is expected one-sidedly from immigrants – before they can belong to 'the real society' – that they demonstrate *their* personal integration through *cultural* participation by adhering to certain national mores, values, practices and traditions. In contemporary sociological literature, this development has also been described as the 'culturalization of citizenship'. For example, Jan Willem Duyvendak et al studied moments in which 'essentialist' views on culture play a central role in debates on citizenship (Duyvendak et al 2008, 2010). In these studies, the culturalisation of citizenship involves that instead of presenting the national cultures of European receiving states as inclusive and fluid, they are portrayed as fixed unities – and as something that *they*, immigrants, have to learn, embody and accept. Along these lines, Mouritsen observes that in Denmark the national culture is described as being connected to 'universal civic values', while immigrants – above all Muslim immigrants – are perceived as the embodiment of inherently 'un-civic' cultures (Mouritsen 2006: 83). In this way, Mouritsen describes, Denmark would (allegedly) have a form of 'particular universalism' tied to a non-negotiable Danishness. And in this particular Danish version of universalism, Christianity, and more specifically Lutheranism, is important (even though in the country religiosity is generally declining), which is defended as giving children the foundations for personal autonomy and responsibility in a democratic society (Mouritsen & Olsen 2013: 703). Moreover, it is suggested that there would be an intrinsic relationship between the 'Danish identity' and the values of democracy, liberal tolerance and redistribution. To illustrate this, Mouritsen quotes the party manifesto of the Danish social-democratic party that states: 'People develop their personality through upbringing and in the meeting with other people in society. As Danes we have Danish culture in common' (Mouritsen 2006: 81). In addition, Mouritsen and Olsen observe that the 'civicness' of the Danes is not only expressed in the adherence to democracy and freedom, but also in the 'smallness, cultural homogeneity and tight-knit "cosiness" of Danish society' (Mouritsen & Olsen 2013: 97). As such, Lea Klarenbeek and Majukka Weide (2020) conclude that in integration programs in Europe, including those in Denmark, a paradox can be observed: the participation of (culturally different) immigrants is both demanded and feared. On the one side, it is emphasised that these immigrants need to be active to be deemed as integrated, but, on the other side, their participation is also seen as an 'illiberal threat' to society (214).

Be that as it may, similar developments are visible in other European countries, in which politicians of different ideological backgrounds referred to the relationship between universal values and the particular (Judeo-)Christian identities and cultures of their countries or their specific *Leitkultur* (see, eg, Joppke 2008a; Pautz 2005).

If we look, for example, at Italy, we see that the preamble of their Charter of Values for immigrants states 'Christianity [...] together with Judaism, has paved the way to modernity and acquiring the principles of freedom and justice' (Cuttitta 2016: 297). To explicate the necessity of the Charter with this preamble, the Italian Minister Amato also declared that he was particularly inspired by the awareness that there are 'specific problems with Muslims' and that 'the question of women is the most crucial issue when we are confronted with the entry of communities arriving from backward countries' (Cuttitta 2016: 295). Moreover, the chair of the committee that drafted the Charter spoke of 'cultures or religions that have not experienced the Western evolution', which are therefore 'antithetical' to the Italian culture (Cuttitta 2016: 295).

In Germany, new naturalisation policies have been defended by the Minister of the Interior Jörg Schönbohm by pointing out that 'those who come here have to adopt the German *Leitkultur*. Our history has developed over a thousand years. We cannot allow that this basis of our community will be destroyed by foreigners' (Orgad 2009: 726). Moreover, the law states that naturalisation should only be possible for spouses of German citizens if 'it is ensured that they will conform to the German way of life'. On that account, Orgad writes that Germany has modified its immigration and integration laws by asking every immigrant 'to conform culturally to its way of life before being able to be German' because 'immigrants – notably from Turkish origin – have not always been culturally "Germanized"' (726–727). Although Mouritsen does not fully agree with Orgad, as he writes that the Germany (political) culture promoted in integration programs has an emphasis on constitutional principles, he does note that 'controversies over citizenship acquisition' often tie in with the question: 'Can newcomers – Muslims particularly – be trusted as democrats?' (Mouritsen 2013: 92). Along the same lines, Daniel Williams concludes that, within integration programmes he observed in Germany, materials and lessons at times suggest that immigrants are 'prospective citizens' – which seems good from a social equality perspective, as it indicates that immigrants are on a pathway to equal citizenship – but at other times they are also 'suspect outsiders' (Williams 2018). Williams observes that this latter 'outsiderhood' is often constructed in relation to certain universal values, including gender equality, democracy and religious freedom (Williams 2018: 7–13), that would form the boundary between host society and immigrants.

Additionally, De Leeuw and van Wichelen (2012) analysed within the Dutch integration trajectory the visual representation of the Netherlands in the short film *Naar Nederland* ('To the Netherlands'), which is part of the integration exam abroad. They concluded that four cultural tropes – gender equality, sexual freedom, freedom of speech and individualism – were exemplified as emblems of 'Dutchness', leaving little room for cultural or religious variations. The only way to become Dutch, it is suggested in the film, is by adopting these *cultural* characteristics (De Leeuw and van Wichelen 2012: 195).

In the same vein, Elizabeth Onasch concludes that the French civic integration programme represents the French nation as modern, secular and striving towards gender equality, while immigrants are assumed to be traditional with patriarchal gender relations and practices that conflict with the values of the French Republic. On that account, she writes 'it discursively draws racialized boundaries between the French nation and participating migrants based on language, culture and religion' (Onasch 2017). As such, she observes 'integration policies rely on stereotypical representations of immigrants' and that 'frontline workers' insisted on "gender equality" as the pathway to belonging in France (Onasch 2020).

In a study on Belgium (Flanders), Waerniers and Hustinx (2019) observe that, in integration policy documents, immigrants are described as expected to earn 'moral citizenship through […] cultural assimilation' (277) by admitting 'to our Western culture' (Waerniers and Hustinx 2018: 288). For example, the proposed participation declaration starts with 'newcomers, like you, are often from countries with different cultural backgrounds […] The inhabitants of this country are however attached to certain rights, duties, freedoms and values' (NWS, 2016). Based on this and other components of Flemish integration trajectories, Waerniers and Hustinx conclude that due to these discourses, a class of what they call 'virtual-citizen immigrants' emerges, who are formally citizens but are only seen as full Belgian citizens if they are *ideal* citizens. They conclude that a form of 'permanently probationary citizenship status' turns out to be the highest attainable goal for these citizens with immigrant backgrounds (Waerniers and Hustinx 2019: 280).

Lastly, studies that find that the UK is increasingly concerned with 'British values' connected to the 'British culture' are adding up (eg, Anderson 2013; Bartram 2018; Monforte et al 2019; Bassel et al 2020). In particular, Bridget Byrne observes that the need for citizenship tests has been explicitly framed in terms of assessing TCNs 'fitness to be citizens' (Byrne 2017: 1). For this reason, she observes based on surveys with people who had to take the test to obtain citizenship, that for newcomers they 'undermine the idea that they can become citizens "'like any other'" (12–13).

For the purposes of this chapter, this last remark by Byrne hits the nail on the head. It is problematic for standards of social equality if integration and citizenship policies insinuate and contribute to the public perception that a binary opposition exists between a fully integrated society (the native 'Us') and immigrants ('They'), of which the previous group has *cultural and historical* access to the (supposedly) correct interpretation of universal norms that underpin the state, which is a privilege that persons with immigrant backgrounds (supposedly) lack. In other words, it is problematic if state policies suggest that minority groups in society, due to their foreign, cultural or religious identity, must continuously prove that they embody what it culturally requires 'to be like Us' to be accepted as competent equal partners in interpreting universal values, in democratic deliberations and as co-authors of the law.

Of course, this binary opposition distorts a far more complex reality. On the one hand, it is surely the case that the realisation and protection of universal values in specific liberal-democratic countries is a precious and praiseworthy achievement. Such values are also always historically situated and contingent – and at present, in European countries such as the Netherlands, Italy and Denmark, these values are indeed relatively well secured. These countries, therefore, have legitimate interests to defend their basic principles: they have every right to deem it as valuable and important to educate them to both (native born) citizens and newcomers. On the other hand, it must be emphasised as well that these universal values are not the (cultural) *property* of any nation and are also recognised in many other countries (eg Canada, Tunisia, Ukraine). After all, if one truly believes in the validity of *universal* rights, the fact that a particular country or culture manages to protect them does not prove that it is impossible for people from other countries or cultures to equally adopt them. Quite the contrary even: if one truly believes that certain values are universal, one must defend that one can come to understand and accept these values via different cultural and historical paths. Or the other way around, if universal values cannot be separated from specific cultures or cultural backgrounds, the claim to universalism must be abandoned.

Furthermore, it must be noted that in states that promote and protect these values, unfortunately, not all (native) citizens personally endorse them. Nonetheless, these dissenting citizens remain *equal* citizens because disagreement about universal values is allowed based on the value of freedom of conscience – as long, of course, as one abides by the law. In the same vein, liberal-democratic receiving states should not conceal that (some of) their currently celebrated universal values have only relatively recently started to truly characterise their countries. In fact, the history of current-day liberal-democratic countries has not been particularly liberal or democratic at all. Just to name two recent examples, in the Netherlands, same-sex marriage became legal in 2001 and the Italian penal code recognised so-called honour killings until 1981 (Cuttitta 2016: 295). This is relevant, as it corrects the perception that 'Western' cultures are *intrinsically* superior to other cultures (which is increasingly often emphasised by European politicians). By the same token, also today, *all* European liberal- democratic states are, ever so often, criticised by constitutional and international courts, Ombudsmen, NGOs and international organisations such as the Council of Europe, for policies and practices that violate human rights, democracy and the rule of law. Universal values and human rights are therefore not *necessarily* culturally fixed in, for instance, Dutch or Italian culture, nor are these values naturally culturally embodied by native Dutch or Italian citizens.

In addition, in debates on immigrant integration and universal values, it often goes unmentioned that universal values at times clash with each other, that particular societies and their judiciaries can respond differently to those clashes and, moreover, that these responses can change over time. For example, liberal-democratic countries throughout the world decide differently on the issue of euthanasia (and also change their stance on it through time). However, this does not imply that some of these countries ignore universal values while others do not: instead, the universal values of, on the one side, 'individual autonomy' and, on the other side, 'respect for life' are given different priorities. In a similar vein, within debates on immigrant integration and universal values in Member States, some universal values are emphasised more strongly than others. This is, for example, the case for the freedom of speech (see, eg, Røstboll 2010: 405). Often, this value is then presented towards immigrants as a core aspect of the national culture and as entirely static. Nonetheless, in truth the *exact* meaning of this value (and other values) is a topic of long-standing democratic disagreement and debate. For instance, in all European countries, to different degrees, laws on slander or blasphemy are in force, limiting the right to freedom of speech to a certain degree. And periodically, there are (heated) political discussions on the boundaries and desirability of such laws. But within debates on immigration, integration and citizenship in Europe, the universal value of freedom of speech is often invoked as one of *the* national values that non-immigrant citizens (given their culture) always agree upon (and carefully secure), while immigrant citizens (given their cultures) supposedly do not know how to handle it and threaten it.

For this reason, in summary, the only correct way to understand and discuss universal values – in the context of immigrant integration and beyond – is, first, that it is essential that states promote them and politicians emphasise their importance, because their protection in a particular liberal-democratic society is never 'finished' and requires ongoing debate and commitment. Second, the state should invite all citizens to participate in democratic deliberations on the interpretation of the universal values, as these values themselves push states to give all citizens of the political community – irrespective of their backgrounds, ethnicity, gender, religions, etc – equal respect and political voice. For this reason, all citizens should be able to speak freely in political discussions with the aim to solve collective problems and promote justice. After all, again, citizens have the right to co-author the laws they are subjected to.

Third, liberal democracies must accept that the meaning of universal rights is not set in stone, but rather constantly subjected to democratic debate. More particularly, liberal democratic states rest on the conviction that it is always possible that if citizens carefully listen to the perspectives of other citizens, they will acquire a better understanding of what universal values require than before. For this reason, the state should nurture a form of 'reasonableness' in the political arena, defined by Marion Young as, at least, a willingness to listen to others, even if those others think your ideas are incorrect or outright inappropriate (Young 2002: 25). Surely, this reasonableness will not ensure that citizens will always be able to convince each other. Instead, political disagreement will (probably) never disappear. But any political community that genuinely adheres to universal values also adheres to, as Christian F Rostbøll puts it, 'moral fallibilism'. This is *not* a form of cultural relativism (as it is clearly not relativist in defending that certain values are universally applicable), even though it depends on the idea 'that every belief about the validity of norms and principles could, in principle, be mistaken and should hence be seen as revisable in light of further learning' (Røstboll 2010: 408) In the same vein, Martha Nussbaum duly writes that, if it comes to the protection of universal values and human rights, all countries are and will always remain developing countries (Nussbaum 2011: preface). This implies, amongst other things, that no one ever culturally owns universal values (Lefort 2016: Ch 6). In addition, in countries that uphold universal values, this commitment, on the side of all citizens (including both 'native' and 'immigrant' citizens), is not stable. This commitment can always intensify and, crucially, also diminish (again), which should make citizenries vigilant.

That being the case, countries that successfully support universal values should be applauded and are legitimised to engage in all sorts of public strategies to protect their community of equals. However, if the state suggests that citizens with (non-Western) immigrant backgrounds should separate themselves from their history and culture in order to absorb the culture of the non-immigrant majority to be able to discuss what is right and wrong in light of universal values, it misunderstands its own core values and fails to protect social equality. This suggestion namely indeed 'essentialises' cultures (in relation to values), both on the side of the native citizens *with* access to discuss universal values and on the side of the immigrant cultures *without* such access. However, in a community of equals, citizens do not represent their alleged culture and its alleged fixed opinions about certain issues but are individually politically included on equal terms and in political debates and, in principle, can speak for themselves. Or phrased otherwise, in democratic debate it is not important who citizens are (in terms of cultural background), but what they express and how they actually act. After all, this suggestion would imply that native citizens, due to their culture (can) never have opinions that are at odds with universal values, which is factually simply untrue. Particularly in contemporary Europe, there is, for example, a growth of populist (far right) movements with political ideas that manifestly conflict with the universal values of the liberal-democratic state and the rule of law, especially in relation to the freedom of religion of Muslim citizens (Mudde 2019).

Lastly, if a state invokes universal values not as being part of the national culture but *as* the culture of the non-immigrant majority, it fuels a societal hierarchy in which (non-Western) immigrant citizens are marginalised in their status of equal citizens. This signals that when it comes to the interpretation of the core values and the principles of the state, citizens without immigrant backgrounds are *hosts* and citizens with immigrant backgrounds are *guests*, in which the guests are required to behave according to pre-established cultural local rules (Beauchamps 2018: xv). However, in a true community of equals, such an evidently unequal relationship between citizens should be avoided. All citizens should be treated by the state as equally entitled and invited to participate as interpreters of the universal values that underpin it and may equally point out where they believe their implementation can be improved, irrespective of their cultural backgrounds and national origins.[8]

[8] I will return in ch 4 to the more *pragmatic* counterproductive effects for nourishing equal belonging of framing 'universal' values not as a shared seedbed of peaceful co-existence, but as culturalised and nativist concepts to which non-immigrants do not (unconditionally) have access.

V. The Other Side of the Coin: Denaturalisation

Before drawing things to a close, I want to briefly address a possible counterargument that critics might raise in response to the line of reasoning presented in this chapter. The gist of this critique, I presume, would entail that the concern that integration requirements as conditions of residency rights and citizenship would affect relations between citizens is unjustified. Such integration requirements, it could be argued, only affect immigrants on the 'path-to-citizenship' while everyone knows that as soon as naturalisation takes place, in a liberal democracy, strict equal treatment applies to all. Seen this way, there is little reason to fear that integration requirements might reinforce social hierarchies in society. This reassurance is however unwarranted, for two reasons.

First, I believe that in the context of present-day Europe, this analysis is unsustainable in light of the growing prevalence of the individualised conception of integration as described in Chapter 1. This conception, I illustrated, does not only affect how the position of non-citizens and their path to citizenship is understood, but also has the effect that immigrant citizens are constantly framed as deserving their citizenship based on their personal integration. Moreover, research of Monforte et al (2019) on the UK indicates that not only 'natives' internalise these hierarchies, but that also many naturalised citizens 'use narratives in which they distinguish between the "deserving" citizens and the "undeserving Others" when they reflect upon their experience of becoming citizens'. That being the case, the highlighted individualised integration requirements do reproduce social hierarchies between native-born and naturalised citizens, treating the latter's membership as conditional. Of course, as noted in the previous chapter, constitutionalism sets limits on how this hierarchy is (legally) expressed, since equal constitutional rights are guaranteed to all citizens. Yet, the social equality approach emphasises that problematic social hierarchies can exist even when legal rights are formally protected.

Second, there is evidence that this social hierarchy is in fact eroding the constitutional commitment to equal rights in growing trends to contemplate the denaturalisation of (certain) immigrant citizens (ie the revoking of citizenship). It would go beyond the scope of this research to fully flesh out the implications of these laws – often, but not solely, prompted by terrorism – and to demonstrate their current-day prominence in the politics of citizenship or the rule of law (see, eg, Mantu 2015). Nonetheless, I hope that presenting a list of examples already makes clear that European states indeed, and through a variety of political acts and public policies, increasingly reinforce a reward paradigm of citizenship. To be sure, the (expected) number of actual denaturalisations is for the time being relatively low, but these policies do, in addition to their real-world effects, have strong symbolic potency. More and more, a societal atmosphere is nurtured in which it is found acceptable that there are two forms of national citizenship: an irrevocable one for native-born nationals and a revocable one for (certain) immigrant citizens.

Indeed, in recent years, mostly in response to the series of terrorist attacks that hit Europe, individualised integration conceptualisations have led to the adaption and expansion of denaturalisation laws in several European states, including France, the Netherlands, Denmark, Belgium and the UK. These measures have received much (mostly critical) academic attention (Macklin 2014-2015; Boekestein and De Groot 2019; Pélabay and Sénac 2019; Carey 2018). So far, most of the case studies in the scholarship focus on the UK and France, because in both countries these citizenship policies have been at the forefront of political debates and illustrate how far states can go (Mantu 2018; Fargues and Winter 2019; Fargues 2017). In addition to discussing these two countries, I will also discuss the Netherlands.

In France, Marie Beauchamp observes, denaturalisation laws increasingly correspond with a 'differentiated approach to nationality' as the policies and rhetoric concerning denaturalisation do not apply to each citizen in the same way (Beauchamps 2018, 2017). To illustrate this, she quotes President Sarkozy who in 2010 announced his intention to revise the French law on denaturalisation with the words:

> It should be possible to withdraw the French nationality of any person of foreign origin who has deliberately attempted to take the life of a police officer or a member of the military police, or any other representative of a public authority. French nationality must be earned, and one must demonstrate one's self to be worthy of it. When one shoots at a public authority agent, one is no longer worthy of being French. (cited in Beauchamps 2018: xiv-xv)

Differently put, Sarkozy contends that the acquisition of citizenship should not be seen as in principle non-reversible for citizens with 'foreign origins'. For this reason, Beauchamp analyses on the ramifications of denaturalisation policies heavily resonate with mine on the integration requirements for TCNs as conditions for attaining increased rights. She writes that behind the formal narrative of equality before the law, denaturalisation policies are an 'Orwellian concept' that imply that 'all people are equal, but some are more equal than others' (xviii). Considering the denaturalisation laws that were eventually enacted in France, she concludes that the formal citizenship of naturalised citizens is in France viewed as 'a reward from the state to individuals: it is granted on the basis of a distinctive apprehension of an individual's behaviour and follows a pre-determined set of performances' (xv). Along similar lines, Émilien Fargues concludes that denaturalisation policies (on grounds of fraud) in France strengthen and create a division between 'accidental' and 'essential' citizens – in my terms conditional and unconditional citizens – of which the membership of the latter group is never called into question. Moreover, he observes that the 'moralising and responsibilising function of deprivation' is mostly targeted on African immigrants, which, he contends, turns them into second-class citizens (Fargues 2019: 257).

In the UK, the government has been reviving the policy instrument of the deprivation of citizenship over the last 20 years. Currently, this is a power that a government minister can invoke without the need for a trial or criminal conviction related to terrorism and it can target citizens whose behaviour may endanger 'the public good' (Choudhury 2017) or is 'seriously prejudicial to the vital interests of the United Kingdom' (Gibney 2020). The objective of punishment of this measure has shifted towards prevention. Initially, the citizenship could not be revoked if it rendered a person stateless. However, today, in certain circumstances, the Home Secretary can denaturalise British citizens who do not have another citizenship (and thus will become stateless), but who the government believes are eligible for another nationality. Given the current laws, denationalisation measures in the UK virtually always apply to dual citizens, naturalised citizens and citizens with immigrant backgrounds, who have or can (it is then assumed) reclaim their former citizenship or that of their parents. Based on this latter ground, British citizenship was revoked in the much-discussed Shamima Begum case, in which the government claimed that Begum is entitled to Bangladeshi citizenship.

In addition to several legal justifications of these measures, the UK Government also argued that these types of measures are reasonable because: 'naturalised citizens have chosen British values and have been granted citizenship on basis of their good character, and it is therefore appropriate to restrict a measure with such serious consequences as becoming stateless to naturalised citizens' (Fargues 2017: 922). On that account, Tufyal Choudhury (2017) concludes that immigrant citizens and particularly Muslims are 'tolerated citizens' at best, contingent on their commitment to 'British values' (225). Those who hold unacceptable extremist views, he argues, are seen as 'failed citizens', whose 'failure as a citizen is enough to justify the deprivation of citizenship'. Along the same lines, also Matthew J Gibney (2020) concludes that denaturalisation laws in the UK are 'still a powerful tracer of groups within the polity who, despite holding formal citizenship, are viewed as foreign' because their focus on the denaturalisation of 'dual nationals creates a minority holding an inferior form of citizenship' (2566).

Lastly, in the Netherlands, since 2010 an irrevocable conviction for certain terroristic acts became a ground for withdrawing someone's nationality, which only applies to Dutch citizens with dual or multiple nationalities, who are virtually always citizens with immigrant backgrounds (De Hart and Terlouw 2015). Moreover, since 2017 the Dutch minister of justice became legally authorised to revoke citizenship of citizens with dual or multiple citizenships who are suspected of being a member of terroristic organisations such as IS (by traveling to Syria or joining a training camp for example). There is thus no full criminal conviction required. As such, the Netherlands now states to have both 'reactive' denaturalisation that seeks to punish those who engage in or facilitate terrorism, and 'proactive' denaturalisation that specifically targets 'foreign fighters' abroad by revoking their right to return. Tom L Boekestein and Gerard-René de Groot (2018) claim that these policies fuel 'us-versus-them' narratives due to the normative conceptions of citizenship underlying them. More specifically, they observe they promote 'discriminatory narratives' that imply that dual-nationals – in particular Dutch Moroccans – possess 'loyalty-based concepts of citizenship', while this is not the case for 'mono-nationals' (331–332).

These are a few examples, but altogether I think it is clear these denaturalisation policies nurture the same forms of social inequality between citizens as the integration requirements discussed in this chapter. In the legal scholarship, these denaturalisation policies are described as part of the 'unmaking' of citizenship which involves that for dual nationals the significance of their citizenship is eroded and that they are seen as potential 'enemy citizens' (Nyers 2006). Less drastically formulated, these requirements have the effect that non-immigrant citizens (who are accused of), for example, participating in terroristic activities will always remain national terrorists, whereas immigrant citizens (most often those with double passports) are also denounced as terrorist *outsiders*. This is problematic, because, as Patti Tamara Lenard states, democratic citizenship is 'commonly understood to be egalitarian', that is, protecting exactly the same equal package of rights and status for all citizens (Lenard 2016: 73).

On that account, the political discourses that surround the growth of denaturalisation laws in EU Member States are in alignment with my analyses in Chapter 1 on how integration requirements for persons with immigrant backgrounds became individualised and contractualised. If immigrant citizens engage in terrorist activities, this is seen as proving that they are not individually integrated (based on images of compatibility with their societies) and, therefore, do not belong. Indeed, their sympathies and actions are interpreted as a breach of their 'integration contracts' that underlies their citizenship, which gives their states the right to revoke their side of the contract, that is, protecting secure and equal rights.

Therefore, both integration and denaturalisation policies increasingly communicate that immigrant citizens will never obtain the same type of citizenship that non-immigrant citizens have, as the immigrant citizens will never be fully released from the burden of proof that they need to provide to deserve their national citizenship (see, eg, Gibney 2020; Pélabay and Sénac 2019; Carey 2018; Fargues and Winter 2019). However, the social equality literature suggests that liberal-democratic states should in fact preclude from communicating such a division between citizens in their status as equal citizens.

VI. Conclusion

In this chapter, I evaluated the increase of integration requirements in several EU Member States through the lens of social equality. I raised the question: which integration measures symbolically suggest that the receiving society is no community of equals, that is, a political community in which no objectionable social hierarchies and social divisions of superiority and inferiority exist between citizens in terms of their status of equal citizens? With my answer I aimed, on the one side, to further our normative understanding of these integration policies. On the other, my aim was to contribute to the social equality literature by explaining what the ideals of social equality concretely imply for political practices related to integration and equal citizenship.

My normative starting point was that immigration triggers a variety of challenges for receiving liberal democratic states from the perspective of social equality, especially in relation to their ambition to uphold a community of equals that cherishes the value of equal citizenship, not only in a formalistic but also in a substantive sense. Receiving states that offer immigrants a path to citizenship should combat the growth of structural inequalities between non-immigrant citizens and immigrant citizens and, where possible, enable a social ethos in which no superior and inferior citizens exist.

At the same time, I observed that the quality and shape of the social ethos of a liberal-democratic country is never entirely in the power of the state. Numerous factors – historically grown societal patterns, psychological dispositions, global developments, unexpected current events, etc – contribute to the formation of social hierarchies between citizens and the extent to which these promote or diminish the ambitions of liberal democracy. Nonetheless, the liberal state does have an impact on these attitudes, and it falls normatively short if it, on top of all these dynamics, entrenches symbolic double standards that deprive members of certain (minority) groups of opportunities for equal participation while privileging others, thus reinforcing status hierarchies.

From this angle, I drew attention to two types of integration requirements introduced in European states today, which I contend are objectionable. First, I discerned the type of integration requirements that convey the symbolic message that (certain) immigrants and forms of diversity are unwelcome and unsuited for territorial or civic inclusion. This leads to state endorsed social divisions between citizens that are preferred and 'wanted', and citizens with (certain) immigrant backgrounds who are unpopular and 'unwanted'.

The second type of integration requirement I highlighted involves the message that persons with immigrant backgrounds have to *earn* their national citizenship. This cultivates public perceptions and societal standards in which immigrant citizens have to demonstrate their entitlement to their equal citizenship. This mechanism has multiple manifestations. On the whole, however, through certain integration and citizenship programs, Member States contribute to a structural social class division between citizens that formally share equal citizenship. More specifically, they fuel a social inequality between first-class native citizens who *are* citizens irrespective of their behaviour and second-class and immigrant citizens who only have citizenship but can lose this entitlement. As a result, citizens that are perceived as native automatically belong, while immigrant citizens are perceived as conditionally deserving belonging. In this context, I gave extra attention to state-backed discourses of integration that emphasised the historical and cultural embedment of universal values in the 'native' majority culture of the receiving state. This inculcates that immigrant citizens are not naturally regarded as equal political members but must culturally adapt before they may be recognized as equals in democratic deliberations and equal co-authors of the laws.

Moreover, I showed that the social hierarchy between superior and inferior citizenship is also increasingly promoted, and legally enshrined, through denaturalisation policies in a number of Member States. In this context, European states also send the message that the citizenship of citizens with immigrant backgrounds remains revocable on standards of deservingness, while that of non-immigrant citizens is irrevocable.

To end, I believe the analysis in this chapter forms a contribution to the normative social equality literature. Based on its (negative) methodology of highlighting social inequalities that communities of equals should avoid, this case study of immigration, integration and naturalisation made apparent an additional source of illegitimate social inequalities. For standards of social equality, a class division between those who are perceived as unconditional members of a group and those who, at best, can only conditionally earn membership of it, is troublesome. Further research on this social inequality may include investigating its examples of (state backed) forms of 'natural belonging' versus 'conditional belonging'.

4

Disconnecting Integration from Rights

So far in this book, I have explored a variety of legal, theoretical and empirical perspectives in order to understand and evaluate the recent growth of (mandatory and formalised) integration requirements in EU Member States for TCNs as conditions for obtaining increased rights (see Chapter 1). In Chapter 2, I examined theories of national liberalism and social science literature on the rise of integration requirements in Europe, together with the political and societal dynamics that shape public policies affecting immigration and immigrants in liberal-democratic states. In Chapter 3, I reviewed the normative debate on social equality and justice and applied it to integration and citizenship laws in Europe.

In this chapter, I will return to the main question of this book and combine the relevant insights I collected in the previous chapters and formulate a normative response to the increase of these integration requirements in EU Member States. This response follows from the observation that none of the existing academic literature I have explored thus far have provided a conclusive normative answer to this development, even though it is often observed that the manner in which EU countries increasingly enact integration requirements for TCNs is problematic. Therefore, in this chapter I pick up the challenge by answering the question: how can we ensure that EU states do not misuse integration requirements for TCNs for exclusionary and counterproductive purposes?

In response to this question, I will argue that the use of (mandatory) integration measures by Member States is permissible, with the important stipulation that a so-called 'firewall' should be implemented between, on the one hand, laws that regulate the access to residency and naturalisation rights for TCNs and, on the other hand, policies and programs promoting integration. This proposal, crucially, does not deny that receiving EU states may indeed have legitimate interests to enact constructive integration schemes for newcomers in their societies. Instead, the normative crux of the argument is that a fundamental problem arises if laws monitoring residency and citizenship rights of TCNs are *connected* to integration policies (and, for example, integration requirements are prescribed as a necessary precondition for obtaining permanent residency).

My proposal to establish a firewall between integration strategies and the allocation of residency and citizenship rights is based on a combination of principled and pragmatic arguments. First, I argue that the firewall is normatively desirable because it prevents states from misusing the stark asymmetry in power relations between them and TCNs. Second, I defend that a benefit of the firewall is that it curbs the ability of states to reinforce a reward paradigm of naturalisation and citizenship, by framing residency and citizenship rights as something to be *earned* through demonstrating the ability to pass the hurdles of integration requirements. Third, I explain that if the firewall would be in force, receiving EU states will be inclined to adopt a broader perspective on the purposes of integration policies. In particular, it will pressure them to assess the success of these public policies based on, what I will describe as a 'disaggregated' perspective on integration. This perspective sees integration as a multidimensional societal process (eg, economical, linguistic, attitudinal, etc) that involves and affects both immigrant and non-immigrant members of society. As a result, it will become likely that integration policies will be evaluated based on their actual societal outcomes within a set timeframe. Moreover, I believe that through this disaggregated perspective on integration, several innovative and constructive integration strategies will become imaginable that are worth considering.

There are hence a variety of reasons that support this firewall, and each of these reasons raises a number of particular questions and issues. I will therefore start with listing the main failings of the current integration requirements in Member States, considering my analysis in the previous chapters. Next, I will present my firewall solution and explain how it can address the problems in the current integration requirements in EU countries. Subsequently, I will examine the additional advantages of making residency and citizenship laws independent of integration strategies, by exploring several possible integration measures that could be considered if the firewall would be installed. Lastly, I will discuss four potential counterarguments against my firewall strategy.

Before further unfurling this line of thought, I will start off with a clarification. In this chapter, I thus defend that a firewall should separate laws that distribute residency and citizenship rights and public strategies to further integration of TCNs. However, as discussed in Chapter 2 (section IV.B), there are multiple types of TCNs (refugees, family migrants, labour migrants, etc). Their legal, political and personal situations differ and, with that, their normative situations. In that light, I contend that the firewall solution clearly should govern the allocation of residency and citizenship rights to *refugees* and *family migrants*. As discussed in Chapter 1, these two groups of TCNs possess strong residency rights and protection against expulsion, and in principle have a right to become permanent residents after five years of residency in a Member State based on the LTR Directive. It is therefore particularly counterproductive to politically communicate what Permoser has labelled 'a myth of sovereignty' regarding the admission of these TCNs (2012). For this reason, it is crucial that *integration* strategies for these groups do not erroneously suggest that they can function as prolonged *immigration* policies – that is, yield the power to reject these TCNs after many years of residency – if they fail to complete certain integration conditions.

That said, I acknowledge that the normative necessity of the firewall for other groups of TCNs such as labour migrants is more open for debate, because they do not reside on humanitarian permits and they were admitted to the territory for temporary purposes (or even stronger, often admitted explicitly without the permission to settle permanently). In addition, degrees of precarity of TCNs are also determined by the circumstances in their countries of origin, for example in terms of protection of human rights and citizenship rights arrangements. However, in my personal view, the firewall should apply to all TCNs (and, for that matter, internal EU migrants that seek full citizenship after five years of residence in another Member State as well). In short, I believe that in all these contexts, the benefits of the firewall outweigh the disadvantages of losing some political discretion on questions of admission, in particular, losing the option to make the (civic) inclusion of TCNs contingent on 'integration' conditions. I believe this, because, as also explained in Chapter 2 (section IV.B), *all* TCNs are confronted with forms of precarity that create the risks that integration requirements are used or start to exploit power inequalities, inculcate hierarchical conceptualisations of citizenship and become counterproductive. Moreover, the additional benefits of severing admission from integration apply to all groups of migrants. In any case, my aim is to demonstrate that the instalment of the firewall is a *normative imperative* in relation to refugees and family migrants (that happen to be the groups towards who these policies are primarily targeted) and *seems normatively appropriate and pragmatic* in relation to other migrants such as expats or internal EU immigrants as well.

I. The Problems of the Current Integration Requirements in European Member States

I will start with briefly enumerating the failings of the integration requirements in Member States for family migration, permanent residency and naturalisation. Delineating their particular flaws is useful for pointing to suitable countermeasures and determining the appropriate normative response. Indeed, drawing on the previous chapters, as I see it, four main issues require normative attention with regard to the proliferation of integration requirements in EU Member States over the last two decades.

A. Abuse of Precarity

To begin with, I argued that a serious risk of imposing integration requirements on legal immigrants (TCNs in EU states) as conditions for obtaining increased rights, is that they are prone to exploit the inherent power imbalance between receiving states and their legal newcomers. This results from the fact that newcomers – whose legal and political situations differ, but who often have relatively strong residency permits – are not (yet) equal members of the political and legal order, but that state policies and public strategies are nonetheless applied to them.

Migrant groups can be especially vulnerable to the extent that they form, in certain contexts, a relatively unpopular minority in society. They are often confronted with language barriers, lack strong social and professional networks and have an interest in or are obliged to obtain secure and/or equal rights. For this reason, I concluded that, normatively seen, the weak point of the integration requirements in EU countries is not that they promote forms of integration (although one must of course have an appropriate conception of what 'integration' then is). Instead, the problem of these policies is that they give Member States the power to constantly redefine a set of performances, achievements and costs that TCNs must fulfil to obtain more secure legal statuses, while anti-immigrant attitudes can (easily) lead to exclusionary and counterproductive integration requirements. Furthermore, I determined that the contractualisation and individualisation of the concept of integration in Europe blur the risks of these integration requirements even more, because these requirements in fact grant the *strong* party (the state) of the alleged contractual relationship between the state and TCNs, the power to constantly change the conditions for legal inclusion (upwards). The *weak* party (the TCN) has no other option than to accept and fulfil these requirements in order to be fully released from residential unpredictability.

On that account, this analysis indicates that an adequate measure to counterbalance this institutional weakness should recognise that TCNs reside in positions of precarity – and should hence be treated as individuals who deserve special protection against state power.

B. Decreased Naturalisation Rates

I found that it is problematic that empirical studies demonstrate that the current growth of integration requirements in Europe reduces numbers of naturalisation (Van Oers 2013, 2020). For example, recent research on Denmark (Jensen et al 2019) demonstrated that the high language requirement for naturalisation in this country (B1/B2) excludes more migrants from naturalisation than self-support and non-criminality requirements (14). Moreover, it indicated that education level at entry is strongly associated with passing this requirement, meaning that the capacity to become a citizen in Denmark increasingly depends on educational background and intelligence (16). Other strong indicators of passing the requirement are age and gender; for example, older and female refugees experience more challenges (11).

However, normative literatures suggest that it is desirable that all long-term immigrants, after a reasonable time-threshold is passed, obtain full citizenship. More particularly, I discussed migration theorists who argue that long-term immigrants should naturalise, because the inner logic of liberal-democracies mandates that all individuals who are perpetually subject to the political and coercive powers of the state should be enabled to have a voice in the processes of law-making. In addition, I deduced that social equality theories also push towards the position that it should be a state priority that de facto members of society obtain equal rights, to uphold a societal ethos that promotes values such as equality and fair treatment. For this reason, an adequate normative response should neutralise potential legal exclusionary effects of integration strategies of receiving states that hamper access to citizenship.

C. Inculcating Hierarchies in Citizenship

I examined potential problematic social 'spill-over' effects that Member States may inculcate through certain (mandatory) integration requirements. I determined that several European countries currently intensify problematic social hierarchies between citizens, mostly by suggesting that gaining access to secure residency and citizenship are *rewards* reserved for persons with immigrant backgrounds who display certain desirable efforts, attitudes and characteristics (framed as standards of personal integration). As a result, these policies (either intentionally or inadvertently) can contribute to a ranked society. In this society, citizens with non-immigrant backgrounds are perceived as *being* citizens (irrespective of their behaviour, attitudes, characteristics, success, etc) and immigrant citizens as *having* a form of citizenship that can be revoked, or at least, to which they can be deemed as undeserving of (as a consequence of undesirable behaviour, attitudes, characteristics, deeds, etc). Moreover, I described that in certain instances, integration requirements suggest that the universal values that underpin EU states are culturally 'nativist' notions, in the sense that they are presented as exclusively, or at least most accessible, through the dominant culture of the receiving state. Following from this, adequate countermeasures to combat such stigmatising integration requirements must restrict the ability of states to suggest that the access to increased rights or equal citizenship is something that must be (culturally or otherwise) *earned*.

D. Ineffective Integration Strategies

Lastly, in Chapter 1, I gave descriptive analyses of the spread of integration requirements in Member States and the conceptual shift that reinforced it. These showed, I believe, that integration requirements in several EU countries are supported by 'individualised' integration conceptualisations, which tend to have counterproductive integration outcomes seen from a more long-term and broader societal perspective. Essentially, if integration requirements start to narrowly assess the deserved belonging of individuals to (an idealised image of) society, they are predisposed to increasingly disregard – and therefore carry great risk of conflicting with – facilitating desirable societal outcomes (eg, enhance language levels and equal opportunity in society). From an individualised integration perspective, it might seem reasonable to *first* determine whether a person 'fits' society and deserves to stay, as this question precedes and subsumes all other concerns. However, from a societal perspective this is often puzzling and at times even nonsensical, because integration requirements should evidently not undermine desirable societal outcomes, not the least because most TCNs – and in particular refugees and family migrants – will most likely eventually remain members of society. For example, in several EU countries fulfilling integration policies has become increasingly burdensome and expensive. As a result, we have seen, lower percentages of TCNs succeed in completing integration requirements. The other, less successful, TCNs are now confronted with prolonged provisionality, and possibly even with fines and having to pay back debts for their (privatised) integration education. Arguably, these integration requirements thus increase rather than decrease the chances that (vulnerable) TCNs will get stranded in the margins of society (eg, Netherlands Court of Audit 2017; Jensen et al 2019). Additionally, if integration requirements for TCNs are ineffective or even prevent the inclusion and participation of newcomers, this may also be problematic from a legal perspective. In Chapter 1, I established that the mandatory integration requirements for family migration and permanent residency are permitted by EU directives, but *only* if they promote the inclusionary objectives of these directives and are in line with the general EU principles of effectiveness and proportionally.

Lastly, perspectives on integration and integration requirements that entail that only those immigrants who are integrated deserve secure rights and citizenship, ignore the pragmatic possibility that naturalisation can in fact serve as a tool to achieve certain integration outcomes. Indeed, multiple empirical research suggest that naturalisation has positive effects on certain integration outcomes, for example because it grants better access to the labour market, stimulates belonging and has the potential to increase earnings (eg, Bloemraad 2017; Bakker et al 2017; Bakker 2016; Steinhardt 2012).

Accordingly, my examinations revealed that an institutional response to the current integration requirements in Member States should aim to prevent that they become ineffective or even counterproductive. Or, to be more precise, they should stimulate that integration measures are less associated with the question 'Who belongs here?' and are redirected towards the pro-active question 'If newcomers join society, what public challenges might this raise, and what state policies would demonstrably work to adequately address these?'

II. The Firewall Solution

I believe these (exclusionary) outcomes and effects of current integration requirements in Europe can be counterbalanced with an institutional precaution. To be sure, I do not argue that this solution is a panacea for all societal challenges that come with incorporating (large influxes of) immigrants into society. Yet I do argue it is normatively desirable and practically helpful to install it. Moreover, I see it as paramount for all receiving liberal democracies, and of special interest for EU Member States given the ongoing influx of refugees into Europe.

I propose that receiving EU liberal democracies should establish a new principle, namely, to place a firewall between, on the one side, laws that regulate the allocation of rights to legal residency and citizenship to TCNs and, on the other side, public strategies that monitor, promote and encourage integration. The institutional attributes of this firewall are therefore quite straightforward: integration measures are in principle legitimate, but they should institutionally and legally be decoupled from laws that supervise the residential inclusion and the naturalisation of TCNs. The outcomes of this institutional separation are, I think, subtler than they may seem. The point is not that newcomers in society do not deserve or should not receive targeted public attention. In fact, the firewall permits receiving states to install all sorts of participation workshops, language education and integration trajectories for TCNs in society and also allows these to be obligatory. Indeed, it should not be automatically assumed that if public integration trajectories such as language education are not connected to the access of rights, they cannot be made *mandatory*. All liberal-democratic states in the world already have forms of education that involve mandatory school attendance, mostly by children, which are imposed by law. In general, most citizens agree and comply with such public systems. However, if needed, it is upheld through school attendance enforcement and municipal courts. Penalties for non-compliance can (in exceptional circumstances) include fines if administrative measures prove unsuccessful. A similar system is imaginable for monitoring the enforcement of mandatory integration measures for newcomers. In this context it is noteworthy that, to my knowledge, no empirical study on integration programs in Member States observes that newcomers are (generally) demotivated or principally object to taking (mandatory) forms of education such as language and civic classes. In fact, the opposite appears to be true: virtually all of them understand and agree they have to complete such requirements and in principle see them as important and helpful for starting their new life in their new home country (see, eg, Kahmann et al 2018). Nonetheless, to make integration trajectories available but optional is surely also a permissible option under the firewall. This option would be in line with what Carrera and Vankova (2019) propose in their Issue Paper for the Council of Europe, in which they conclude that 'promoting voluntary integration are preferable to obligatory integration policies because the latter may restrict immigrants' and refugees' human rights, increase the insecurity of residence for applicants and their families and present some discriminatory effects' (5).

In any case, the firewall proposal is sympathetic to the assumption of liberal nationalists that well-designed integration policies can be beneficial to society as they can, amongst other things, promote strategies of nation building, nurture broader projects of communal democratic socialisation, have emancipatory effects and stimulate senses of belonging. However, receiving states cannot demand the demonstration of degrees of 'integration' by individual TCNs as preconditions for obtaining increased legal status, in which the ('open-ended') standards of integration can be specified by the receiving state and must be delivered by these newcomers.

The firewall could be respected in EU Member States in two ways. The first option would be through legal reforms at the level of EU law. It must be noted that this solution is in conflict with the chosen methodological approach of this book that, as explained in the Introduction (section II), aims to understand the proliferation of integration requirements in EU Member States within their current legal and political frameworks. However, I do believe it informative to explore this option a bit further, because it would not require fundamentally changing migration and integration laws and practices in the EU, but amending or abolishing Article 7.2 of the Family Directive and Article 5.2 of the LTR Directive. These Articles grant Member States respectively the option to enact integration requirements as conditions for family migration and permanent residency. Furthermore, EU harmonisation of naturalisation would be required, minimally to ensure that for Member States it would be prohibited to demand certain degrees of integration in order to become a citizen with equal rights.

Although the EU has thus far largely avoided the issue of naturalisation given its political sensitivity – notwithstanding certain exceptions, for example in relation to children and stateless persons – I believe there would be advantages to enacting some sort of European Citizenship Directive. For example, Orgad argues that it 'can prevent part of the mistreatment of resident aliens and abuse of power in citizenship allocation' (2019: 539). Orgad also notes that common EU rules can also be in the interest of states as it would, amongst other things, give them more guidance on how to legitimately restrict access to citizenship in certain cases.

The second option would not necessitate changing EU law but would involve the voluntary commitment of Member States to enact this firewall at the domestic level by disconnecting their integration policies from laws regulating the territorial and civic inclusion of TCNs. This option is feasible in the short-term, as both the Family and the LTR Directives do not insist that Member States should connect integration requirements to increased rights for TCNs, but only give the option to enact such policies. Hence, Member States could also opt out. Regarding naturalisation, given that there is no EU harmonisation in this policy field, Member States can also simply decide not to link integration requirements to citizenship. Obviously, the weakness of this second option is that the commitment to the firewall diminishes as soon as political parties come into power that are convinced that family migration, permanent residency and/or naturalisation by TCNs should be earned (or even prevented). Nonetheless, perhaps in response to the arguments provided in this this book, it is not inconceivable that the firewall principles would eventually become accepted in certain Member States or even across the board, without the need to adjust the current EU legal framework.

Yet either way, the firewall would not radically transform the current legal obligations Member States have towards admitting individuals with bona fide claims to family migration or granting TCNs permanent residency access to permanent residency after a given number of years of uninterrupted residency. These legal obligations rest upon EU and international law, with or without such a firewall installed. However, in relation to naturalisation the firewall would limit the discretion of Member States to install integration requirements as conditions for access to citizenship.

III. The Problem-Solving Capacity of Disconnecting Rights from Integration Strategies

In this section, I will explain how the firewall proposal will address the four main problems I enumerated in section I of this chapter.

A. Counterbalancing Precarity

The firewall proposal entails the commitment to deliberately limit state powers towards migrants, offsetting the structural risk of misuse that stems from the inherent unequal power relationship between the receiving European states and TCNs. More precisely, by making integration policies completely independent of laws that regulate the territorial and societal inclusion of TCNs, the firewall would simply curtail the possibility that Member States might take advantage of their vulnerable position (through integration requirements).

This line of reasoning might sound radical, but it is not unprecedented. In the migration literature, Joseph Carens for instance also proposes to create a firewall between, on the one side, the enforcement of immigration and deportation laws and, on the other, social policies to secure fundamental human rights (Carens 2013: 133). His firewall would make it possible for undocumented immigrants (who are in a highly vulnerable position) to seek healthcare, as it would forbid hospital officials to report them to immigration authorities. On that account, Carens mostly focuses on passing information about the identity of undocumented immigrants from doctors to immigration officials, to prevent that undocumented immigrants refrain from seeking medical care if they need it. The firewall solution I propose is of a different nature and based on different considerations, but it rests on the same core idea. It involves that states purposely constrain their potential influence in certain policy fields, as part of the commitment to protect individuals who are in precarious positions.

Furthermore, it is worth considering a parallel legal principle illustrating that this proposal is not unprecedented, by considering an example from another part of the legal system. On an abstract level, the firewall for integration requirements is comparable with the 'presumption of innocence' principle as it exists in criminal law. I realise this is quite a tricky comparison, as it might seem to suggest that immigrants are comparable with persons who are accused of an offence or crime. This is of course not what I mean to imply. The comparison is relevant because *conceptually seen* the same justification applies to both institutional precautionary measures: the state should limit its procedural and political powers in contexts in which the power imbalance between the state and individuals is so extreme, that the risk of misconduct on the part of the state is impermissibly high. If we look more specifically at criminal proceedings, we see that liberal democracies decide to lay the burden of proof fully and unequivocally on the prosecution (ie the state). This means that the prosecution has the obligation to prove each element of the offence or crime beyond reasonable doubt. Moreover, it restrains the state from engaging in intrusive investigation and surveillance methods to find evidence of offences of crimes persons allegedly committed (Shahidullah 2012: 160). This is required, this principle holds, as individuals deserve protection 'against specific dangers inherent in being subject to the powers of the state in the criminal process' (Weigend 2013: 204). The presumption of innocence is therefore deemed indispensable for fair trials, given the enormous power inequality that exists between the state and criminal suspects, together with the persistent latent possibility of the gradual installation of a police state or the orchestration of fake trials to single out people as scapegoats for political interests. On that account, as with my firewall solution, it provides a crucial institutional safeguard to prevent that public policies are put to wrong use. It neutralises the risk that the virtually omnipotent state exploits persons who are placed in defenceless positions (for political interest or otherwise).

In addition, the comparison between my firewall proposal and the presumption of innocence also shows well, in line with my discussion of liberal nationalism in Chapter 2, that for normative assessments of state policies it is not always enough to establish whether these policies could *in principle* be legitimate. In the context of criminal proceedings, it is conceivable that these can also have fair outcomes in hypothetical situations in which the presumption of innocence is not an established principle. This could be the case, I imagine, if the law enforcement and judiciary in a specific country are trustworthy and the evidence (or the lack of it) in a particular case is evident. Nonetheless, this does not affect the normative core of arguments in favour of the presumption of innocence: it is a safeguard against the misuse of power towards individuals in those instances in which the intentions of the powerful state are not, or at least not fully, benign but biased, one-sided or even outright menacing towards (certain) persons.

Put differently, the argument in favour of the principle of innocence does obviously not implicate for liberal-democratic states that having a criminal system is problematic *as such*. Instead, the presumption of innocence is a remedy to prevent that state policies that are in principle legitimate and, if well-functioning, even highly beneficial or crucial to society, are not utilised for the wrong purposes. Analogously, my defence for the firewall solution does not imply that receiving states would never benignly stimulate TCNs to participate in language and civic education, if they link integration measures to the obtainment of rights. Nor does it imply that integration strategies are not valuable as such. Instead, the firewall is required to prevent that, in principle, legitimate public policies are not utilised for the wrong purposes, given that they are applied to individuals who are to an exceptional high degree subject to the discretionary powers of the state.

B. Enabling Naturalisation

The firewall can serve to negate potential exclusionary effects of integration requirements on the number of TCNs that eventually naturalise. Research indicates that European countries have increasing integration obligations for naturalisation but provide weak support (Huddleston 2013; EMN 2020). On that account, the firewall is a response to the final analysis of Van Oers that I quoted in Chapter 1, in which she concluded that integration requirements such as citizenship tests are 'destined' to lead to lower numbers of citizenship acquisitions (Van Oers 2013: 277). Based on empirical research, she writes, it seems that integration requirements for citizenship simply always reduce naturalisation numbers to a certain extent, compared to when they were not installed. For this reason, to recall, Van Oers observed that integration requirements such as citizenship tests have 'inherent limits to achieve the [… integration …] goals for which they are introduced' (2013: 278). One such an inherent limit, I explored in depth in Chapter 2 and is connected to counterbalancing precarity as discussed under section III.A of this chapter. There I highlighted that 'integration' is a problematic standard for obtaining rights and citizenship, because the content of 'integration' that must be completed by newcomers is open-ended and arbitrary – especially if integration regimes become underpinned by individualised conceptualisations of integration (and politicians start to refer to naturalisation as being 'too easy' or 'given away for free' (Van Oers 2013: 249)). The firewall will therefore be helpful in this regard, as it will make it impossible for states to use the notion of 'integration' to allocate citizenship rights. This applies to all integration requirements discussed in this book – and also to integration requirements abroad and for permanent residency, because these also determine who can obtain naturalisation eventually. As a result, it will necessitate that Member States use more neutral and objective requirements for citizenship that will have less selective or discriminatory effects, for which reasonable residency requirements seem to me as most appropriate (if applicable, limited by the European Convention on Nationality to a maximum of 10 years).

C. Counteracting Conditional Belonging

The firewall will also form an antidote against the current European tendency that Member States inculcate standards of earned citizenship for immigrant citizens through integration requirements. In Chapter 3, I already touched upon the argument that from a social equality perspective, arguably *any* integration requirement as a condition to obtain increased rights and citizenship could be qualified as a step in the wrong direction. Their mere existence will always reinforce a dissimilarity between non-immigrant citizens who received their citizenship as a natural entitlement and immigrant citizens that obtained it later in life.

Indeed, considering social equality concerns, the firewall would limit the capacity of states to nurture, whether deliberately or accidently, symbolic differences between those who gain citizenship as a birth right, and newcomers who became citizens later in life (which may also, as Blake (2005) reasoned, negatively impact citizens with the same backgrounds as newcomers that must earn their citizenship).

In relation to refugees and family migrants, it is particularly beneficial that states are pressured to explain that these TCNs do not have to 'earn' secure rights based on standards of personal integration or merit. Rather, they must be transparent that their state powers in the context of these types of immigrants are to a large degree 'self-limited' as Joppke described it (1998). More precisely, states will have to explain that these immigrants are admitted based in human rights standards and that therefore the allocation of rights to them is not determined on standards of integration or merit. Instead, these allocations are based on questions of law (eg, does this person have a right to family reunification or a humanitarian status?) and time (has this person resided for the prescribed amount of years to obtain secure rights and obtain access to equal rights?).

In addition, if receiving states decide to make integration trajectories under certain circumstances mandatory for migrants, this duty to integrate is less stigmatising if it is not connected to 'deserving' certain rights. Providing language education or civic classes for newcomers would become merely one example of public education, in the same way that all born citizens have been provided with education. Of course, a difference between the public education for non-immigrant citizens and newcomers is that they are confronted with it at different points in their lives. Born citizens undergo public education in their younger years, and immigrant citizens shortly after their arrival. However, the public objectives and normative state justifications of these (mandatory) educational state programs are exactly the same – and ideally, this should be made explicit by politicians, policy makers and the like. All these policies involve facilitating desirable societal and emancipatory outcomes (not to measure 'who belongs').

The firewall will also make it more difficult to suggest through integration requirements that newcomers have to culturally embody the majority culture of their receiving country in order to have access to the universal values of the state. This is valuable, as when the entitlement to citizenship underpinned by universal rights is 'culturalised' (eg, portrayed as 'our' values), they fail to provide a solid basis for a society grounded in social and political equality. That is, if receiving European states perceive and frame their equal citizenship and values increasingly as 'nativistic' notions, it is harder for persons with immigrant backgrounds to feel as 'real citizens' of the nation and it is also less likely that other citizens will perceive them as such. This is unfortunate, as in fact universal values have the power to function as common fertile grounds for cultivating a political community based on peaceful co-existence. Essentially, when the state is committed to these values, given their universalistic aspirations, it enables citizens – regardless of their background, personal perspectives and life decisions – to commit themselves to them as equals. In this context, carefully taking into account empirical research that indicates that integration policies shape and influence societal norms, particularly on the side of the receiving majority, these values are highly relevant. For example, Schlueter et al (2013) demonstrated that non-restrictive integration requirements – in their terms 'permissive' integration policies, defined as 'equal rights are relatively easily granted' – are 'associated with decreased perceptions of group threat from immigrants' (670). Additionally, a recent study (Green et al 2020) also found that such integration schemes (in their terms 'tolerant' policies) foster higher everyday contact and lower 'national majority members associations of immigration-related threat' (642).

That said, it must be noted that the firewall is surely not a magic silver bullet to secure the value of equal citizenship (for immigrant citizens) and nurture equal relationships in society. The state and politicians in power can still stigmatise immigrant citizens through, for example, public statements (such as the statements of Dutch Prime Minister Rutte discussed in Chapter 2). Furthermore, also within integration education that is disconnected from the obtainment of rights, the national culture or *Leitkultur* of the receiving country can be portrayed as intrinsically superior, unchangeable, fully coinciding with the 'universal' values underpinning the state and/or even inherently in clash with the 'non-Western' cultures. Nevertheless, the firewall irrefutably restricts the ability of states to publicly inculcate the idea that immigrants must deserve to legally belong (while this is not the case for non-immigrant citizens). Both immigrant and non-immigrant citizens do not earn or deserve their residency or citizenship based on completing certain integration standards. On the contrary, both are equal citizens regardless of those things, receiving their legal citizenship (and are provided emancipatory public schooling) simply by virtue of being long-term members of a society that strives to be a community of equals.

D. Avoiding Ineffective Integration Strategies

Seen from a more long-term and societal perspective, the firewall will also be valuable in preventing counterproductive integration outcomes that integration requirements for TCNs may have. It namely counteracts that EU states can treat these TCNs as being required to go through some sort of 'test phase' to demonstrate their personal integration, before they are perceived as deserving secure residency rights, citizenship and public concern. As a result, it will shift the focus of public integration measures away from questions of earning rights or belonging towards addressing public issues that are elicited by migration. After all, the firewall will preclude that states can organise their integration strategies based on the assumption that TCNs must personally 'fit in' to merit belonging. That narrative is simply less available now in the context of integration policies. Therefore, it pressures EU states to rethink their conceptions of both integration and integration policies. If integration is *not* about individual belonging, then what is it about?

Most likely (and perhaps even inevitably) states will shift to redefining integration in terms of a set of desirable societal outcomes. With the firewall in force, states can namely not maintain that integration is only the sole problem of TCNs, pressuring *them* to integrate to avoid deportation. Instead, if policies that facilitate integration are totally disconnected from laws determining the residency and citizenship rights of TCNs, it is unconvincing to suggest that there is no public responsibility, or at least, public *interest*, to install integration policies that are measurably effective in achieving their policy objectives. In particular, in relation to family migrants and refugees, if it is transparent from the start that a large share of migrants in principle will have a right to permanent residency after five years, I contend that it will become clear that the EU societies receiving them should carefully invest in their incorporation process and actual inclusion.

On a more theoretical level, I believe the firewall will therefore stimulate that integration will become understood in a more 'disaggregated' fashion such as described by Gary Freeman in his article *Immigration Incorporation in Western Democracies* (2004). This conceptualisation does not hold that newcomers ('they') should integrate in a supposedly fully fixed and pre-existing real society ('we'). Instead, it works with an image of society that exists of 'ramshackle, multifaceted, loosely connected sets of regulatory rules, institutions, and practices in various domains […] that together make up the frameworks within which migrants and natives work out their differences' (2004: 946). Accordingly, this view on integration does not match with either 'holistic' integration as developed by functionalist sociologists that works with the fiction that societies can be fully integrated, or with 'individualised' integration as increasingly prevalent in Europe today. Rather, 'society' is perceived as fragmented and decentred, with the result that the 'incorporation process must also be fragmented' (947). It involves a complex interaction of several societal dynamics, that could be labelled as economic, social and cultural processes, all interacting with each other (see, eg, Entzinger and Biezeveld 2003).

On that account, the firewall will prompt states to change *the order in which* issues of integration are approached. Currently, EU states increasingly first lump together all public challenges and potentially public issues that surround the arrival of newcomers in society under the unspecific diagnosis of 'integration issues' on the part of those who 'stand outside of society', and then install punitive measures to exclude those immigrants that supposedly cause them. However, the firewall will force receiving states to be more transparent with what is actually at stake. They must *first* acknowledge that, if migrants arrive in society, the best strategy is to pro-actively specify the disaggregated issues that need public attention (considering liberal-democratic values) and *then* enact appropriate public policies to address these challenges (which, if desired, can be labelled as integration policies). So, for example, if one worries about the language proficiency in society and thus also of newcomers, it is important to craft public policies that enhance these levels and evaluate them based on their actual outcomes. Additionally, in the face of migration, one could also be concerned with stimulating senses of belonging, democratic socialisation, offsetting the increase of inequality in education, unemployment, social isolation, spatial segregation, undemocratic attitudes, and so forth. It should be politically decided upon what the exact focus of policies for newcomers should be, but in principle all these issues deserve public attention and well-crafted state policies. Yet, all things being equal, not much is gained if we amalgamate all these public concerns and problems together, in all their complexity, and then roughly label them as 'integration issues' that newcomers must solve (on their own) in order to (allegedly) deserve to belong. Instead, integration policies should be installed that have specific policy objectives to uphold specified societal outcomes, which can be evaluated based on whether they effectively promote the intended aims. For this reason, it is useful that the firewall will help provide that the benchmark for assessing the quality of integration measurements will no longer be testing on whether individual TCNs *integrated enough* to belong and obtain secure and equal rights, but based on *comparing their measurable effects on the societal outcomes that are specified as their policy objective(s) within a given timeframe.*

As I see it, if this would become the methodological lens based on which the research field of integration policy evaluation is conducted this would enhance this field of study, because it would make what 'integration policies' should causally do more straightforward.[1] Over the last decade, as Garibay and De Cuyper (2018) pointed out, the methodologies used to assess the quality of integration policies have been scattered and therefore difficult to compare, because the conceptual principles of what 'integration' means varies greatly (21–22). However, within this 'disaggregated' view, one could imagine for example a comparative research on language strategies for newcomers between countries (or cities), that compares the effects of these strategies in terms of the relative increase of language levels of new residents over, say, five years.

On that account, this benchmark strategy will also have several beneficial effects on the effectiveness of integration policies. I will briefly highlight four.

First, it will presumably influence what proposals in the first stages of policy making are deemed as acceptable, for example during parliamentary and public debates. If we look at the Dutch case, for example, I think that if the firewall would have been in force in 2013, it would immediately have been obvious that it was an irresponsible proposal to provide TCNs, including refugees and family migrants, with little or no public assistance during their first years of residency and to fully privatise integration education. If it would have been impossible for the Dutch Government to promise that they could 'solve' potential resulting integration issues by deporting TCNs or systematically thwart the possibility of the allegedly unintegrated to belong to society, it would have been (more) difficult to

[1] This argument does not deny that questions of causality will always belong to the hardest questions of empirical research, also if the used indicators for certain phenomena are relatively clear.

convincingly defend the lack of public supervision and support for newcomers. The foreseeable counterproductive outcomes of these policies would immediately have been recognised as a societal risk, as integration would have been understood as a (disaggregated) collective responsibility, requiring effective interventions of public policy. Not surprisingly, the Netherlands Council of Audit (2017) indeed observed that no research had been done on the feasibility of the expected standards of 'self-reliability' of newcomers before the policies of 2013 were enacted (25).[2]

Second, in the same vein, the firewall will also influence how integration requirements are evaluated retrospectively, if their policy outcomes turn out to be disappointing. In the Netherlands, we saw that of the refugees that arrived in 2013, only 30 per cent completed their integration trajectories three years later (Netherlands Council of Audit 2017: 25). In such situations, the firewall would prevent that the state or politicians can 'hide' behind the political narrative that this is the sole problem of the involved refugees, since they will not obtain full rights and will eventually face exclusion. Given that, with the firewall installed, integration is not about earning residency in the first place, it is evident that the installed integration policies for new residents should be improved to attain better policy outcomes, that is, to more constructively facilitate achieving a set of desirable societal goals.

Third, this disaggregated integration approach will also stimulate states to reconsider the relevance and impact of integration policies for those who complete them. For example, the questions in citizenship exams I referred to in the introduction of this book, that test trivial and obscure things about the dominant culture of the receiving country? Are those tests genuinely facilitating integration or do they only form a formal check on whether or not someone is 'integrated', without genuinely assessing whether such integration measures indeed empower newcomers to participate in society? Also, in the Netherlands, recent research indicates that it is possible for TCNs to pass all language and civic requirements, while virtually never leaving home and being socially totally isolated (eg, by preparing for the language and civic exams via the internet) (De Lange et al 2017: 7). This is arguably not the purpose of an integration strategy. Moreover, research shows that since 2013, in the Netherlands, TCNs do not strive to complete the highest possible language education but decide to play it safe and structurally opt for the easiest options (Netherlands Council of Audit 2017: 15). Seen from their perspective, this is understandable, as they are motivated to secure their rights and avoid fines while the integration requirements trigger anxiety by requiring considerable effort, time

[2] With the firewall in place, I think that in the Dutch case, also more attention would have been given to other implications of certain policy changes in 2013. For example, the language and integration education was privatised but no effective public regulation was installed to guarantee the quality of integration schools. As a result, a high number of fraudulent language schools entered the 'integration market'. These schools lured TCNs into buying overly expensive language education packages upfront (eg, by promising free laptops) while the education offered was poor and did not sufficiently prepare them for their prescribed language exams and citizenship tests. See also Dutch House of Audit 2017: 35.

and money. Yet from a disaggregated integration perspective, this demonstrates that punitive measures for the non-fulfilment of integration requirements can lead to substandard societal outcomes – even if newcomers complete all official requirements.

Fourth, if integration is indeed seen as a multidimensional process in which both persons with and without immigrant backgrounds are involved, it becomes visible that not only policies that are formally labelled as 'integration' policies (and are specifically targeted at newcomers) influence whether the objectives of integration policies are realised (Entzinger 2000). Instead, to meaningfully facilitate and assess integration, other public and social institutions should be considered as well, such as the structure of the labour market, the educational system, cultural dynamics, etc – together with how all these institutions interact with each other, as well as with the formal integration policies. On that account, it is also relevant that research suggests that obtaining citizenship is a resource for successful socio-economic integration, especially for refugees (Bakker 2016: 41–42). Accordingly, with this mindset, it becomes clear that specific integration measures for TCNs are only one piece of the puzzle of how to build and maintain a flourishing society, while receiving newcomers. Surely, it can be a valuable piece, if it enables TCNs to participate more successfully (and more rapidly) in several societal spheres. Nonetheless, if integration measures are enacted, states should ensure that they are in line with the objectives of other state policies, and do not (unexpectedly) undercut general societal concerns. For example, in the Netherlands, it appears that for people with a refugee status, the strict language requirements at times make it more difficult for them to hold a stable job or to structurally participate in the labour market (De Lange et al 2017: 60). From a disaggregated perspective, it seems therefore most reasonable that states should be more flexible in such situations, for example by offering evening courses or by being more lenient with language requirements if migrants have a job, in order to avoid that their language policies undermine participation in the labour market, instead of supporting it.

In this context, also a study of Dirk Gebhardt (2016) on the manner in which effective integration strategies of cities in the Netherlands, Germany and Sweden have been undermined by enacted integration strategies at the state level is of great interest. In short, he shows that the integration requirements in Member States installed at the national level increasingly focus on 'control and coercion' instead of on pragmatic results and, with that, increasingly jeopardised the capacity of cities to 'respond to concrete integration needs' (2015: 742). Put differently, his work shows, in my understanding, that given that the growth of state-level integration requirements that have been underpinned by individualised integration strategies – that makes these policies first and foremost about measuring individual belonging – the leeway of cities to install pro-active, context-sensitive and pragmatic integration policies are diminished. However, from a disaggregated integration perspective, state policies should naturally not hinder (but only boost) measurably effective city policies that welcome and support their newcomers.

IV. More Innovative Integration Strategies

In the previous section, I explored how the firewall would address the main negative effects and problems of the integration requirements in Member States under current EU and domestic laws, as analysed in this book. However, I hold that if the disaggregated perspective would become more prevalent in Europe, it has the potential to also more generally lead to a more enriched and constructive perspective on the potential of integration policies. If the benchmark for the quality of integration measures indeed becomes to compare the measurable effects of state policies on a number of societal outcomes, a variety of innovative and effective integration strategies become conceivable. This section presents some of the possible policy directions.

A. Customised Integration Approaches

If integration policies are disconnected from laws distributing residency permits and citizenship rights to TCNs, the question arises why all newcomers should be provided or expected to complete the same integration trajectory. Within the current institutional configuration, when integration requirements are connected to the gaining of access to increased rights (family migration, permanent residency and citizenship) they are bound to be the same for all. Any other arrangement would be unfair, as people should be able to obtain such rights under the same conditions. But this understandable concern with fairness limits and narrows our constructive thinking on possible integration strategies. Therefore, the firewall – disconnecting residency rights and integration – unlocks the possibility to explore the untapped potential of developing customised approaches to integration. This is advantageous, as research on the current integration requirements in Member States demonstrates that their exclusionary effects chiefly affect the more vulnerable groups of TCNs. In her research, Van Oers (2013) therefore draws an 'integration spectrum'. On the one side, there is the 'Top End' existing of immigrants who are already highly educated or who have strong social networks. For this group, she writes, citizenship tests are 'insultingly easy' and 'belittling' (270). On the other side, there is the 'Bottom End' that consists of 'elderly, low educated and illiterates, women in disadvantaged positions and traumatized refugees' (271). For this group, it is often very difficult or simply impossible to pass integration requirements such as a citizenship test. As a result, they often abstain from applying for increased rights altogether, have to undergo the humiliation of multiple failed attempts to pass all requirements and/or fall under an exemption clause without actually improving their language skills. Along the same lines, we have seen, the study of Jensen et al (2019) shows that 'ostensibly "contractual" criteria', constitute 'overwhelming obstacles for some groups' for which 'class differences' in terms of education level, gender and age 'very significantly affect the very capacity to become a citizen' (16). Amongst other things, this research mentions that the chance that a refugee with little education (and who starts her integration trajectory with taking the most basic Danish course) will fulfil the residency requirement for naturalisation within 13 years of residence is 2.5 per cent (16).

By installing the firewall, the selective legal exclusion of these integration requirements for, in Van Oers' terminology, the 'Bottom End' could effectively be counteracted. This would address the concern that TCNs do not succeed in obtaining secure residency rights or naturalisation. Yet, on top of that, it would also make it possible to provide TCNs with customised forms of integration education and supervision. For instance, in relation to language acquisition one could try to provide, say, different trajectories, adjusted to the needs of specific immigrant groups and their didactical needs. There is simply no one who benefits from putting immigrants who finished university degrees and those who are illiterate together in the same language class, or to expect them to (always) eventually achieve the same language level after they completed their language education programs.

In this context, the UNHCR also gave two important recommendations in its report *A New Beginning; Refugee Integration in Europe*. First, it recommends not collating integration policies for refugees and other TCNs such as family migrants, because they have different backgrounds, reasons for migration and (psychological) needs. Second, however, it also warns to neither fully standardise integration policies for people entering the EU on humanitarian grounds, as the challenges that the influx of refugees pose can 'only be addressed if refugees are recognised as individuals, rather than as a homogenous group for whom the same interventions are envisaged' (UN Refugee Agency: 118).

From this angle, the best approach to integration strategies seems to be built on a dialogue between the state and newcomers. For example, a possibility could be that municipalities receive an allotted personal budget per newcomer who can indicate what they think would be the most effective method to learn the language, culture, history, political system and to obtain access to the labour market. Moreover, if, for example, a refugee battles severe trauma, it should also be an option to postpone her integration trajectory (without delaying the moment she has access to secure rights), because enforcing certain educational progress or activities at that stage would be ineffective and also, under the circumstances, inhumane (Magro 2007). In a sense, one could therefore say that the firewall would lead to a radically different 'individualised' approach to integration policies than I observed in Chapter 1, in the sense that the provided education and supervision is customised to the personal needs of *individual* migrants. To adjust to this intervention by states requires acknowledging that integration is not an individual responsibility, but a matter of adequate public policy design that takes into account the talents, needs and potential of individual persons. (I will continue using the term 'customised' integration to avoid any confusion).

In any event, if integration policies are seen as a public responsibility and in its interest and meant to enable all members of society to participate to the best of their abilities (instead of being a personal condition to be achieved by individual immigrants to prove that they deserve citizenship), a whole catalogue of possible customised integration strategies becomes realisable, most likely with much better outcomes than the current policies which are not customised to the specific needs and capacities of immigrants.

B. Other Groups

If integration policies are indeed understood as facilitating a set of desirable societal outcomes, integration trajectories can also be provided as a response to internal EU migration. Within the currently growing individualised perspective on integration under EU law, fellow EU citizens cannot be obliged to complete integration standards in order to deserve belonging (eg, obtain, renew and increase their residency rights). As a result, in Member States there is less public attention for citizens from, for example, Eastern European countries that move to Western Europe to live and work: often, they are simply not perceived as an immigrant group that should be offered integration or language education. Nonetheless, the Dutch Scientific Council of Government Council (WRR) wrote in a report on internal EU migration that if Polish and Bulgarian immigrants that (most probably) settle are offered 'education, language training and labour market supervision', unemployment could be prevented (WRR 2012: 10). In fact, literally *all* arguments in favour of (disaggregated) integration measures for TCNs, also apply to internal EU migrants. To be sure, if the firewall disconnects integration policies from laws distributing residency and citizenship rights, this will not change the legal position of EU-citizens. As a result, it will remain impossible to make language courses mandatory for them. However, it will become possible to offer voluntary courses (at low cost).

Along the same line, the firewall might also lead to paying attention to the needs of *citizens* who are disadvantaged due to low language levels. For example, in the Netherlands over 12 per cent to 18 per cent of the population is functionally illiterate, which can be roughly defined as being ill-equipped to participate in society and particularly in the labour market due to being able to read or write individual phrases but not a longer text.[3] From a disaggregated integration perspective, illiteracy in citizens is problematic for the same reasons as low language levels on the side of newcomers. For this reason, if the firewall would abolish the current individualised integration perspective in EU countries that only perceives integration as a pressing issue in relation to assessing the belonging of persons with (non-EU and non-Western) immigrant backgrounds, this might lead to the launch of a broader public investment in language levels. For example, (customised) language courses could be made available for all residents in society, citizen or not, that

[3] Stichting Lezen en Schrijven, n.d., Laaggeletterheid in Nederland [Retrieved from:.www.lezenen-schrijven.nl/informatie-over-laaggeletterdheid-nederland].

might benefit from them. In addition, one could think of other measures such as public funding for an (online) TV channel continuously offering (free) lessons on the national language.

C. Trajectories for Asylum Seekers

The disaggregated integration perspective also casts new light on the best institutional treatment of asylum seekers who must wait (often in the context of isolated asylum centres) for the outcomes of their individual procedures. In virtually all European countries, these individual procedures are periodically subject to tremendous delays due to a sudden influx of migrants who apply for asylum, leading to a bureaucratic backlog. Over the last decade, this happened in several Member States because of the destabilisation in the Middle East, but also as a consequence of increased arrivals of asylum seekers from Balkan countries (who virtually never actually received asylum). In Chapter 1, I mentioned that in France recommendations from civil society to open up language courses for asylum seekers were ignored, despite long waiting times (NIEM 2018). In the Netherlands the average waiting time for asylum seekers was 15 months in 2015. Nonetheless, during this period, the newcomers were only permitted to participate in the labour market to a limited degree (on a volunteer basis). Moreover, they could only start with their integration and language trajectories *after* their humanitarian permits were granted. The political reasoning behind this legal arrangement is, I presume, that receiving states do not want to invest in persons, or let persons participate and merge into society, who eventually have no entitlement to stay. This is to a degree understandable. However, research shows that if asylum seekers must wait and are 'forced to do nothing' for prolonged periods of time, this is harmful for their mental health (ACVZ 2013). Also, if they eventually do receive a permit, this prolonged period of forced inactivity negatively impacts on their motivation for building up a new life (WRR 2015). For this reason, if their individual legal procedures take time, it is pragmatic that asylum seekers in the meanwhile are allowed to engage in activities, such as language lessons, education and participate in civil society.

On that account, if the firewall would be installed, it could still be reasonable to limit public integration trajectories and participation to qualified refugees, yet *only if* asylum procedures are efficient and short. Then rejected asylum seekers can be sent back to their countries of origin and the accepted refugees can quickly start building up their life in their new country. Nevertheless, if asylum procedures become clogged, it is crucial that receiving states are willing to open up their integration strategies for asylum seekers to prevent that they do not suffer due to enduring inactivity (particularly not if these asylum seekers are, for example, from Syria or Eritrea and will almost certainly eventually receive a refugee status anyhow). However, existing integration policies only reluctantly allow for this flexibility, due to the individualised perception on integration. This perspective makes it counterintuitive to already enable and support asylum seekers to start with their integration trajectory, as it is unclear whether they deserve a 'test phase' at all. Yet from a disaggregated perspective, this is the wrong approach: for matters of integration, there is no problem if asylum seekers have participated in integration education, the labour market or civil society for a period of time and are still rejected, if this risk overall facilitates desirable societal outcomes in the long term (UN Refugee Agency 2013: 118).

V. Possible Counterarguments against the Firewall

Despite the different, both principled and pragmatic, arguments in favour of the firewall presented in the previous sections, there are, as I see it, at least four possible arguments against it. The first is that it would be too costly, the second is that it removes the punitive powers that receiving states can use to force TCNs to integrate, the third is that it will be detrimental to the symbolic value of naturalisation and the fourth is that it is reasonable to demand of immigrants a minimal degree of civic knowledge and language levels before they are given political membership. I will discuss these possible counterarguments below.

A. Limitations of Public Spending

One could argue that my firewall proposal and all the integration trajectories that would follow from it would simply be too costly. It could then be said that it is financially unrealistic to increase public spending on integration by: (1) providing integration trajectories that are customised to the needs of individual newcomers; (2) offer language courses to citizens and internal EU immigrants that might benefit from them; and (3) give asylum seekers access who did not (yet) receive a residency permit access to integration courses. And of course, there are limits to the public resources available for integration strategies such as language education, in the same way that funding for all public policies is limited. In this chapter, I therefore mainly explored what the potential is of installing such a legal firewall, henceforth adopting a more effective perspective on the purposes of disaggregated integration policies.

However, it should be emphasised that from an economic perspective, it could also be argued that it is in fact most sensible to invest adequately in integration strategies for newcomers (and citizens) as this prevents negative societal consequences and hence public costs in the future. Essentially, it is better for everyone if (particular groups of new) residents are not banished to the margins of society, potentially resulting in increased welfare dependency, unemployment, crime (etc), which may potentially cause costs for society. For this reason, it seems that to install measurably effective integration trajectories for different (new) groups in society is in fact economically most lucrative and the best strategy for society as a whole.

B. Enforcing Integration

Another possible argument is that the firewall would dangerously remove the 'big stick' that receiving states can yield, compelling TCNs to integrate and forcing them to, for example, learn the national language and the basics of the political system. In weighing the importance of this argument, it is important to recall the legal and normative differences between different groups of TCNs.

i. Refugees and Family Migrants

For refugees and family migrants, as we have seen in Chapter 1, integration requirements formally do not serve to select their eligibility for residency rights. Furthermore, if refugees and family migrants do not complete integration requirements, this virtually never leads to their physical removal from the territory. For this reason, the main effect of the current integration requirements in Member States in relation to these groups is that these TCNs remain within society in positions of 'prolonged provisionality' with limited packages of rights, and less socio-economic perspectives. Therefore, the mechanisms of control that result from the connection between integration policies and laws that regulate the residency and citizenship rights for family migrants and refugees are mostly counterproductive. Indeed, as long as the firewall is lacking, the formation and structure of the integration requirements in Member States for family migrants and refugees structurally carries the risk of becoming heavily based on the assumption that the alleged 'unintegrated' can be removed from the territory, if it turns out (after years) that they cannot or do not want to integrate.

ii. Other Groups of TCNs

The residency rights of other groups of TCNs such as labour migrants are less strongly protected and their (normative and legal) right to civic inclusion is less straightforward. However, it must be noted that they as well often reside in territories of Member States for extensive periods of time based on their work visas, which are not withdrawn or directly affected if they do not, or fail to, complete integration requirements. For this reason, it could be argued that these groups, after a reasonable time period has passed, should also develop a right to access full (democratic) inclusion based on the inner logic of democracy and social equality concerns. Nonetheless, as stated in Chapter 2 (section IV.B) and the introduction of this chapter, in their case installing integration requirements as conditions to attain rights is more defendable, although I contend these should then be combined with comprehensive supporting structures that provide everyone a fair chance.

The drawback of this set-up, in my view, is that as soon as integration requirements built on individualised conceptions of integration take root – after all, in this scenario not all but particular types of TCNs must *earn* their permanent residency rights or citizenship by completing integration conditions – it is likely that adequate public support for these groups will diminish. In other words, in order to work this institutional set-up requires that Member States can deem integration requirements to measure *individual* belonging of (particular) migrants while they simultaneously continue to recognise that to install and invest adequately in comprehensive integration programs is a *public* responsibility. However, my analyses have shown that this is an unlikely scenario. The shift towards individualised integration in Europe in fact triggers a trend in exactly the opposite direction: it leads to undermining and decreasing public support for newcomers.

For this reason, again, to me it seems prudent to completely severe integration requirements from decisions on territorial and civic inclusion in relation to all groups of migrants (while acknowledging that reasonable disagreement can exist on this issue). This will best secure that disaggregated perspectives on integration will become prevalent and integration strategies, for all possible groups that might benefit from them, become more pro-active and enabling than they are now. The risk of establishing connections between residency rights and integration policies is that it obscures the purpose of these integration measures in general – that is, promote the idea that they measure who should belong. This might lead across the board to less innovative and less adequate public policies to uphold certain political and societal goals, in the context of the arrival and incorporation of newcomers, but also beyond.

C. The Ritual of Becoming a Citizen

Still, one could argue that the firewall should be rejected, because the connection between integration standards and access to rights for TCNs is important for more *symbolic* reasons. For example, Randall Hansen argues that a citizenship test enhances the 'transformative nature' of integration requirements and naturalisation. If citizenship is obtained too easily, he writes, 'it means little' as human beings throughout their lives 'take pride in accomplishments for which we have prepared and on which we have been tested' (Hansen 2010: 26). And many people intuitively seem to agree with this point; for example, recent research (on Norway) indicates that both natives and immigrants in principle agree that receiving countries can demand (moderate) integration requirements for citizenship (Brochmann and Midtbøen 2020). In response to this claim, I would say that the idea that ceremonies and rituals can indeed have transformative effects and can matter to people has merit. Moreover, empirical research indicates that (moderate) integration conditions such as language requirements as conditions for naturalisation can motivate migrants to invest in their linguistic skills, if they decide that they want to naturalise – in the literature this is called 'the anticipation effect'. (Peters et al 2018).

This argument therefore has a kernel of truth. However, in my view its weakness is that it seems to suggest that the *only* or *best* way to give integration meaningful symbolic weight is by installing integration requirements as conditions for residential and civic inclusion, potentially also connected to the non-obtainment of rights or the imposition of fines. This seems unwarranted to me. European states are powerful institutions and possess many alternative tools for promoting education, celebrating citizenship, nation building and cultivating senses of belonging. To be sure, this is not to downplay the importance of what Irene Bloemraad calls 'the context of reception' that provides immigrants with symbolic or interpretative resources, or said simpler, to communicate the benefits and interests in acquiring nationality, but in fact strongly supporting it. Building on Bloemraad (2006, see also Huddleston 2020), research suggests that administrative practices of receiving states can act as a 'signalling' function that can (re)shape the social identity of immigrants. Therefore, it is valuable that states structurally take promotional measures for nationality and publicly support integration strategies, such as (mandatory) courses and trajectories, TV-shows, national holidays, ceremonies and websites to make it possible for migrants. These options, and many others, make it attractive and possible for migrants to learn how things work in their new country, to hear about the national traditions, the nation's history and traditions and its language(s), and, ultimately, to feel welcome, feel motivated to acquire citizenship and to be able to fully participate in society.

Seen this way, it is doubtful whether the current integration requirements in Europe have the *best* effects on both newcomers and the receiving societies (form the best 'ritual'). Put differently, even if an 'anticipation effect' can be observed under certain circumstances if integration requirements are connected to the acquisition of full citizenship (ie naturalisation seems valuable and feasible to migrants), such requirements tend to escalate and become punitive and hostile instead of enabling and welcoming. In my opinion, the potential benefits of a firewall-based policy design therefore strongly outweigh the structural risks. For this reason, institutional set-ups that take into account the symbolic importance of the shaped 'context of reception' for immigrants but respect the firewall proposal are more attractive.

D. Having the Competency to Vote

A final possible argument against the firewall is that it is most reasonable to ask newcomers (basic facts) about the political system and to expect minimal language levels on their side, before they should be allowed to naturalise and, with that, to vote and thereby influence the political system. In this context, a citizenship test for obtaining political rights is often compared to obtaining a driver's licence. What is wrong (or discriminatory) with demanding certain knowledge and competences before being allowed to drive on the highway or to participate in the political realm?

This argument is not convincing for a number of reasons. First, throughout history, additional requirements for voting rights have often been used as a mechanism of racial exclusion and disfranchisement. For example, in the American states of Mississippi and Connecticut a literacy test was put into practice in the mid-nineteenth century to specifically disfranchise African Americans (Kostakopoulou 2010a). Similarly, in the Canadian province of British Columbia, immigration from China, Japan and India was effectively curbed under the slogan 'White Canada Forever' through, amongst other things, literacy tests (Backhouse 1996: 322). Moreover, in Australia during the White Australia policy, comparable forms of racial exclusion took place (Willard 1967). The shared strategy behind all these tests was to demand exactly those levels of knowledge and literacy of which it was anticipated that it would be impossible for specific certain (racial) groups to pass in order to acquire admission, civic membership or suffrage. It is therefore not unreasonable to conclude that testing competences for political membership risks having discriminatory intentions and affects and therefore does not deserve recommendation.

Nonetheless, from a more principled and theoretical point of view, such historical examples do not conclusively establish that all tests for political rights are wrong. For this reason, it is also important to consider that the link between democratic and political membership and standards of knowledge is not invoked in relation to non-immigrant citizens. Indeed, if the rights of 'native' citizens would be made contingent on, say, passing public or high school exams, this would certainly result in revoking the voting rights of major portions of (often more vulnerable) citizens in society. This would be unequivocally criticised as compromising universal suffrage. Seen this way, the firewall importantly erases an institutional double standard. It prevents that completing certain (mandatory) public (integration) education becomes a *prerequisite* of political membership for members of society with immigrant backgrounds, while this is not the case for non-immigrant citizens who may also not meet certain basic standards of (political) capabilities.

Of course, in response to this argument, it could be pointed out that instead of opening up the right to vote to newcomers without educational conditions, we should move in the opposite direction, also requiring non-immigrant members of society to complete civic and language tests to exercise their citizenship and have voting rights. To fully address this argument leads beyond the scope of this book. In brief, I believe it fails because it rests on an impoverished and narrow conceptualisation of citizenship. Liberal-democratic states (committed to individual freedom, equality, the rule of law, etc), are, first and foremost, inclusive and protective political projects. This means that their core ambition is to offer individuals maximum protection in terms of rights, even if their individual characteristics and competences do not coincide or even contrast with those of the majority. The best understanding of citizenship is therefore that certain levels of knowledge, skills, language levels and dispositions are unquestionably important to factually exercise citizenship. On that account, the state has the crucial task to facilitate and enable citizens to acquire these competences, inter alia, through providing public education. However, it is undesirable and unjust if certain competences or skills *serve as tools for selecting* whom the state recognises as citizens in the first place. Otherwise, if the notion of citizenship would indeed only be granted to individuals who are able to live up to certain (idealised) standards required to contribute to democratic deliberations, this would immediately dangerously affect the political membership of many more citizens than only newcomers (Wong 2009). Indeed, in contemporary citizenship theory there is a strong consensus that the idea of citizenship is deeply committed to the full political agency of citizens – such as the capacity to rationally deliberate and to speak and understand the national language – but that degree of political agency indeed should not determine who is a citizen. From this theoretical angle, approaches have been explored to enable the citizenship of all members of society through 'dependent', 'assisted' or 'interdependent' agency (Silvers and Francis 2005; Kymlicka and Donaldson 2014). This may sound as applying only to exceptional cases, but in fact all citizens throughout life go through stages in which they are in need of assisted agency, for instance in childhood, due to temporary illness or often increasingly with old age, *without* their national citizenship being questioned.

Lastly, a more practical argument is that being allowed to vote actually promotes engagement in public discourse. If individuals (including immigrants) are given political responsibility, they are stimulated to think about civic matters and to follow public debates. In this sense, inviting people into the political realm is in fact an educational opportunity to engage in a better understanding of a particular political community. Put differently, granting citizenship and voting rights can (better) be used as an instrument to promote integration, not a reward for having already done so.

VI. Conclusion

In this chapter, I have suggested that EU Member States should install a firewall between laws that regulate residency and citizenship rights for TCNs (especially if they are refugees and family migrants) and public policies that promote integration. I have argued that this approach has several normative and pragmatic benefits. On the one hand, it counteracts the most prominent issues of the current integration requirements as conditions to attain increased rights in Member States as analysed in the different chapters of this book. These risks and problems involve: (1) the potential exploitation of the precarious legal and political position of TCNs; (2) a decrease in newcomers who have access to naturalisation; (3) susceptibility of jeopardising the ambition of European states to uphold a 'community of equals'; and (4) proclivity to lead to ineffective or even counterproductive integration outcomes, from a long-term societal perspective (which might result in integration requirements contradicting EU laws).

On the other hand, I explained that the firewall solution would also lead to an improved perspective on the purpose and possible applications of integration trajectories and make a number of innovative, flexible and demonstrably effective integration strategies conceivable that are worth giving consideration to. Amongst other things, it makes customised integration strategies imaginable that address the specific needs of individual TCNs, but also other groups in society such as internal EU-migrants, disadvantaged citizens and asylum seekers.

Conclusion

This book has been devoted to comprehending and assessing the burgeoning growth of integration requirements for TCNs as conditions for attaining increased rights in several EU Member States over the last two decades. As a starting point, it set out to examine the relationship and potential tensions between the proclaimed commitment of EU states to the core liberal-democratic values of the EU as listed in the Lisbon Treaty (democracy, rule of law, equality, respect for human rights, etc) and their actual integration and naturalisation practices. Within this endeavour, my main question has been: How to ensure that EU states do not misuse integration measures for TCNs for exclusionary and counterproductive purposes?

To answer this question, this research has adopted an interdisciplinary approach, as it combined legal analysis, political and legal theory and social science research on integration requirements in contemporary Europe. In Chapter 4, I summarised my main findings on the problematic aspects of these integration requirements in section I. To avoid repetition, I will not again give a summary of my findings here in the conclusion. In the closing pages of this inquiry, I will draw conclusions based on its results and explore possible directions for future research.

I. Conclusions

While in all European countries immigrant integration became one of the most significant and hotly debated features of political life over the last quarter of a century, a growing number of EU Member States increasingly install(ed) public policies that invest *less* rather than *more* in integration, also, or even in particular, in relation to newcomers that they are required to admit (or at least cannot expulse) based on EU and international laws. The most important contribution of this book is that it has disentangled this paradoxical development. Indeed, despite the concerns of a majority of European citizens about immigrant integration, the public response of Member States has been to delay the legal inclusion of TCNs, to jeopardise the value of equal citizenship and to enact integration requirements that increasingly hamper, rather than facilitate, integration processes.

In other words, integration measures have proliferated across European states. Yet, taking a closer look, these policies have only to a limited extent been the result of careful policy making with the purpose to genuinely promote the integration – in terms of a set of societal processes – of newcomers who will most likely permanently settle.

This outcome, at the core, is the result of the underlying development discussed in Chapter 1. European countries have started to discuss and conceptualise (potential) public problems that arise if newcomers arrive in society, through individualised integration conceptualisations: TCNs must first 'integrate' to be seen as full members of society and therefore meriting (full) public concern. This development increasingly connects societal challenges related to immigration to matters of personal identity and belonging (eg, 'Has Farid became a real Dane or not?'), instead of recognising integration as a societal process, that is, as a set of shared issues that require proactive public attention.

For this reason, the findings of this book are critical of the current developments concerning integration in Europe, on multiple levels: regarding the political and rhetorical tendency to operate from individualised understandings of integration, as well as the societal ramifications of the implementation of public policies based on this understanding. It indicates that EU states should fundamentally rethink growing perceptions of what 'integration' is and who is responsible for it. Currently, integration policies, especially at the level of Member States, are increasingly framed as the sole responsibility of individuals with non-EU and non-Western backgrounds (instead of a shared responsibility of the receiving state *and* the newcomer). However, one of the societal results of this integration strategy is that it preserves a subclass of vulnerable TCNs (eg, traumatised refugees, illiterates), who remain within society, but without equal rights and the public supervision that could ameliorate their positions of disadvantage and enable their integration processes. Moreover, this group is stigmatised as having personally failed to integrate.

A case in point is the frame of mind that integration requirements are public instruments to select 'integrated immigrants', a rigid attitude which limits the imagination and capacities of receiving states to implement customised integration strategies for different types of newcomers. If integration policies are installed as an examination after a prescribed 'test phase', this pressures states to install standardised integration requirements for all newcomers, as all people should obtain rights (to belong) under the same conditions. However, if we relinquish the idea that public strategies of integration focus on whether individuals merit inclusion, customised integration policies become conceivable that are adjusted to the needs of particular newcomers, immigrant groups and citizens. (For example, a broader language policy could also address functional illiteracy at the side of citizens.) Seen this way, from a more pragmatic and consequentialist perspective, it is even pivotal that European countries will soon recognise that the shift towards individualised integration (has) led to integration programs that are ineffective and even counterproductive – or, at least, that most of their current integration policies are not as effective as they could potentially be. This will allow installing integration policies based on their actual effects on broader policy objectives (eg, increasing language levels, stimulating participation in the labour market, nurturing senses of belonging, etc).

In this context, it is important to point out that if the firewall solution I propose (separating, on the one side, laws that regulate access to residency and citizenship rights and, on the other, policies and programmes promoting integration) would be installed, it is quite likely that European states will spend *more* public supervision and budgets on integration than they do within their current policy schemes. Since, as I see it, one of the aspects that make this firewall an appealing institutional measure, is that it straightforwardly forces European states to shift from individualised to disaggregated conceptualisations of integration and integration policies. Nonetheless, prima facie, I can image that people might fear that if states disconnect their integration strategies from laws regulating the residency rights and citizenship rights of newcomers, this will make integration policies too 'soft'. However, I hope to have convincingly demonstrated that this perspective is misguided. First of all, integration trajectories can still be made mandatory under certain conditions. Moreover, I contend that if it becomes impermissible for states to suggest that (alleged) unintegrated TCNs can be directly removed from their territory, this will in fact lead to better monitored, customised and measurably more effective integration strategies. After all, expulsion based on the non-fulfilment of integration requirements is virtually impossible in the case of family migrants and refugees (the two groups of TCNs that can be mandated to integrate). Moreover, in the context of other groups of migrants such as labour migrants, residency rights are also not (fully) contingent on passing integration requirements, so without completing them they will potentially be part of the population of the country for extensive periods of time.

Therefore, essentially, the crux is that if it is clear from the outset that there is a good chance that newcomers remain for longer periods of time or even permanently settle in society, this demands a proactive stance on the part of the receiving state to make sure their incorporation process turns out well, adopting the shared responsibility to create the conditions that will optimally enable them to flourish.

In addition, a further advantage of the firewall is that it will make it more difficult for European states to cultivate forms of 'earned citizenship', for example by suggesting that the universal values that underpin their liberal-democratic states are only accessible through the dominant majority culture of the receiving state. In other words, it takes away an instrument for states to suggest that newcomers must culturally adapt to the 'native' culture before they may be recognised as 'real' citizens and equal political members and co-authors of the law. This is important, as if European countries genuinely want to promote the liberal-democratic values underpinning their states as universal, they, and their policies, should never deviate from the firm commitment to endorse and foster equal citizenship for all citizens, irrespective of their (cultural, religious, ethnic, etc) backgrounds. Integration requirements should therefore not reinforce problematic status hierarchies between citizens. In particular, they should not nurture the social perception that the entitlement of citizens with (non-EU, non-Western) backgrounds to their legal citizenship is conditional and contingent on certain desirable competences, attitudes and efforts, while citizens without immigrant backgrounds are perceived as having a natural right to the legal status of unconditional citizenship. Moreover, from a practical point of view, if a state promotes its values as inclusive and equally accessible to all citizens, this can help create the conditions under which all citizens can be(come) committed to nurturing a shared society and can recognise each other as equally belonging to it.

In sum, this book signals the warning that integration strategies in Europe are under the influence of societal and political forces that tend to make them deficient and skew their social impact in ways that are undesirable, both for newcomers and for born citizens. Moreover, it showed that the current legal and political configuration of EU legislation structurally provides Member States with the opportunity to install counterproductive integration requirements. For this reason, this admonishment applies both to Member States that already enacted (excessively individualised) integration requirements connected to rights, as well as to Member States that did not (yet) enact such requirements. The tendency in Europe to invest less in integration trajectories (because it is increasingly seen as the contractual personal duty of newcomers to integrate) is a public strategy that will lead to a variety of negative consequences that are prone to require public investments in the future. More particularly, if integration requirements are broadly ineffective or even have negative impacts on societal processes, this will potentially result in increased poverty, crime, welfare dependency, unemployment, deficient language skills and potentially even to distrust between newcomers and citizens and segregation. For this reason, to invest in (disaggregated) integration programs – in times of a humanitarian refugee crisis but also in general – is by no means a 'soft' policy. Instead, it is enacting public policies that are in accordance with the long-term interests of receiving EU states.

However, the prevalence of the individualised conceptualisation of integration clouds this pragmatic perspective on integration policies and, with that, also draws public and political discussions away from the fundamental shortcomings of current integration measures in EU Member States. Within this individualised framework, disappointing policy outcomes of integration strategies can be defended with the explanation that these policies merely indicate the personal failings of certain newcomers. Additionally, installing additional (arbitrary) integration requirements as conditions for attaining rights remains attractive as it accommodates voters, while TCNs are not in a position to object to the terms imposed on them for obtaining full residential security.

II. Future Research

A variety of possible future work arises from the investigations of this project. Given the predominately legal-philosophical approach of this book, I contend that this book could be most strongly enriched by researches with a more empirical focus.

For example, a fascinating opening for further research could involve cost-profit analyses of different integration strategies. Indeed, in Chapter 4 and in this Conclusion, I introduced the hypothesis that pro-actively and publicly investing in integration in an inclusive manner is likely to be *economically* lucrative on the long term (compared to when individualised integration requirements are defective). It would be valuable to gather data to fully flesh out if and how this claim would be substantiated according to evidence-based research.

In addition, if feasible, it could be of value if more empirical research (see already, eg, Monforte et al 2019; Green et al 2020) would be conducted on the attitudinal ramifications of the reward paradigm of naturalisation on senses of belonging, the self-image of political communities and migrants themselves, levels of generalised trust, levels of trust in public institutions, etc. If states increasingly treat certain citizens as having conditional citizenship and others having unconditional citizenship, what will be the consequences in the long term?

Moreover, it could be useful to examine further the potential links and reinforcing relationship of the shift towards individualised integration with wider 'neoliberal' tendencies in welfare states (see, eg, Borevi 2010 on Scandinavia; Bassel et al 2020). Notwithstanding that the shift towards individualised integration has particular consequences for TCNs given, in Bosniak's terminology, the Janus face of citizenship, there is undeniably a broader trend in developed states to assume that citizens are responsible for their own better participation, for example in relation to the labour market and education. What is the exact relation and impact of this trend on designing effective integration strategies?

Finally, I believe the firewall proposal would deserve a full study of its own, in which all questions linked to it can be addressed. For instance, it would be of interest to investigate in more detail under which political, legal and societal circumstances it is likely to be adopted. Given that this book argues that integration requirements should be assessed not only based on whether they can be justified *in principle*, but instead by scrutinising their actual political dynamics and electoral mechanisms that shape them, it is crucial to also determine the empirical preconditions for the firewall. Moreover, it could be described in more detail how the firewall exactly applies to different migrant groups on European soil (eg, family migrants, refugees, students, perhaps also undocumented migrants or disadvantaged minorities).

Lastly, it could be explored to what extent the arguments presented in this book in favour of separating integration strategies from laws monitoring the allocation of residency and citizenship rights to TCNs, also apply to other requirements for territorial or civic inclusion. For instance, prima facie, it seems that my normative and empirical arguments suggest that there is also something wrong with income requirements (eg, for family migration). However, possible countervailing considerations – such as that a minimum income for inclusion is a less 'open-ended' requirement than asking 'personal integration' – should be carefully explored.

BIBLIOGRAPHY

Abizadeh, A (2008) 'Democratic Theory and Border Coercion: No Right to Unilaterally Control Your Own Borders' 36 *Political Theory* 37.

Abou-Chadi, T (2016) 'Niche Party Success and Mainstream Party Policy Shifts – How Green and Radical Right Parties Differ in Their Impact' 46 *British Journal of Political Science* 417.

ACVZ (2013) 'Verloren tijd' (Adviescommissie Vreemdelingenzaken) publicatie www.adviescommissievoorvreemdelingenzaken.nl/publicaties/publicaties/2013/3/22/verloren-tijd accessed 18 November 2020.

Adam, I and Jacobs, D (2014) 'Divided on Immigration, Two Models for Integration. The Multilevel Governance of Immigration and Integration in Belgium' in E Hepburn and R Zapata-Barrero (eds), *The Politics of Immigration in Multi-Level States: Governance and Political Parties* (Palgrave Macmillan UK).

Akkerman, T (2012) 'Comparing Radical Right Parties in Government: Immigration and Integration Policies in Nine Countries (1996–2010)' 35 *West European Politics* 511.

Alaoui MH, 'L'immigration familiale: une obligation d'« intégration républicaine ». Le cas du Contrat d'accueil et d'intégration' (2016) 13 *Recherches familiales* 79.

Alarian, HM and Neureiter, M (2019) 'Values or Origin? Mandatory Immigrant Integration and Immigration Attitudes in Europe' 0 *Journal of Ethnic and Migration Studies* 1.

Allan, K (2005) *Explorations in Classical Sociological Theory: Seeing the Social World* (Pine Forge Press).

Anderson, B (1983) *Imagined Communities: Reflections on the Origin and Spread of Nationalism* (Verso).

—— (2013) *Us and Them?: The Dangerous Politics of Immigration Control* (Oxford University Press).

Anderson, E (2013) *The Imperative of Integration* (Princeton University Press).

—— (1999) 'What Is the Point of Equality?' 109 *Ethics* 287.

Arcarazo, DA (2015) 'Civic Citizenship Reintroduced? The Long-Term Residence Directive as a Post-National Form of Membership' 21 *European Law Journal* 200.

Arneson, RJ (1989) 'Equality and Equal Opportunity for Welfare' 56 *Philosophical Studies* 77.

Arribas Lozano, A and others (2014) 'Revisiting the European Union Framework on Immigrant Integration: The European Integration Forum as a Technology of Agency' 14 *Ethnicities* 556.

Backhouse, C (1996) 'The White Women's Labor Laws: Anti-Chinese Racism in Early Twentieth-Century Canada' 14 *Law and History Review* 315.

Badenhoop, E (2017) 'Calling for the Super Citizen: Citizenship Ceremonies in the UK and Germany as Techniques of Subject-Formation' 5 *Migration Studies* 409.

Bader, V (2001) 'Cohesion, Unity and Stability in Modern Societies' in Anton van Harskamp and AW Musschenga (eds), *The Many Faces of Individualism* (Peeters).

—— (2005) 'The Ethics of Immigration' 12 *Constellations* 331.

Bakker, L (2016) *Seeking Sanctuary in the Netherlands* https://repub.eur.nl/pub/79617 accessed 5 September 2020.

Bakker, L, Dagevos, J and Engbersen, G (2017) 'Explaining the Refugee Gap: A Longitudinal Study on Labour Market Participation of Refugees in the Netherlands' 43 *Journal of Ethnic and Migration Studies* 1775.

Baldi, G and Goodman, SW (2015) 'Migrants into Members: Social Rights, Civic Requirements, and Citizenship in Western Europe' 38 *West European Politics* 1152.

Ballin, EH (2014) *Citizens' Rights and the Right to Be a Citizen* (Martinus Nijhoff Publishers).

Bartram, D (2018) 'The UK Citizenship Process: Political Integration or Marginalization?': *Sociology*.

Bassel, L, Monforte, P and Khan, K [2020] 'Becoming an Active Citizen: The UK Citizenship Test' *Ethnicities.*
Bauböck, R (1994) *Transnational Citizenship: Membership and Rights in International Migration* (Edward Elgar).
—— (2009) 'Global Justice, Freedom of Movement and Democratic Citizenship' 50 *European Journal of Sociology / Archives Européennes de Sociologie* 1.
——, 'The Rights and Duties of External Citizenship' (2009) 13 Citizenship Studies 475.
Bauböck, R, Groenendijk, K, Ersb, E and Waldrauch, H (2006) *Acquisition and Loss of Nationality. Policies and Trends in 15 European Countries. Volume 1: Comparative Analyses* (Amsterdam University Press).
Bauböck, R and Goodman, S (2011) 'Naturalisation' EUDO Citizenship [GLOBALCIT] 2011/2 https://cadmus.eui.eu//handle/1814/51625 accessed 2 July 2020.
Bauböck, R and Joppke, C (2010) 'How Liberal Are Citizenship Tests?' (Robert Schuman Centre for Advanced Studies) info:eu-repo/semantics/report https://boris.unibe.ch/3879/ accessed 27 May 2019.
Beauchamps, M (2017) 'Perverse Tactics: "Terrorism" and National Identity in France' 58 *Culture, Theory and Critique* 48.
—— (2018) *Governing Affective Citizenship: Denaturalization, Belonging, and Repression* (Rowman & Littlefield).
Benhabib, S (2004) *The Rights of Others: Aliens, Residents, and Citizens* (Cambridge University Press).
Besselsen, E and De Hart, B (2015) 'Verblijfsrechterlijke Consequenties van de Wet Inburgering' (Amsterdam Centre for European Law and Governance) www.researchgate.net/publication/292565302_E_Besselsen_B_de_Hart_'Verblijfsrechterlijke_consequenties_van_de_Wet_Inburgering'_Wolf_Legal_Publishers_2014 accessed 29 June 2020.
Blake, M (2005) 'Immigration' in Christopher Wellman (ed), *The Blackwell Companion to Applied Ethics* (Blackwell).
Bloemraad, I (2006) *Becoming a Citizen: Incorporating Immigrants and Refugees in the United States and Canada* (University of California Press).
—— (2016) 'The Politics of Immigration By James Hampshire' 95 *Social Forces* e23.
—— (2017) 'Does Citizenship Matter?' (*The Oxford Handbook of Citizenship*) www.oxfordhandbooks.com/view/10.1093/oxfordhb/9780198805854.001.0001/oxfordhb-9780198805854-e-23 accessed 18 September 2020.
Böcker, A and Strik, T (2011) 'Language and Knowledge Tests for Permanent Residence Rights: Help or Hindrance for Integration' 13 *European Journal of Migration and Law* 157.
Boekestein, TL and Groot, G-R de (2019) 'Discussing the Human Rights Limits on Loss of Citizenship: A Normative-Legal Perspective on Egalitarian Arguments Regarding Dutch Nationality Laws Targeting Dutch-Moroccans' 23 *Citizenship Studies* 320.
Bonjour, S (2014) 'The Transfer of Pre-Departure Integration Requirements for Family Migrants Among Member States of the European Union' 2 *Comparative Migration Studies* 203.
Bonjour, S and Duyvendak, JW (2018) 'The "Migrant with Poor Prospects": Racialized Intersections of Class and Culture in Dutch Civic Integration Debates' 41 *Ethnic and Racial Studies* 882.
Borevi, K (2010) 'Dimensions of Citizenship: European Integration Policies from a Scandinavian Perspective' in B Bengtsson, Per Strömblad and A-H Bay (eds), *Diversity, Inclusion and Citizenship in Scandinavia* (Cambridge Scholars Publishing).
Borevi, K Jensen, KK and Mouritsen, P (2017) 'The Civic Turn of Immigrant Integration Policies in the Scandinavian Welfare States' 5 *Comparative Migration Studies* 9.
Bosniak, L (2008) *The Citizen and the Alien: Dilemmas of Contemporary Membership* (Princeton University Press).
Brettschneider, C (2016) *When the State Speaks, What Should It Say?: How Democracies Can Protect Expression and Promote Equality* (Princeton University Press).
Brochmann, G and Midtbøen, AH [2020] 'Philosophies of Integration? Elite Views on Citizenship Policies in Scandinavia' *Ethnicities.*

Brubaker, R (1992) *Citizenship and Nationhood in France and Germany* (Harvard University Press).
Byrne, B (2017) 'Testing Times: The Place of the Citizenship Test in the UK Immigration Regime and New Citizens' Responses to It' 51 *Sociology* 323.
Carens, J (2010) 'The Most Liberal Citizenship Test Is Non at All' in R Bauböck and C Joppke (eds), *How Liberal are Citizenship Tests?* (Robert Schuman Centre for Advanced Studies) https://boris.unibe.ch/3879/ accessed 27 May 2019.
—— (2013) *The Ethics of Immigration* (Oxford University Press).
Carey, B (2018) 'Against the Right to Revoke Citizenship' 22 *Citizenship Studies* 897.
Carrera, S and Vankova, Z (2019) 'Human Rights Aspects of Immigrant and Refugee Integration Policies' (Council of Europe) Issue Paper https://edoc.coe.int/en/migration/7908-human-rights-aspects-of-immigrant-and-refugee-integration-policies.html accessed 17 June 2020.
Castles, S (1985) 'The Guests Who Stayed – The Debate on "Foreigners Policy" in the German Federal Republic' 19 *International Migration Review* 517.
Cavallar, G (2017) *The Rights of Strangers: Theories of International Hospitality, the Global Community and Political Justice since Vitoria* (Routledge).
Chemin, JE and Nagel, AK (2020) 'Integration Policies, Practices and Experiences – Germany Country Report' Horizon 2020 Respond 2020/51 www.academia.edu/43243737/Integration_Policies_Practices_and_Experiences_Germany_Country_Report accessed 3 August 2020.
Choudhury, T (2017) 'The Radicalisation of Citizenship Deprivation' 37 *Critical Social Policy* 225.
Cohen, GA (1997) 'Where the Action Is: On the Site of Distributive Justice' 26 *Philosophy & Public Affairs* 3.
Cooke, M (2009) 'Barrier or Entitlement? The Language and Citizenship Agenda in the United Kingdom' 6 *Language Assessment Quarterly* 71.
Cuttitta, P (2016) 'Mandatory Integration Measures and Differential Inclusion: The Italian Case' 17 *Journal of International Migration and Integration* 289.
Dahl, RA (2000) *On Democracy* (Yale University Press).
de Groot, GR, Kuipers, J and Weber, F (2009) 'Passing Citizenship Tests as a Requirement for Naturalisation: A Comparative Perspective', *Illiberal Liberal States. Immigration, Citizenship and Integration in the EU* (Ashgate) https://cris.maastrichtuniversity.nl/en/publications/11070bf2-d488-4565-a0e8-6bae1fd89659 accessed 12 June 2020.
de Hart, B and Terlouw, AB (2015) 'Born Here. Revocation and the Automatic Loss of Dutch Nationality in Case of Terrorist Activities.' in M van den Brink, S Burri and J Goldschmidt (eds), *Equality and human rights: nothing but trouble.* (SIM) https://research.vu.nl/en/publications/1f2e1068-0126-44f6-864e-985f0644f1a9 accessed 9 August 2020.
de Lange, T, Besselsen, E, Rahouti, S and Rijken, C (2017) *Van azc naar een baan* (Universiteit van Amsterdam) https://dare.uva.nl/personal/pure/en/publications/van-azc-naar-een-baan(f0d64912-bad7-466f-b7ea-f33f43f5458a).html accessed 23 June 2020.
De Leeuw, M and Van Wichelen, S (2012) 'Civilizing Migrants: Integration, Culture and Citizenship' 15 *European Journal of Cultural Studies* 195.
de Vries, K (2013) *Integration at the Border: The Dutch Act on Integration Abroad and International Immigration Law* (Bloomsbury Publishing).
—— (2017) 'Integratie en de onzekere verwachting van gelijke behandeling van derdelanders. Great Expectations' 2017 *Asiel&Migrantenrecht* 257.
—— (2019) 'Reactie: Inburgering, wat mag en wat werkt?' https://repository.ubn.ru.nl/handle/2066/215056 accessed 17 June 2020.
De Waal, T (2020) 'Conditional Belonging: Evaluating Integration Requirements from a Social Equality Perspective' 41 *Journal of Intercultural Studies* 231.
—— (2018) 'Make Sure You Belong: A Critical Assessment of Integration Requirements for Residential and Citizenship Rights in Europe' 25 *Buffalo Human Rights Law Review* 37.
Debruyne, P (2019) 'Inburgering en integratie zijn gewoon instrumenten van migratiebeheer geworden' www.mo.be/mopaper/inburgering-en-integratie-zijn-gewoon-instrumenten-van-migratiebeheer-geworden accessed 19 August 2020.
Durkheim, É (2018) *Le Suicide* (Books on Demand).

Driouichi, F (2007) *De Casus Inburgering en Nationaliteitswetgeving* (Amsterdam University Press).
Duyvendak JW, Geschiere P and Tonkens E, *The Culturalization of Citizenship: Belonging and Polarization in a Globalizing World* (Springer 2016).
Duyvendak, JW, Hurenkamp, M and Tonkens, E (2010) 'Culturalization of Citizenship in the Netherlands' in AC d'Appollonia and S Reich (eds), *Managing Ethnic Diversity After 9/11: Integration, Security, and Civil Liberties in Transatlantic Perspective* (Rutgers University Press).
Dworkin, R (1981) 'What Is Equality? Part 1: Equality of Welfare' 10 *Philosophy & Public Affairs* 185.
Elias, SB (2016) 'Testing Citizenship' 96 *Boston University Law Review* 2093.
EMN (2020) 'Study on Pathways to Citizenship in the EU' (EMN) EMN Synthesis Report for the EMN Study https://ec.europa.eu/home-affairs/content/emn-study-pathways-citizenship-eu_en accessed 13 July 2020.
Entzinger, H (2000) 'The Dynamics of Integration Policies: A Multidimensional Model' in R Koopmans and P Statham (eds), *Challenging Immigration and Ethnic Relations Politics* (Oxford University Press).
Entzinger, H and Biezeveld, R (2003) 'Benchmarking in Immigrant Integration' (European Research Centre on Migration and Ethnic Relations 2003) European Commission No DG JAI-A-2/2002/006 https://ec.europa.eu/migrant-integration/librarydoc/benchmarking-in-immigrant-integration accessed 5 September 2020.
Ersanilli, E and Koopmans, R (2011) 'Do Immigrant Integration Policies Matter? A Three-Country Comparison among Turkish Immigrants' 34 *West European Politics* 208.
Ersbøll, E (2015) 'Report on Citizenship Law: Denmark' http://cadmus.eui.eu//handle/1814/36504 accessed 5 June 2019.
ESRI & Department of Justice and Equality, 'Supporting Integration? International Practices on Civics and Language Requirements Linked to Naturalisation: Policy Implications for Ireland' (ESRI & Department of Justice and Equality 2020) Report www.esri.ie/publications/supporting-integration-international-practices-on-civics-and-language-requirements accessed 16 October 2020.
Eurobarometer, (2019) 'Eurobarometer: Immigration and Climate Remain Main Concerns' (Eurobarometer) Text https://ec.europa.eu/commission/presscorner/detail/en/IP_19_6839 accessed 24 July 2020.
—— (2018) 'Integration of Immigrants in the European Union' Text Special Eurobarometer 469 https://ec.europa.eu/home-affairs/news/results-special-eurobarometer-integration-immigrants-european-union_en accessed 24 July 2020.
EWSI, (2020) 'Governance of Migrant Integration in Denmark' (*EWSI*) https://ec.europa.eu/migrant-integration/governance/denmark accessed 16 July 2020.
Fargues, É (2017) 'The Revival of Citizenship Deprivation in France and the UK as an Instance of Citizenship Renationalisation' 21 *Citizenship Studies* 984.
—— (2019) 'Simply a Matter of Compliance with the Rules? The Moralising and Responsibilising Function of Fraud-Based Citizenship Deprivation in France and the UK' 23 *Citizenship Studies* 356.
Fargues, É and Winter, E (2019) 'Conditional Membership: What Revocation Does to Citizenship' 23 *Citizenship Studies* 295.
Fiss, OM (1999) *A Community of Equals: The Constitutional Protection of New Americans* (Beacon Press).
FitzGerald, DS and others (2018) 'Can You Become One of Us? A Historical Comparison of Legal Selection of "Assimilable" Immigrants in Europe and the Americas' 44 *Journal of Ethnic and Migration Studies* 27.
Fourie, C (2012) 'What Is Social Equality? An Analysis of Status Equality as a Strongly Egalitarian Ideal' 18 *Res Publica* 107.
Fourie, C, Schuppert, F and Wallimann-Helmer, I (2015) *Social Equality: On What It Means to Be Equals* (Oxford University Press).
Fraser, N (2001) 'Recognition without Ethics?' 18 *Theory, Culture & Society* 21.
Fraser, N and Honneth, A (2003) *Redistribution Or Recognition?: A Political-Philosophical Exchange* (Verso).
Freeman, GP (1979) *Immigrant Labor and Racial Conflict in Industrial Societies: The French and British Experience, 1945–1975* (Princeton University Press).

—— (2004) 'Immigrant Incorporation in Western Democracies' 38 *International Migration Review* 945.
Garibay, MG and Cuyper P, de (2018) 'Is There an Evidence Basis for Immigrant Integration Policies?: A Methodological Enquiry' 8 *Nordic Journal of Migration Research* 15.
Gebhardt, D (2016) 'When the State Takes over: Civic Integration Programmes and the Role of Cities in Immigrant Integration' 42 *Journal of Ethnic and Migration Studies* 742.
Gerhardt U, *The Social Thought of Talcott Parsons: Methodology and American Ethos* (Routledge 2016).
Gibney, MJ (2020) 'Denationalisation and Discrimination' 46 *Journal of Ethnic and Migration Studies* 2551.
Goldring, L, Berinstein, C and Bernhard, JK (2009) 'Institutionalizing Precarious Migratory Status in Canada' 13 *Citizenship Studies* 239.
Goodman, SW (2010a) 'Integration Requirements for Integration's Sake? Identifying, Categorising and Comparing Civic Integration Policies' 36 *Journal of Ethnic and Migration Studies* 753.
—— (2010b) 'Naturalisation Policies in Europe: Exploring Patterns of Inclusion and Exclusion' (Robert Schuman Centre for Advanced Studies).
—— (2011) 'Controlling Immigration through Language and Country Knowledge Requirements' 34 *West European Politics* 235.
—— (2012) 'Fortifying Citizenship: Policy Strategies for Civic Integration in Western Europe' 64 *World Politics* 659.
Goodman, SW and Howard, MM (2013) 'Evaluating and Explaining the Restrictive Backlash in Citizenship Policy in Europe' in A Sarat (ed), *Special Issue: Who Belongs? Immigration, Citizenship, and the Constitution of Legality*, vol 60 (Emerald Group Publishing Limited).
Goodman, SW and Wright, M (2015) 'Does Mandatory Integration Matter? Effects of Civic Requirements on Immigrant Socio-Economic and Political Outcomes' 41 *Journal of Ethnic and Migration Studies* 1885.
Grande, E, Schwarzbözl, T and Fatke, M (2019) 'Politicizing Immigration in Western Europe' 26 *Journal of European Public Policy* 1444.
Green, EGT and others (2020) 'When Integration Policies Shape the Impact of Intergroup Contact on Threat Perceptions: A Multilevel Study across 20 European Countries' 46 *Journal of Ethnic and Migration Studies* 631.
Green-Pedersen, C and Mortensen, PB 2015) 'Avoidance and Engagement: Issue Competition in Multiparty Systems' 63 *Political Studies* 747.
Groenendijk, K (2006) 'Family Reunification as a Right under Community Law' 8 *European Journal of Migration and Law* 215.
—— (2011) 'Pre-Departure Integration Strategies in the European Union: Integration or Immigration Policy?' 13 *European Journal of Migration and Law* 1.
—— (2019) 'Nederlands inburgeringsbeleid en het Unierecht 2009–2019. Nederlandse strengheid en wetgevend perfectionisme werken contraproductief' https://repository.ubn.ru.nl/handle/2066/215056 accessed 17 June 2020.
Guild, E Groenendijk, CA and Carrera, S (2009) *Illiberal Liberal States: Immigration, Citizenship and Integration in the EU / Edited by Elspeth Guild, Kees Groenendijk and Sergio Carrera* (Ashgate).
Gutmann, A (1995) 'Civic Education and Social Diversity' 105 *Ethics* 557.
Hajjat, A (2012) *Les frontières de l'"identité nationale": L'injonction à l'assimilation en France métropolitaine et coloniale* (La Découverte).
Hachimi-Alaoui, M (2016) 'L'immigration familiale une obligation d'*«intégration républicaine»*. Le cas du Contrat d'accueil et d'intégration' 13 *Journal-recherches-familiales* 79.
Hampshire, J (2011) 'Liberalism and Citizenship Acquisition: How Easy Should Naturalisation Be?' 37 *Journal of Ethnic and Migration Studies* 953.
—— (2013) *The Politics of Immigration: Contradictions of the Liberal State* (Polity).
Hansen, R (2009) 'The Poverty of Postnationalism : Citizenship, Immigration, and the New Europe' 38 *Theory and Society* 1.
—— (2010) 'Citizenship Tests: An Unapologetic Defense' in R Bauböck and C Joppke (eds), *How Liberal are Citizenship Tests?* (Robert Schuman Centre for Advanced Studies) https://boris.unibe.ch/3879/ accessed 27 May 2019.

Hernes, V (2018) 'Cross-National Convergence in Times of Crisis? Integration Policies before, during and after the Refugee Crisis' 41 *West European Politics* 1305.

—— (2020) 'Convergence, Centralization and Change: Immigrant Integration Policies in West-Europe, 1997–2017' (University of Oslo) www.duo.uio.no/handle/10852/79316 accessed 14 October 2020.

—— (2020) 'Policy Preferences and Ministerial Structures: Immigrant Integration Governance in Western Europe, 1997–2017' n/a Governance https://onlinelibrary.wiley.com/doi/abs/10.1111/gove.12481 accessed 26 October 2020.

Hobbes T, *Hobbes's Leviathan* (1651).

Howard, MM (2006) 'Comparative Citizenship: An Agenda for Cross-National Research' 4 *Perspectives on Politics* 443.

—— (2009) *The Politics of Citizenship in Europe* (Cambridge University Press).

—— (2010) 'The Impact of the Far Right on Citizenship Policy in Europe: Explaining Continuity and Change' 36 *Journal of Ethnic and Migration Studies* 735.

Huddleston, T (2011) 'Family Reunion: Confronting Stereotypes, Understanding Family Life' (Migration Policy Group).

—— (2011) 'Migrant Integration Policy Index 2011' (British Council and Migration Policy Group).

—— (2013) 'The Naturalisation Procedure: Measuring the Ordinary Obstacles and Opportunities for Immigrants to Become Citizens' https://cadmus.eui.eu//handle/1814/28122 accessed 18 September 2020.

—— (2020) 'Naturalisation in Context: How Nationality Laws and Procedures Shape Immigrants' Interest and Ability to Acquire Nationality in Six European Countries' 8 *Comparative Migration Studies* 18.

Huddleston, T and Vink, MP (2015) 'Full Membership or Equal Rights? The Link between Naturalisation and Integration Policies for Immigrants in 29 European States' 3 *Comparative Migration Studies* 8.

Human Rights Watch, (2008) 'The Netherlands: Discrimination in the Name of Integration' (Human Rights Watch) www.hrw.org/report/2008/05/13/netherlands-discrimination-name-integration/migrants-rights-under-integration accessed 25 June 2020.

Huntington, SP (2005) *Who Are We?: America's Great Debate* (Free Press).

Ipsos, (2017) 'Global Views on Immigration and the Refugee Crisis' (Ipsos) www.ipsos.com/en/global-views-immigration-and-refugee-crisis accessed 24 July 2020.

Jacobson, D (1996) *Rights Across Borders: Immigration and the Decline of Citizenship* (BRILL).

James, JS and Janmaat, JG (2019) 'Understanding Variation in Approaches to Immigrant Integration' in JS James and JG Janmaat (eds), *Civil Disorder, Domestic Terrorism and Education Policy: The Context in England and France* (Springer International Publishing).

Jensen, KK and others (2019) 'Roadblocks to Citizenship: Selection Effects of Restrictive Naturalisation Rules' 0 *Journal of Ethnic and Migration Studies* 1.

Joppke, C (2008b) 'Comparative Citizenship: A Restrictive Turn in Europe?' 2 *Law & Ethics of Human Rights* 1.

—— (1998) 'Why Liberal States Accept Unwanted Immigration' 50 *World Politics* 266.

—— (2006) 'Citizenship between De- and Re-Ethnicization' in YM Bodemann, YM and G Yurdakul (eds), *Migration, Citizenship, Ethnos* (Palgrave Macmillan).

—— (2007) 'Beyond National Models: Civic Integration Policies for Immigrants in Western Europe' 30 *West European Politics* 1.

—— (2008a) 'Immigration and the Identity of Citizenship: The Paradox of Universalism' 12 *Citizenship Studies* 533.

—— (2009), 'Limits of Integration Policy: Britain and Her Muslims' (2009) 35 *Journal of Ethnic and Migration Studies* 453.

—— (2010) 'How Liberal Are Citizenship Tests?', *How Liberal are Citizenship tests?*.

—— (2013) *Citizenship and Immigration* (Polity).

—— (2017) 'Civic Integration in Western Europe: Three Debates' 40 *West European Politics* 1153.

Joppke, C and Eule, T (2016) 'Civic Integration in Europe: Continuity versus Discontinuity' in GP Freeman and N Mirilovic (eds), *Handbook on Migration and Social Policy* (Edward Elgar Publishing).

Joppke, C and Morawska, E (2003) 'Integrating Immigrants in Liberal Nation-States: Policies and Practices' in C Joppke and E Morawska (eds), *Toward Assimilation and Citizenship: Immigrants in Liberal Nation-States* (Palgrave Macmillan UK).

Kahmann, M and others (2018) 'Vluchtelingenwerk Integratiebarometer 2018' (Verwey-Jonkers 2018) www.verwey-jonker.nl/publicaties/2018/vluchtelingenwerk-integratiebarometer-2018 accessed 6 January 2021.

Kernohan, A (1998) *Liberalism, Equality, and Cultural Oppression* (Cambridge University Press).

Kiwan, D (2008) 'A Journey to Citizenship in the United Kingdom' 10 *International Journal on Multicultural societies* 60.

Klarenbeek, LM and Weide, M (2020) 'The Participation Paradox: Demand for and Fear of Immigrant Participation' 14 *Critical Policy Studies* 214.

Koopmans, R, Statham, Passy, F and Giugni, M (2005) *Contested Citizenship: Immigration and Cultural Diversity in Europe* (University of Minnesota Press).

Kostakopoulou, D (2010b) 'The Anatomy of Civic Integration' 73 *The Modern Law Review* 933.

—— (2008) *The Future Governance of Citizenship* (Cambridge University Press).

—— (2009) 'Citizenship Goes Public: The Institutional Design of Anational Citizenship' 17 *Journal of Political Philosophy* 275.

—— (2010a) 'What Liberalism Is Committed to and Why Current Citizenship Policies Fail This Test' in R Bauböck and C Joppke (eds), *How Liberal are Citizenship Tests?* (Robert Schuman Centre for Advanced Studies) https://boris.unibe.ch/3879/ accessed 27 May 2019.

Kymlicka, W (1995) *Multicultural Citizenship* (Clarendon Press).

—— (2001) *Politics in the Vernacular: Nationalism, Multiculturalism, and Citizenship* (Oxford University Press).

—— (2002) *Contemporary Political Philosophy: An Introduction* (Oxford University Press).

—— (2012) 'Multiculturalism: Success, Failure, and the Future | Migrationpolicy.Org' (Migration Policy Institute) www.migrationpolicy.org/research/TCM-multiculturalism-success-failure accessed 11 June 2020.

Kymlicka, W and Donaldson, S (2014) 'Animals and the Frontiers of Citizenship' 34 *Oxford Journal of Legal Studies* 201.

Lægaard, S (2010) 'Immigration, Social Cohesion, and Naturalization' 10 *Ethnicities* 452.

—— (2012) 'Naturalisation, Desert, and the Symbolic Meaning of Citizenship', *Territories of Citizenship* (Palgrave Macmillan, London).

Larin, SJ (2020) 'Is It Really about Values? Civic Nationalism and Migrant Integration' 46 *Journal of Ethnic and Migration Studies* 127.

Lefort, C (2016) *Wat is politiek?* (Pol van de Wiel and Bart Verheijen trs, Boom Amsterdam).

Lenard, PT (2016) 'Democracies and the Power to Revoke Citizenship' 30 *Ethics & International Affairs* 73.

Lipsky, M (1980) *Street-Level Bureaucracy: Dilemmas of the Individual in Public Services.*, vol 10 (Russell Sage Foundation) https://doi.org/10.1177/003232928001000113 accessed 17 June 2020.

Lucassen, L and Lucassen, J (2011) *Winnaars En Verliezers* (Prometheus).

Macionis, JJ and Gerber, LM (2010) *Sociology* (Pearson Education Canada).

Macklin, A (2014) 'Citizenship Revocation, the Privilege to Have Rights and the Production of the Alien' 40 *Queen's Law Journal* 1.

Magro, K (2007) 'Overcoming the Trauma of War: Literacy Challenges of Adults Learners' 47 *Education Canada* 70.

Manatschal, A Wisthaler, V and Zuber, CI (2020) 'Making Regional Citizens? The Political Drivers and Effects of Subnational Immigrant Integration Policies in Europe and North America' 0 *Regional Studies* 1.

Mantu, S (2015) *Contingent Citizenship: The Law and Practice of Citizenship Deprivation in International, European and National Perspectives* (BRILL).

—— (2018) '"Terrorist" Citizens and the Human Right to Nationality' 26 *Journal of Contemporary European Studies* 28.

Marx, K (1844) *Economic and Philosophical Manuscripts.*

Mazouz S, *La République et ses autres: Politiques de l'altérité dans la France des années 2000* (ENS Éditions 2017).

Meijers, MJ (2017) 'Contagious Euroscepticism: The Impact of Eurosceptic Support on Mainstream Party Positions on European Integration' 23 *Party Politics* 413.

Michalowski, I (2011) 'Required to Assimilate? The Content of Citizenship Tests in Five Countries' 15 *Citizenship Studies* 749.

—— (2004) 'Integration Programs for Newcomers–A Dutch Model for Europe?'

Mill, JS (1859) *On Liberty* (Independently Published).

—— (1861) *Considerations on Representative Government.*

Miller, D (1997) 'Equality and Justice' 10 *Ratio* 222.

—— (1995) *On Nationality* (Clarendon Press).

—— (2008) 'Immigrants, Nations, and Citizenship' 16 *Journal of Political Philosophy* 371.

—— (2016) *Strangers in Our Midst: The Political Philosophy of Immigration* (Harvard University Press).

Modood, T (2019) 'A Multicultural Nationalism' 25 *Brown Journal of World Affairs* 233.

Monforte, P, Bassel, L and Khan, K (2019) 'Deserving Citizenship? Exploring Migrants' Experiences of the "Citizenship Test" Process in the United Kingdom' 70 *The British Journal of Sociology* 24.

Morris, L (2002) *Managing Migration: Civic Stratification and Migrants' Rights* (Psychology Press).

Mouritsen, P (2006) 'The Particular Universalism of a Norfic Civic Nation' in T Modood, A Triandafyllidou and R Zapata-Barrero (eds), *Multiculturalism, Muslims and Citizenship: A European Approach* (Routledge).

—— (2013) 'The Resilience of Citizenship Traditions: Civic Integration in Germany, Great Britain and Denmark' 13 *Ethnicities* 86.

Mouritsen, P, Kriegbaum, JK and Larin, SJ (2019) 'Introduction: Theorizing the Civic Turn in European Integration Policies' 19 *Ethnicities* 595.

Mouritsen, P and Olsen, TV (2013) 'Denmark between Liberalism and Nationalism' 36 *Ethnic and Racial Studies* 691.

Mudde, C (2019) *The Far Right Today* (John Wiley & Sons).

Nationale Ombudsman, (2018) 'Een valse start: een onderzoek naar behoorlijke inburgering' (Nationale Ombudsman) www.nationaleombudsman.nl/onderzoeken/2018065-onderzoek-naar-behoorlijke-inburgering accessed 13 July 2020.

Netherlands Court of Audit, 'First Results of the Civic Integration Act 2013' (Algemene Rekenkamer 2017) rapport https://english.rekenkamer.nl/publications/reports/2017/01/24/civic-integration accessed 20 July 2020.

NIEM (2018) 'Integration of Beneficiaries of International Protection in France' National Report www.forintegration.eu/pl/pub/poland-national-report-2018/dnl/24 accessed 6 January 2021.

Nussbaum, MC (2001) *Women and Human Development: The Capabilities Approach* (Cambridge University Press).

—— (2011) *Creating Capabilities* (Harvard University Press).

Nyers, P (2006) 'The Accidental Citizen: Acts of Sovereignty and (Un)Making Citizenship' 35 *Economy and Society* 22.

Nygren-Junkin, L (2009) 'Language, Migration and Citizenship in Sweden: Still a Test-Free Zone' in G Extra, M Spotti and PVan Avermaet, *Language Testing, Migration and Citizenship: Cross-National Perspectives on Integration Regimes* (A&C Black).

Onasch, E (2020) 'Framing and Claiming "Gender Equality": A Multi-Level Analysis of the French Civic Integration Program' 34 *Gender & Society* 496.

Onasch, EA (2017) 'Lessons on the Boundaries of Belonging: Racialization and Symbolic Boundary Drawing in the French Civic Integration Program' 64 *Social Problems* 577.

Oomen, B and Leenders, E (2020) 'Symbolic Laws, Street-Level Actors: Everyday Bordering in Dutch Participation Declaration Workshops' in M Ambrosini, M Cinalli and D Jacobson (eds), *Migration, Borders and Citizenship: Between Policy and Public Spheres* (Springer International Publishing).

Orgad, L (2009) '"Cultural Defence" of Nations: Cultural Citizenship in France, Germany and the Netherlands' 15 *European Law Journal* 719.

—— (2010) 'Illiberal Liberalism Cultural Restrictions on Migration and Access to Citizenship in Europe' 58 *The American Journal of Comparative Law* 53.

—— (2019) 'The Citizen-Makers: Ethical Dilemmas in Immigrant Integration' 25 *European Law Journal* 524.

Oudejans, N (2011) *Asylum: A Philosophical Inquiry Into the International Protection of Refugees* (Tilburg University).

Paquet, M (2012) 'Beyond Appearances: Citizenship Tests in Canada and the UK' 13 *Journal of International Migration and Integration* 243.

Pascouau, Y (2014) 'Measures and rules developed in the EU member states regarding integration of third country nationals – Comparative Report' (European Policy Centre) www.europeanmigrationlaw.eu/en/articles/papers/measures-and-rules-developed-in-the-eu-member-states-regarding-integration-of-third-country-nationals-comparative-report.html accessed 27 May 2019.

Pautz, H (2005) 'The Politics of Identity in Germany: The Leitkultur Debate' 46 *Race & Class* 39.

Pélabay, J and Sénac, R (2019) 'Citizenship Revocation: A Stress Test for Liberal Democracy' 23 *Citizenship Studies* 388.

Perchining, B (2010) 'Country Report Austria: Integration and Naturalisation Tests: The New Way to European Citizenship' The INTEC Project https://bim.lbg.ac.at/en/access-justice/integration-and-naturalisation-tests-new-way-european-citizenship-intec accessed 29 June 2020.

Permoser, JM (2012) 'Civic Integration as Symbolic Politics: Insights from Austria' 14 *European Journal of Migration and Law* 173.

Peters, F, Vink, M and Schmeets, H (2018) 'Anticipating the Citizenship Premium: Before and after Effects of Immigrant Naturalisation on Employment' 44 *Journal of Ethnic and Migration Studies* 1051.

Peucker, M (2008) 'Similar Procedures, Divergent Function: Citizenship Tests in the United States, Canada, Netherlands and United Kingdom' OPEN FORUM UNESCO 240.

PEW, (2016) 'Europeans Fear Wave of Refugees Will Mean More Terrorism, Fewer Jobs' (PEW Research Center) www.pewresearch.org/global/2016/07/11/europeans-fear-wave-of-refugees-will-mean-more-terrorism-fewer-jobs/ accessed 24 July 2020.

Pierik, R (2012) 'Burgerschap En Inburgering' 1 *Recht der Werkelijkheid.*

Prins, dr B (Baukje) (2011) 'How (never) to become Dutch: testing the civic integration test', *Strangeness and familiarity: global unity and diversity in human rights and democracy* (Forum) https://surfsharekit.nl/publiek/hh/5778729f-5382-46a1-b7a1-d7f55c7a94e4 accessed 22 June 2020.

Putnam, RD Leonardi, R and Nanetti, RY (1994) *Making Democracy Work: Civic Traditions in Modern Italy* (Princeton University Press).

Radoilska, L (2014) 'Immigration, Interpersonal Trust and National Culture' 17 *Critical Review of International Social and Political Philosophy* 111.

Rawls, J (1971) *A Theory of Justice* (Harvard University Press).

Regioplan, (2005) 'Vluchtelingenwerk IntegratieBarometer 2005' Vluchtelingenwerk IntegratieBarometer: www.regioplan.nl/project/vluchtelingenwerk-integratiebarometer-een-onderzoek-naar-de-integratie-van-vluchtelingen-in-nederland/ accessed 13 July 2020.

Repstad, PP and Furseth, API (2013) *An Introduction to the Sociology of Religion: Classical and Contemporary Perspectives* (Ashgate Publishing Ltd).

Rostbøll, CF (2010) 'The Use and Abuse of "Universal Values" in the Danish Cartoon Controversy' 2 *European Political Science Review* 401.

Rubio-Marín, R (2000) *Immigration as a Democratic Challenge: Citizenship and Inclusion in Germany and the United States* (Cambridge University Press).

Rytter, M (2013) *Family Upheaval: Generation, Mobility and Relatedness among Pakistani Migrants in Denmark* (Berghahn Books).

Sassen, S (2004) 'The Global City: Introducing a Concept' 11 *Brown Journal of World Affairs* 27.

Scheffler, S (2003) 'What Is Egalitarianism?' 31 *Philosophy and Public Affairs; Hoboken* 5.

Scheid DE, (1795) 'Perpetual Peace: Kant' in DK Chatterjee (ed) https://doi.org/10.1007/978-1-4020-9160-5_763 accessed 5 August 2020.

Schinkel, W (2018) 'Against "Immigrant Integration": For an End to Neocolonial Knowledge Production' 6 *Comparative Migration Studies* 31.
—— (2008) 'The Moralisation of Citizenship in Dutch Integration Discourse' 1 *Amsterdam Law Forum* 15.
—— (2010) 'The Virtualization of Citizenship' 36 *Critical Sociology* 265.
—— (2017) *Imagined Societies: A Critique of Immigrant Integration in Western Europe* (Cambridge University Press).
Schinkel, W and Houdt, FV (2010) 'The Double Helix of Cultural Assimilationism and Neo-Liberalism: Citizenship in Contemporary Governmentality' 61 *The British Journal of Sociology* 696.
Schlueter, E, Meuleman, B and Davidov, E (2013) 'Immigrant Integration Policies and Perceived Group Threat: A Multilevel Study of 27 Western and Eastern European Countries' 42 *Social Science Research* 670.
Schmid, SD [2021] 'Stagnated Liberalization, Long-Term Convergence, and Index Methodology: Three Lessons from the CITRIX Citizenship Policy Dataset' *Global Policy*.
Scholten, PWA and others (2012) 'Integration From Abroad? Perception and Impacts of Pre-Entry Tests for Third Country Nationals' (PROSINT).
Schutter, HD and Ypi, L (2015) 'Mandatory Citizenship for Immigrants' 45 *British Journal of Political Science* 235.
SCP, (2015) 'Werelden van Verschil' (Sociaal en Cultureel Planbureau) www.scp.nl/Publicaties/Alle_publicaties/Publicaties_2015/Werelden_van_verschil accessed 28 July 2020.
Sen, A (1980) 'Equality of What?' I *The Tanner Lecture on Human Values* 197.
Sen, AK (2009) *The Idea of Justice* (Harvard University Press).
Shachar, A (2009) *The Birthright Lottery: Citizenship and Global Inequality* (Harvard University Press).
Shahidullah, SM (2012) *Comparative Criminal Justice Systems: Global and Local Perspectives* (Jones & Bartlett Publishers).
Significant, (2018) 'Inburgering: Systeemwereld versus Leefwereld. Evaluatie Wet Inburgering 2013' (Significant) www.eerstekamer.nl/overig/20180627/inburgering_systeemwereld_versus/meta accessed 13 July 2020.
Silvers, A and Francis, LP (2005) 'Justice through Trust: Disability and the "Outlier Problem" in Social Contract Theory' 116 *Ethics* 40.
Simbartlová, A (2019) 'Civic Integration Policies in Central Europe: The Case of the Czech Republic' 59 *Der Donauraum* 73.
Solano, G and Huddleston, T (2020) 'Migrant Integration Policy Index 2020' (Migrant Policy Group and Barcelona Centre for International Affairs).
Soysal, YN (1994) *Limits of Citizenship: Migrants and Postnational Membership in Europe* (University of Chicago Press 1994).
Steinhardt, MF (2012) 'Does Citizenship Matter? The Economic Impact of Naturalizations in Germany' 19 *Labour Economics* 813.
Strik, MHA, Hart, B de and Nissen, EJW (2013) *Family Reunification. A Barrier or Facilitator of Integration?* (Wolf Legal Publishers) http://hdl.handle.net/2066/126552 accessed 27 May 2019.
Strik, MHA and Pascouau, Y (2012) *Which Integration for Migrants? Interaction Between the EU and Its Member States* (Nijmegen Legal Publishers 2012).
Strik, T, Luiten, M and Van Oers, R (2010) 'Country Report The Netherlands' (European Integration Fund) https://ec.europa.eu/migrant-integration/librarydoc/the-intec-project-integration-and-naturalisation-tests-the-new-way-to-european-citizenship accessed 24 June 2020.
Stronks, M (2017) 'Grasping Legal Time' PhD dissertation.
—— (2022) *Grasping Legal Time: Temporality and European Migration Law* (Cambridge University Press).
SUO, (2020) 'En Långsiktigt Hållbar Migrationspolitik' (SUO) Betänkande av Kommittén om den framtida svenska migrationspolitiken (Migrationskommittén) 54.
Suvarierol, S and Kirk, K (Kate) (2015) 'Dutch Civic Integration Courses as Neoliberal Citizenship Rituals' 19 *Citizenship Studies* 248.

Tamir, Y (1995) *Liberal Nationalism* (Princeton University Press).
Taylor, C (1994) *Multiculturalism: Expanded Paperback Edition* (Princeton University Press).
Tocqueville, A de (1838) *Democracy in America* (Alfred A Knopf).
Triadafilopoulos, T (2011) 'Illiberal Means to Liberal Ends? Understanding Recent Immigrant Integration Policies in Europe' 37 *Journal of Ethnic and Migration Studies* 861.
Turner, J (2014) 'Testing the Liberal Subject: (In)Security, Responsibility and "Self-Improvement" in the UK Citizenship Test' 18 *Citizenship Studies* 332.
UN Refugee Agency (2013) 'A New Beginning: Refugee Integration in Europe' (UN Refugee Agency) www.refworld.org/docid/522980604.html accessed 23 June 2020.
UNCHR (2019) 'Figures at a Glance' (*UNHCR*) www.unhcr.org/figures-at-a-glance.html accessed 23 November 2020.
Valentini, L (2012) 'Ideal vs. Non-Ideal Theory: A Conceptual Map' 7 *Philosophy Compass* 654.
Van der Brug, W, D'Amato, G, Ruedin, D and Berkhout, J (2015) *The Politicisation of Migration* (Routledge).
Van Houdt, F, Suvarierol, S and Schinkel, W (2011) 'Neoliberal Communitarian Citizenship: Current Trends towards "Earned Citizenship" in the United Kingdom, France and the Netherlands' 26 *International Sociology* 408.
Van Oers, R (2013) *Deserving Citizenship: Citizenship Tests in Germany, the Netherlands and the United Kingdom* (Martinus Nijhoff Publishers).
—— (2020) 'Deserving citizenship in Germany and The Netherlands. Citizenship tests in liberal democracies' *Ethnicities*.
Van Spanje, J (2010) 'Contagious Parties: Anti-Immigration Parties and Their Impact on Other Parties' Immigration Stances in Contemporary Western Europe' 16 *Party Politics* 563.
Vassalo, K (2019) 'The Implementation of the Integration Polic for Third Country Nationals in Malta' (Bachelor dissertation).
Verkuyten, M (2013) *Identity and Cultural Diversity: What Social Psychology Can Teach Us* (Routledge).
Vink, MP (2007) 'Dutch "Multiculturalism" Beyond the Pillarisation Myth' 5 *Political Studies Review* 337.
Waerniers, R and Hustinx, L (2019) 'The Labyrinth towards Citizenship: Contradictions in the Framing and Categorization of Immigrants in Immigration and Integration Policies' 26 *Identities* 270.
Waldron, J (2011) 'Does "Equal Moral Status" Add Anything to Right Reason?' (Social Science Research Network) SSRN Scholarly Paper ID 1898689 https://papers.ssrn.com/abstract=1898689 accessed 3 June 2019.
Walzer, M (1983) *Spheres Of Justice: A Defense Of Pluralism And Equality* (Basic Books).
Weigend, T (2013) 'There Is Only One Presumption of Innocence' 42 *Netherlands Journal of Legal Philosophy* 193.
Wellman, CH (2008) 'Immigration and Freedom of Association' (2008) 119 *Ethics* 109.
Wieviorka, M (2014) 'A Critique of Integration' 21 *Identities* 633.
Wilde, M de (2017) 'Offering Hospitality to Strangers: Hugo Grotius's Draft Regulations for the Jews' 85 *Tijdschrift voor Rechtsgeschiedenis / Revue d'Histoire du Droit / The Legal History Review* 391.
—— (2019) 'Seeking Refuge: Grotius on Exile, Expulsion and Asylum' 20 *Journal of the History of International Law / Revue d'histoire du droit international* 471.
Willard, M (1967) *History of the White Australia Policy to 1920* (Psychology Press).
Williams, D (2018) 'Suspect Outsiders or Prospective Citizens? Constructing the Immigrant/German Boundary in Germany's Integration Courses' 7 *Social Sciences* 61.
Wolff, J (1998) 'Fairness, Respect, and the Egalitarian Ethos' 27 *Philosophy & Public Affairs* 97.
—— (2015) 'Social Equality and Social Inequality' in C Fourie, F Schuppert and I Wallimann-Helmer (eds), *Social Equality: On what it Means to be Equals* (Oxford University Press).
Wong, SI (2009) 'Duties of Justice to Citizens with Cognitive Disabilities' 40 *Metaphilosophy* 382.
WRR, (1989) 'Allochtonenbeleid' (Ministerie van Algemene Zaken) rapport www.wrr.nl/publicaties/rapporten/1989/05/09/allochtonenbeleid accessed 13 July 2020.
—— (2012) *In betere banen* (WRR) https://library.oapen.org/handle/20.500.12657/33942 accessed 5 September 2020.

—— (2015) 'Geen tijd verliezen' (WRR) http://resolver.tudelft.nl/uuid:b1b323e3-1936-4039-ba63-a3563d0fa5ce accessed 5 September 2020.
Xhardez, C (2019) 'From Different Paths to a Similar Road? Understanding the Convergence of Subnational Immigrant Integration Policies in Belgium' 0 *Regional Studies* 1.
Young, IM (2001) 'Equality of Whom? Social Groups and Judgments of Injustice' 9 *Journal of Political Philosophy* 1.
—— (1990) *Justice and the Politics of Difference* (Princeton University Press).
—— (2002) *Inclusion and Democracy* (Oxford University Press).
Zuber, CI (2019) 'Explaining the Immigrant Integration Laws of German, Italian and Spanish Regions: Sub-State Nationalism and Multilevel Party Politics' 0 *Regional Studies* 1.

INDEX

P

  - 'in-group orientations' 63–4
  - need for migrant labour 71
  - negative opinions of immigrants 64
  - potency and limits of constitutionalism 72–5

R

S

www.ingramcontent.com/pod-product-compliance
Ingram Content Group UK Ltd.
Pitfield, Milton Keynes, MK11 3LW, UK
UKHW020820290926
15470UKWH00003B/1277